A Daoist Alchemy
Self-Discovery Journey

THROUGH THE
MYSTERY GATE

Leta Herman
& Jaye McElroy

Born Perfect ink
ANCIENT WISDOM FOR MODERN TIMES
NORTHAMPTON, USA

Important: The information and techniques discussed in this book are based on the personal and professional experiences and research of its authors. The information contained in this book is not meant to be a substitute for medical care by a physician or other healthcare provider(s). Any diagnosis or medical care should be done under the guidance of a healthcare professional. The publisher does not promote the use of specific healthcare protocols but believes the information in this book should be made available to the general public. Neither the authors nor the publisher assume any liability whatsoever for the use of the information contained in this book. The authors and publisher strongly suggest consulting a professional healthcare provider about the appropriateness of any technique or procedure mentioned in this book.

Through the Mystery Gate: A Daoist Alchemy Self-Discovery Journey

Contents

Acknowledgments

We are grateful to all who helped make this book come to life. As people who aren't originally from thc Chinese Daoist culture, we want to acknowledge with deep gratitude all those (living and ancestral) who have generously shared their teachings and gifts with us.

Our heartfelt appreciation goes to Master Jeffrey Yuen, an 88th generation Daoist priest, who has inspired us to expand and seek more in this lifetime. He has taught us how to cultivate Le or happiness in our lives. Le is the kind of joy that makes us want to get out of bed in the morning with the desire to seek expansion on Earth while, at the same time, reaching upward toward something greater than ourselves (what the Chinese often refer to as Heaven) for the betterment of all. Our intention is to carry this wisdom forward in a good way and share it with others.

We also want to express our deep appreciation for all those who have embarked on the path of Alchemy with us. It takes courage to enter the mystery, and we feel blessed to be companions and guides along their journeys. It's a true joy to share in the excitement of profound personal change with those brave enough to embrace their own transformation. Thank you, thank you, thank you. Our wish is that every person can find their personal transformation path. And a little laughter along the way always helps! Here's to a path of loving, laughing, learning, and finding your Le every day.

What you seek is seeking you.

—Rumi

Preface

Before we (Jaye and Leta) encountered Alchemy, we were "normal" people, looking to grow and evolve in order to find happiness in our lives.

We were trying our best to navigate the ups and downs of this crazy world as best we could, just like everyone else. We lived as healthy a lifestyle as we could: we exercised, ate organic food when we were able to, did some yoga, and meditated a little. We loved, cried, worked, and slept like everyone else, but something was missing. We asked ourselves, "Is there more to life than this?" Although we had travelled different paths, those paths met in the junction of wanting more, seeking more, and searching for deeper meaning.

Then we discovered Alchemy—Leta first, with Master Yuen, and Jaye some years later, after meeting Leta.

Today, we are still ordinary people, just with an Alchemical twist that has radically transformed our lives. We try to live a simple life though we like to think of it as a perpetual work in progress! We certainly aren't smarter than anyone else in the world, nor do we have any special or secret knowledge. We just have had access to some really cool teachers and their teachings, read a lot of books, and have worked diligently to understand Alchemical concepts as they apply to our own lives and our clients' lives. We want to share what we are doing and all we have learned. We may be a little farther down the path than some people—or just starting out compared to others!

We believe that everyone has the power to improve their own lives, even though it can sometimes seem like healers belong to a secret wisdom society, which we don't believe is the case! Instead we want to open doors to anyone who wants to learn more about Alchemy and how it can transform lives.

This book is humble and simple. We made it this way with clear intention and direction. There is so much more to Alchemy than what we've put into the pages of this book —lifetimes' worth of words and wisdom. This book represents our own interpretation through our cultivation of the ancient wisdom, knowledge, and information that we received from our teachers, taking into account both our studies and experiences over the past 20 years.

We have only been on this planet for a little over 50 years each—a blink in time for an immortal. We plan on being here a very long time to come. So this knowledge will definitely change and grow as we change and grow, and as we expand and go in and out of other dimensions and realities.

> We are living as Alchemists in our own lives. As such, we always reserve the right to change our minds as our minds change us.

We wrote this book for our clients who are currently walking the Alchemical path with us as well as for anyone who might be inspired by some of the ideas in this book. We are also excited for people to discover the wonders of Alchemy for the first time.

This book can be used as a guide for walking through your life in a very awake and aware state of consciousness.

We will explain some ideas that can show you how to remove obstacles to spiritual evolution while opening up portals to new ways of experiencing reality, which from a Daoist perspective is ultimately an illusion.

Alchemy is something that you can do for this lifetime or for many lifetimes. We hope it becomes something you engage in for many years to come, if you choose.

We have discovered one thing for certain: you can't force or rush Alchemy. Alchemy has no timetable except your own. You can walk this path as quickly or as slowly as your destiny allows. You can't speed it up, but you also can't slow it down if it seems to be moving very quickly. It just happens to you once you let it. You can study theory for years and years and never fully get the lightning bolt or the aha moment. Then one day, it just happens, and that is where your Alchemical transformation begins.

This book can also be a study companion to whatever spiritual path you have been on, are currently on, or plan to embark upon. The Alchemical path is not the only path, and this book is simply an explanation of Alchemy from our experiences and joint perspectives. If you would like to incorporate these ideas into your life, whether you're a lifelong learner, healer, spiritual teacher, or energy worker, we wrote this book for you—as a welcome invitation to Daoist Alchemy.

If you have a strong affinity with Alchemy and feel inspired, you can choose to work with a teacher or practitioner to help guide you along this path. We all need guides and teachers. They are the people who help us avoid the ditches of self-deception and denial we may fall into, and at the same time, they gently encourage us to seek without self-judgment. The Alchemists of antiquity helped each other through their transformational journeys, too. Having a mentor can be just as valuable for us today. We have created our own Alchemy Healing Center for this exact purpose.

We think of this book as a mentoring guidebook more than a do-it-yourself book. Think of it as an opportunity to begin to find out everything you'd want to know about an ancient Alchemical path to personal transformation—even immortality in this lifetime—but didn't know how or what to ask!

We are both teachers, and we love to teach. Alchemy, self-cultivation, and Chinese Medicine—these are our passions. We've truly enjoyed bringing this spark of hope to others through our work in our clinic, our friendships, our workshops, our podcast, and in the books we've written or published for others. We sincerely hope that what we are writing here, or maybe we should say, what you are reading at this very moment in time, may give you the motivation, inspiration, and impetus to *ask*, to *pursue*, and to *awaken* to your own life. That is indeed the ultimate goal of this book.

> We *did not invent, create, or discover the ancient secrets of Alchemy. It is vast, ancient, and wise. We are just on our own journeys of transformation and loving every minute of it!*

We believe that *you*—not your healers, teachers, psychologists, parents, siblings, doctors, or neighbors—are ultimately in charge of *your own* destiny. While others can certainly help you on your path, if you are willing to claim ownership of your own life and be accountable for your own choices, then knowledge and wisdom can be key factors that can help move you forward. Buddha walked this earth for a long time gaining wisdom and knowledge from everyone and everything he encountered before he sat under the Bodhi tree and attained enlightenment all on his own.

> *Alchemy is a journey of one that can be shared with others along the way.*

We are hopeful that you will want to know more about this magical path. And, well, why not start here? We suggest you strap on your seatbelts because humble though our intentions may be, this book is going to be a wild, fun, and amazing ride! Let's set out to learn more about this Alchemical journey—each of us alone—yet together. We believe our personal stories are a good place to start to help you understand what this book is going to be about... so here goes!

Leta's Story

I knew my life had suddenly changed in a direction that I didn't even know was possible. "Are you alright, sweetie?" the flight attendant asked me, leaning over to get closer to me. "I really don't know" was all I could squeak out, as she handed me a small pack of tissues and a bag of nuts.

Apparently that was the remedy for sobbing on a plane —a few tissues and a salty snack. My whole existence, my whole perspective on life was being called into question at that very moment. I was about to radically alter my life and my young family's forevermore—all because of a small book that I was holding in my hands.

It wasn't even my book! Less than 24 hours before, as I finished packing up for our giant move from California to Massachusetts, my friend Jill simply handed me a book and said, "This is for the plane ride."

That was it. No warning, no heads-up, not even a little pack of tissues from her! My friend's well-worn book landed in my lap during a huge transition in my life. I was leaving my beloved home in California with my four-year-old child and my spouse to return to New England where I grew up.

The small book was entitled *Plant Spirit Medicine*, and the author's name was Eliot Cowan. I was crying because his words touched things inside me that I thought I had lost —an innocent love of nature and a sense of something magical in the world. They'd been bred out of me by years of schooling. In addition, I'd been raised by highly educated parents, whose religion was, basically, academia.

I also wept that day because I realized I was careening at 500 miles per hour to a destination 3000 miles *away* from where the author of this book lived. It felt like I was going to somehow miss my calling! Had I made the wrong decision to move? Now I was in doubt and panic.

This is insane! We need to go back. Maybe we can somehow make it work back in California, I thought. But no, in fact, it was too late. The house was bought, our son was enrolled in his new school, and the plane was hurtling me through time and space.

Still, I knew I had to know more about Plant Spirit Medicine. After all, the book had reduced me to tears in public at 30,000 feet above the earth.

The day after we settled into our new house, the universe delivered my wish. I called the office of the book's author in California and explained that I wanted to know more, to take a class, to read another book—to somehow study more of what he was teaching. To my great relief and complete astonishment, he was starting a brand new class in a couple of months in Massachusetts, right near where I lived! What good luck! Thank you, universe!

And so my life took a hard right turn, away from my fancy corporate tech job and right into unlocking and unfolding the deeper realms of the great mystery of life. Even with a very supportive partner and a wonderful child, I had been conflicted about my road in my life. For the first time in my life, this new path would require me to be my authentic self. I was terrified.

But before continuing, I must go back in time a bit—back to the days when I was carefree and in love with nature and my life. I grew up in New Hampshire in an idyllic setting on a lake surrounded by gardens and evergreen trees everywhere. My parents were extremely loving and present in my life, both graduate students on their way to getting their PhDs and becoming college professors. But I was very young and more interested in being outside playing in nature than anything else at the time. I spent entire days in the tops of the tall pine trees that grew next to my house, or tending to my tomato plants in the yard. Curious and eager to learn just about everything, I was a very happy child.

That is, until it was time for me to go to kindergarten. Though I had clearly inherited my parents' aptitude for studies, school was a social disaster for me. I was a friendly, outgoing child, but on my first day of school, a bully targeted me and made my life suddenly miserable. This painful event started me on a path of social awkwardness that seemed to attract bullying from other children as well, for most of my grammar school years. To make matters worse, my parents had to move us several times in the next few years.

They say that bullying is one of the worst things that can happen to a human being because our dependence on each other is actually built into our genes. Humans are inherently a social species. On an emotional and even on a bodily level, being cast out means we have to figure out how to survive on our own physically but also emotionally. The damage of my early experiences was longterm. It took me years to process the social shunning and to return to my true nature—an essentially happy, loving, and very social person.

Today I work with people who have had devastating traumas in their lives—much worse than anything in my story. Yet I've learned that the effect of trauma on a person varies widely depending on the person and the circumstances. One person might tell you the most horrific story you've ever heard, but the effect on them is less than the effect of some other person's seemingly mild story. I know my trauma was not horrifying, but it did affect me deeply. After all, I'm what we call in Chinese Medicine, a Fire Element person. This means my natural temperament is outgoing, friendly, and fundamentally happy. Fire people like to be friendly because they want to be liked. They are the people pleasers in the world. They are the social butterflies that we all know and love. That's Fire's true nature! So being an outcast is a Fire person's nightmare, which was surely the case for me.

When I read that Plant Spirit Medicine book on the plane that day, it touched a giant wound deep inside of me that I'd somehow learned to ignore. Unconsciously I knew that maybe, just maybe, the plants and the mystery of the world that he so eloquently wrote about would help me heal and change my life. Subconsciously, I was still that little girl being shunned on the first day of school.

Eliot Cowan's new class in Massachusetts was a year-and-a-half-long program. I was both excited and terrified. I was the least likely participant of all of the students who attended! I wasn't one of these new-age, yoga, herbalist, Reiki-practicing spiritual people who had signed up and seemed so at home in this class. I was a hard-core brainiac, a Smith College graduate, a system engineer at a software firm, raised by academic atheists! I felt as if I really had no business being in that class at all. I had no clue what I was in for, and I didn't realize the reality of that fact until we started doing Plant Spirit Shamanic journeys. I didn't even know what a Shaman was before I started the class, and until we began to journey, I only knew what I read in the book.

The class progressed along. My classmates seemed to accept me, but I definitely felt like an outsider looking into this new world. I tried to keep an open mind, but I soon came to the realization that I was really, really bad at this shaman business. I mean, really bad.

It reminded me of the incredible frustration I had felt at Smith when I took a prerequisite class in drawing. Academically, I was a straight-A student, but I was terrible at drawing. As the semester began, I was facing the real possibility of getting my first not-an-A-but-an-F grade in my entire schooling career! I was desperate to succeed, but the more my mind tried to solve the problem of how to draw, the worse I got at it. My boyfriend was a wonderful artist and would spend hours trying to help me, but that only seemed to make it worse. I could see that his mind just worked differently than mine! I just couldn't draw!

Finally, he stopped trying to teach me and handed me a book called *Drawing on the Right Side of the Brain*. Once I understood that the "problem" was in my brain and that there was a way to learn how to "see" differently with the right side of my brain, I actually learned how to draw. And I was pretty good! I think I even managed to eke out a solid B in that class—and I eventually enjoyed drawing.

I needed to experience this same type of transition in the Plant Spirit Medicine class, but I hadn't figured that out yet. I got more and more frustrated at trying so hard to *do* it, but somehow failing miserably. It was very disheartening. Then one day while we were doing a shamanic exercise in class, I remembered that *Drawing on the Right Side of the Brain* book. Unfortunately there was not a book entitled *Easy Shamanic Journeys for Any Side of Your Brain*. There still isn't! However, I remembered its theory, and I just relaxed. I closed my eyes, took a deep breath, and I let my mind go—or to be exact, I let my left brain go. And suddenly, it began to work. I was able to access something other than complete darkness, which had been the extent of my skills up until that point. Within a short time after this successful moment, I was on my shamanic way.

However, I still felt skeptical under the surface, and I felt oddly on the outside of both worlds—my old Western thinking world and my new Plant Spirit Medicine world. At that moment in my life, it was just too much of a leap for me to totally believe, coming from my upbringing. I would say I suspended my disbelief during that first year and a half, and just played with the ideas I was learning and exploring without truly committing to any of them.

Fast forward to almost two years after my first reading of the Plant Spirit Medicine book. It was my final graduation "test," when I had to do an actual Plant Spirit Medicine treatment with a client in front of the whole class. I brought in the person I had picked to be my "first client." This person was a friend who kindly agreed to come with me to do this treatment in front of the entire class and had no idea what we were about to do! She was so exhausted, drained, and in pain from multiple surgeries, I think she figured she had nothing to lose. She was such a good friend to even agree to come with me!

As part of the test, students were to be evaluated based on their pulse-taking skills. Chinese Medicine pulses measure the Qi or energy in the body, but when I took her pulses, I couldn't feel a thing. I was stunned. I had never felt no pulse before and immediately assumed I was going to fail the test. I wrote down the notation for no pulses on the board. My teacher then took the pulses and confirmed that I was correct! I hadn't failed after all. The client I had brought had the extremely rare block that made the pulses appear to have disappeared.

Next I had to do the treatment for that incredibly rare case, which I'd barely studied since it was considered so rare. Luckily, I was able to remember! After doing the treatment, I took her pulses again and was absolutely blown away. Not only could I suddenly feel her pulses, but they felt normal! How did that happen? Did the treatment do that to her? How could that be possible?

To this day, I marvel that I asked this particular woman to come for that class. I feel that if I hadn't had such a radical case with such incredible results, I may never have ventured into the world of healing and eventually Alchemy. The fact that I, as a total newbie, could feel such a radical difference proved to me without a doubt that this work was powerful. That day, in that treatment, the transformation was undeniable, powerful, and freeing for BOTH of us. I will never forget it personally. Something magical had occurred. It was as if my friend had woken up from being the walking dead that day. Her pain and exhaustion somehow lifted, and her life then shifted. She had more energy, and she began to make a full recovery.

But *how* had this happened? I HAD to know more. I needed to know more.

I had a similar experience with my next teacher, Niki Bilton, who was the former dean of a renowned graduate school of Five Element Acupuncture in England. She personally studied with the famous J.R. Worsley, the Father and Master teacher of the Five Element Acupuncture tradition in the modern world.

I became involved in her more esoteric teachings, which really were my introduction to Alchemical healing, though we didn't call it that back then. We had week-long training sessions, and each practitioner would do a long treatment that lasted four or more hours and included Alchemical points like the Thirteen Ghost points.

In those trainings, I found myself in the same situation as in my past learning experiences, yet again. My bossy left brain kept getting in the way of trying to learn something that actually seemed unexplainable. I was trying to reason with it and wrestle it to the ground. I wanted to *figure it out.* I had to figure it out, but I was failing, miserably. It would take me twelve hours to do an Alchemical treatment that should have taken four, because I would show up with so many expectations of the way I thought it should be. Niki was very patient with me and would often jump in to save the day and finish the treatments when I could not. It was during this time that I finally learned to let go of that left-brain desire to control everything and instead learned to *allow* the treatments to unfold the way they needed to. Once I finally got it, everything clicked, and I was truly on my Alchemical healer path.

It was Niki who introduced me to Master Jeffrey Yuen's work on Chinese Medicine and Alchemy. And my life once again took a momentous turn—a deep and meaningful turn towards understanding Alchemy.

> *When the student is ready, the teacher will appear. When the student is truly ready, the teacher will disappear.*

—Anonymous

Master Jeffrey Yuen has been my teacher since 2004. He's an 88th generation Daoist Priest, and he teaches acupuncturists and other Chinese Medicine practitioners all over the world about many topics, including my favorite, Daoist Alchemy. He is also one of the most knowledgeable people I have ever met, and one of the kindest humans on the planet. I consider myself blessed and lucky to have found such a wonderful teacher and Master to learn from.

The very first lecture of his that I attended was on Alchemy, and so many of the ideas he discussed that day expanded my belief system, or should I say, blew the doors off of it! I sat in the 100-person audience stunned, much like that day on the plane when I first read the Plant Spirit Medicine book. But thankfully no tears this time. I could feel that this was where my whole life had been leading up to. *This is why I am here on the planet, to learn THIS.* I felt it in my bones.

Master Yuen parted the veil to the mystery and invited me to peek behind the curtain. This unveiled the deep wisdom I'd been seeking, and it was the next turning point in my life. I knew it was my path. And seventeen years later, at this writing, it still is the driving force in my life.

I dove into Master Yuen's work with gusto and glee. I went to every lecture I could get into and travelled with him to many places all over the world, including China three times. I began to incorporate his Alchemical teachings into my own healing practice on a daily basis, and I began to undergo the treatments myself, with a healer friend of mine guiding me and acting as my practitioner. I was also building my Energetic Acupressure practice and gaining more and more experience every day.

Personally undergoing the Alchemy work has been one of the two biggest transitions in my life, second only to the beautiful birth of my child Dunan. Both have been occasions of true joy and transformation, and I've been blessed to have experienced both in the same lifetime. I had been an incredibly anxious person on the whole, probably due to my difficult experiences in grammar school. Through Alchemy, I was able to release my social fears and anxieties and begin to see my life in a whole new way. I felt safe in myself. I felt connected to the "whole," so much so that it felt as if I was sitting in the lap of God. And that's coming from the kid who grew up as an atheist! Life started to feel easy, and big decisions that had seemed impossible now came without struggle. I changed my life in so many ways and in doing so found my true path.

As I began to incorporate Alchemy more and more into my healing practice, I noticed how my clients went through similarly amazing transformations. They became much more effective in their lives. They found momentum where they had felt stuck for years. They became happier, more at ease, and clearer about what they really truly wanted and needed to be and do. They began to *live their life's full potential.*

Because Alchemy transforms life, it does have its challenges. One of those challenges is that if you've been on the ground your whole life, suddenly finding your wings doesn't mean you'll know how to fly! When Jaye began studying Alchemy and became involved with our Alchemy program, our work together helped me solve a significant piece of the Alchemy puzzle that I just hadn't been able to put together before. I was her first Alchemical coaching client, and I like to say that she helped me learn how to metaphorically fly in my life. I was still feeling stuck because even though things were going so well due to Alchemy, I had unfulfilled dreams of writing a book and moving beyond the walls and limitations that I had imposed even on this new life that I had created. I was telling myself a negative story about why I had no time to write that book or do other things.

In a single, powerful four-hour strategy session, Jaye was able to help me remove the mental obstacles that had been in my way for almost a decade. Within six months of that first session, the first book was sold and published by

Llewellyn Publishing. I say the first, because since that book, we've written three books, and this one is the fourth! We also birthed a new media publishing company and have even published other healers' books. We've created a podcast and a community membership site called the Alchemy Learning Center. Our healing clinic, the Alchemy Healing Center, continues to thrive in our community with amazing healers, students, and clients who walk through our doors every day. This is what I call *flying* in my life—having the wings AND the practical knowledge and strength to actually realize dreams. Jaye likes to say it's about being *limitless*, which is easier said than done, until you are doing Alchemy! We will discuss this concept more in Stage Six of this book, but that's the beauty of Alchemy. Understanding the concepts comes when you awaken them inside you.

Realizing your dreams—or what the Daoists would call, your destiny—is only the *outer world* part. The real Alchemy is inside us. How do I want to feel inside myself every day? Is life easy for me? Is life meaningful? Can I find the quiet connection with my higher self? This is what Alchemy really inspires. Alchemy profoundly changed things internally for me. I found peace inside. I found meaning. I began to live life in this new way of being. I began to live life for the transformation itself, the Alchemy process.

I am deeply grateful for all my teachers, both past and present, and for those whom I have yet to meet. I give thanks for all the forces that directed me (willingly or not) on my own path. I am really excited to be traveling this Alchemical road that is so full of a deep wisdom that I get to engage with every day. I appreciate all who come into my life both for what they share and also for challenging my beliefs daily. I have a sincere appreciation for the people who help me avoid becoming stagnant in my life!

I have come to realize that the esteemed title of teacher is not limited to those who work in classrooms: my clients, my students, my friends, and my family are my ongoing teachers in my life and in Alchemy in the truest sense. I can't wait to see what the next 500 years brings!

Jaye's Story

The first thing you need to know about me is that I have lived an ordinary yet extraordinary life. To even be here writing these words is amazing. There are so many roads and paths I have taken over the years—each one leading me, teaching me, showing me the joys of the world. I had a crazy childhood, and a pretty normal adulthood, until I discovered Alchemy—which is exactly what I asked the universe for! Life is good, and it can be even better. For the purpose of this introduction, I will try to give a short "her-story" of my life up to this point. Who knows what the future will bring—more magic, more fun, and more experiences. Limitless options await each of us.

Being the youngest of four children, you wouldn't think that I would have been the responsible one of the family. However, being the "baby" of the family doesn't necessarily have to mean you are immature, and I am living proof of that! For as long as I can remember, I have been the responsible one.

I used to say my childhood ended when I turned 11 and my father walked out on the family. From that day forward, I seemed to be the only one in the family who had any common sense. Now, I realize fully that each person on this planet is walking a unique path. So I am saying these things with no judgment or criticism of any kind.

Growing up in the 1970s and 1980s was a time when teenagers were living for parties, drugs, and rock-n-roll, and my siblings fit right in. We had working parents, so with very limited supervision, my older sister and brothers just fell headfirst into crazy lifestyles. I saw what they were doing, and it was completely the opposite of what I wanted. It seemed like they were on the road to ruining their lives. And frankly, they terrified me. Seemingly every night, there were big parties at my house and the older kids would be running wild—playing loud music, drunk or high, falling down, fighting, bleeding—all while I was tucked away reading a book in my room. Some nights I was lucky enough to stay at the neighbors' house with a friend. I didn't so much see that as a negative thing at the time. That was just the way it was at our house. I loved my brothers and sister but I longed for escape and a quieter family life.

When I wasn't reading, I was throwing myself into sports. The sports teams I belonged to became my home away from home where everyone loved me. Because I am a Wood Element type (Wood Element people are often naturally athletic and good leaders), I was captain of most every one of my sports teams. And I was one of the most talented and energetic members on each team, no matter what sport I played. I guess I was just naturally gifted in sports and felt happy when I was pushing myself physically.

I spent the rest of my time at other friends' houses, where they fed me good food and held kind and intelligent conversations around the dinner table. In fact, although my family members didn't come to any of my games or competitions, my friends' parents did, and they were always watching and rooting for all of us. They took good care of me. Perhaps they even felt bad that no one from my family was that supportive, but they never ever said anything or made me feel bad in any way. They accepted me for me. I just wanted to play and be the best that I could possibly be —all the time. I also liked to help others do the same.

Looking back, I now realize that I wanted structure and to know that someone had my back. I was so lucky to have a person that filled that gap in my life. That person was my Nana. She was my life and my rock. She was the constant factor that drove me to succeed in my life. She made me feel like anything was possible—that I could do anything I wanted to do in my life. She gave me permission to follow my dreams, and I didn't need to get that advice from anyone else. She was a trailblazer and a good person. I miss her every day. As a single parent, my mother was overwhelmed with the other kids, but she always did the best she could, and I love her dearly.

I remember being about eight years old, and my oldest brother wanted to be Evil Knievel, a crazy stunt performer who jumped his motorcycles over cars and buildings in the 1970s. My brother was indeed the daredevil in the family and jumped his dirt bike over anything and everything. One day, he missed, hit a tree in the yard, and his leg got wedged in between the tree's limbs. That was the first of many broken bones for him. That was also the first time I had ever seen an ambulance actually come to someone's house and take someone away with lights flashing and sirens blaring. My parents rushed to the hospital to be with him. I remember them piling all my other siblings into the car and leaving, saying, "Take care of the house and dogs, and we'll be back soon."

There I was, left in the house all alone for the first time. At first I was proud to be the one they chose to be responsible enough to be left home to take care of the animals. But after many hours later, as dark descended, I began to feel a little scared. They hadn't called. No one had checked in on me. In all the drama of the moment, I think they forgot about me. There were no cell phones back then, only land lines, so I couldn't call them. I didn't even know what hospital they'd gone to. I was utterly alone for the first time. I had to make my own dinner, I had to feed the animals and take them outside, and I had to turn on the lights in the house. This was the exact moment I realized something wasn't quite right about the way my family was functioning. Why was the youngest child left home alone? What was wrong with my sister who was 16 years old or my brother who was 14? Why didn't they take me with them to the hospital and leave my sister or brother unattended? I certainly was quite relieved when they all returned late that night. I was sleeping on the couch with our dog by my side and the TV sign-off signal was blaring, which happened back in the day when TV was done broadcasting for the night.

Yet, as my daily life went on, I didn't dwell on this at all. All of it really didn't matter to me. I had plenty to keep me busy. I was a year-round athlete, playing four sports in high school. I simply escaped the craziness at home by running to my friends' houses to be with them and their families. I was raised by the village, and I was, all-in-all, a very happy kid. I was creative, artistic, and athletic. I was even a vegetarian, which was very radical back then. I loved animals and people—I loved to help other people. I just liked to help everyone be happy.

I was the only one in my family interested in attending college. I knew it was my ticket out of the kind of lifestyle I didn't want—my family's chaotic way of being. Their unpredictability was not for me. I wanted to be free to follow my ambition wherever it led me, and academics, like sports, came easy for me. I'm fast on my feet and my mind works pretty fast too. I got a small scholarship to my state college, where I played sports and had fun, and was on my way to my new adult life.

At college I came into my own. I loved to laugh, and make other people laugh. I liked to play games with my friends and entertain them. I loved to learn new things. I was very gregarious. I liked being a part of a community, just interacting with people in general. For me, life was not about being serious. I met and fell in love with my long-term partner, who I shared many adventures with for the next twenty-five years. It was always about being happy and following your bliss.

Right from my childhood on, I always felt driven to do things differently. Even though I was young, after college I got thrown into a rather important and very responsible advertising position. I had a big budget and my own staff, and I was a fast learner. However, when it turned out I wasn't happy working for my bosses, I decided to start my own advertising agency. I thought, like many Wood Element people do, that becoming really successful would be the magic elixir that would make me happy.

The business went well. It should have made me happy, if in fact material wealth can make anyone truly happy. Fast forward 20 years, my niche agency was very successful for a small company. I used to laugh and say that I can teach anyone to make money, because I was indeed in the business of making other people quite wealthy. I wasn't fabulously wealthy like them, but I did alright. I guess in the end, the money didn't really matter to me. Having all the money that I had just gave me this empty feeling inside and left me wanting to know more. But what that more was, I didn't know at the time.

Without really being able to figure the whole thing out, I kept trying to fill that empty space with creative endeavors. It wasn't necessarily a bad thing—I took up painting, photography, and even trained for and completed a triathlon. But nothing seemed to fill this void. Even though I had had a stable and happy life, I needed to figure out how to make myself happier. I think that's when I turned to the sport of golf.

My father loved golf. He had always been a mystery to me growing up. At the time, to me, he was the only one in the family that seemed to have some common sense to him. He worked as an electrical engineer and a successful local politician. But on the other hand he wasn't around much when I was little and then he left when I was still quite young, so I didn't get to have the relationship I'd wanted to have with him until much later in life. I seemed to only get glimpses of him, and they were not always good ones.

I had started playing golf soon after college. In a sense, it was my way of reaching out to my father to have a relationship with him. He'd always wanted my brother to play golf when we were younger. He'd take him golfing, but because I was a girl, he never took me to the golf course. Golf was, as with all sports, easy for me to understand and learn to master. And it did in fact catch my father's interest that his daughter was good at it. We started golfing together.

I chased the golf dream as hard as I could for a few years, part-time and in between work and life. I had a dream of becoming a professional golfer one day, but because of a series of injuries, that dream ultimately slipped away from me. I had debilitating feet and knee pain that would not go away. Every doctor I went to said "surgery, surgery, and more surgery." I knew that wasn't the answer for me. I felt I just needed more time to heal, and more training, which was very expensive, time consuming, and sometimes took me away from my partner and our little family, which was hard for me. My chiropractor told me it was hopeless—I would never be able to stand on my feet and train for hours and hours, which is essential in golf. But believe me, I'm stubborn. I persisted as long as I could bear it.

Finally, I had to decide whether to settle down and buy a house or continue to chase the dream, limping along injured all the time, which was draining my energy and our resources. I chose the first option and did not play golf again until many years later. Once again I felt that deeply empty space, but luckily I did have my many other hobbies and skills and many, many more dreams that I wanted to explore. I had good friends in my life and enjoyed having fun with them. My life kept me busy, so I wasn't just sitting around and thinking about what I was missing. But that was just it! I *was* missing something, and I'd known it since I was a child. Looking back now, I can see that my injuries were a blessing in disguise. If I had continued down the golf road, I would never have met the people I met, had the experiences I had, or probably even discovered Alchemy, which ultimately helped me not only fill that void inside me but remove it completely.

I met Leta by chance through a mutual friend who thought I could help her with some business strategy and marketing coaching. Leta started explaining Alchemy to me in a very gentle and subtle way. Listening to her talk about Alchemy started to tie everything together, so that my life began to make more sense. I began to see why making a lot of money or the chasing the dream of becoming a pro golfer hadn't been my road to happiness. I began to see that the real path to fulfillment, at least for me, was my own internal spiritual journey. And it had nothing to do with the outer world.

In our meetings, Leta also explained to me that the life I had been leading was the natural path for a Wood Element person. Wood people naturally tend to go out to conquer the outer world in their youth. They like to "fight the good fight" on the side of justice and righteousness. They like to help others who can't help themselves. This is often a Wood person's mission. But as Wood Element people grow older, they tend to retreat from that focus on the outer world and turn inward to face their own internal conflicts. They begin battling their own their negative tendencies, regrets, and bad habits. This is often the path of the Wood warrior once the war is over. The warrior retreats and begins to tackle the battles on the inside.

Not long after starting to study Alchemy, I realized I had to leave my career as well as the safety and security of my current life. It wasn't that I didn't love all the work I was doing. I did love helping people in general, but I could see that they weren't actually happier in their lives just because they made tons of money.

The decision to leave was made before I even knew it… Once free from that career, I had an open road before me. I felt scared but at the same time limitless in my choices. It was a dark emotional time, but I was hopeful for the future.

I started to combine my strategic business coaching work with some Alchemy concepts. Alchemy made so much sense! It explained why, even when I could make things happen easily in the world (which had always been my experience), it never seemed to satisfy me. I combined the Alchemical concepts with my innate coaching skills and suddenly the work was inspiring and exciting me! After 20 years in advertising and marketing, I felt motivated again. I said goodbye to the advertising world and entered the mystery of the Alchemical world, becoming an Alchemical Life Strategist, a term that Leta and I made up after trying to explain exactly what I was doing, and how it was different from Life Coaching, therapy, or general advice giving.

Many people have come to me seeking help and guidance as well as answers to questions about their lives. But ultimately, that is not what I offer them. Instead I guide people inward where they will find their own help and guidance, learning to ask themselves better questions. Most people *think* they want to make more money, find a bigger and better job or house, or meet the love of their lives. But I like to help them see what they need most of all—to fall in love with themselves first, which means learning all about their internal world.

For the most part, money and the pursuit of money has always been a prevalent obsession in our culture. I sometimes explain to people that I can show anyone how to make money—that's easy! But it's so much more rewarding to show people how to find happiness in many facets of their lives. True happiness is something that no amount of money could ever buy. My personal opinion and the outcome of my experiences working with so many clients have shown me that to live an authentic life is much cooler than collecting material possessions. I say that completely without judgment because each person's journey is ultimately their own.

In the end, for me, that's really what Alchemy and transformations are about. Each person evolves in their own unique way, according to the path that magically unfolds, just for them. No two people are the same, yet we *are* all the same in that we all are capable of changing our lives. Working on this level of transformation with people is challenging and exciting. I appreciate the time I spend with each client because through this work, I am also transformed. Every day is a gift, and every day is a chance to learn, grow, and expand. The theory of Alchemy is easy enough to learn (hopefully this book will help you understand it better if we did our job well), yet it takes a lifetime, or many lifetimes, to practice and master it. However, more than anything, Alchemy is about being authentic and having fun along the way!

Alchemy is a modality for immortality. If we can return back to the original source, then we can continue to engender life.

—Master Jeffrey Yuen

Introduction

Alchemy is one of those trendy words that's used to describe all sorts of things these days yet has been around for thousands of years. But what exactly is Alchemy, and why are we suddenly so fascinated with this ancient esoteric word? Alchemy restaurants, Alchemy nail salons, Alchemy skin care products, Alchemy apartment buildings, Alchemy tattoo shops...the list goes on and on. Have you ever wondered what ancient Alchemy is *really* about? Have you ever wondered what all the pop culture references to Alchemy really mean? Is Alchemy really real?

If you have ever pondered about what Alchemy actually is, you've come to the right place. This book is about what we think the true meaning of the word Alchemy is, dating back thousands of years: *the transformation of the human spirit.* There are many ancient theories and books on the chemistry of elixirs and the exact firing times and rituals deemed necessary for the practice of Alchemy. This book is not one of those books. However, it is a book about profound transformation on a human scale.

Alchemy is not just a little bit of transformation at a time. It's not about the typical evolution of a human being. We are always, as humans, in a constant state of growth, and it is our inborn nature to change and grow. But the Alchemy we're discussing here is not about this comparatively slow evolution. Rather, it's about radical transformation—the kind that alters the basic fundamental properties of an object, like base metal being turned into gold. Or, in our approach, it's about a person becoming a completely different person. Alchemy is more akin to actual mutation into something new. Transmutation might even be a better word. So in terms of the time it takes for a species to evolve, Alchemy does happen quickly.

When we humans are born, we don't have the wisdom of experience to understand what is happening around us. We are reliant on our guardians, caregivers, our families, or with whatever our environments provide us, to guide our first steps in the world. We have no awareness of the dangers of the world at first. It's all good. But then experiences both good and bad happen, and we begin to form opinions about life and our own identity—who we think we are—based on those experiences and how we react to them. In fact, we are born into this lifetime to have experiences.

The methods we develop for handling the experiences of the outer world can be grouped into three main approaches.

1. The first and most common approach feels like you're all alone in a little boat on a big sea with no rudder, no sail, no oars, no motor. The waves come at you from the left, from the right, from the front and the back, and you get tossed this way and that.

   One minute the waves take you toward something great, amazing, and wonderful, and you never want that experience to end. But then the next waves come and they may take you to something bad, frightening, and terrible, and then you just want it to stop. Then other waves come, and suddenly life isn't so bad again. In fact, it starts to feel so much better. But then another wave comes, and it's not so great again. And so it goes, on and on.

> *In this scenario you are essentially the victim of your own life—a little boat being tossed around. Rudderless. No matter how many plans and goals you have, LIFE is always one step ahead of you. LIFE is happening TO you.*

You may spend your life trying to learn how to tame the rough waters. You may even spend your life trying to feel like you're in a really BIG IMPORTANT boat— trying to feel significant. You may expect and believe that good things will come, even in the bad times, because no matter how bad it gets, experience has proven that good will eventually come again. You think you have to take the bad with the good. Good luck always follows bad luck, and vice versa. Happiness and sadness flow and appear like your music library playing on shuffle for a whole lifetime. You just never know what is coming next, and you have no choice but to just react. These are all the things you tell yourself over time.

2. The second approach is somewhat less common, and results when life simply wears you down. Suffering is the path for you. Perhaps a string of bad experiences

—such as the death of a loved one, losing your job, health crisis, addiction, going into debt—seemingly came all at once, and now you believe that only bad will come your way. You're so depressed about the bad that's happened in your lifetime, you're actually attracting more bad. Perhaps you think you are constantly being tested, or that you are cursed, or that a black cloud has always followed you from birth. Your beliefs on the whole are negative, and the little boat you are in is always sinking. Perhaps you're going down slowly, but you are definitely always going down —not because you have to, but because you believe that only bad is coming to you. You don't know why others always get the good stuff and you get the bad, but there's so much evidence of bad, you're convinced that it's your fate and you keep attracting more and more of it. The other shoe is dropping—always dropping.

3. The third and rarest approach in life, which is certainly the road less travelled, is the Alchemist's way —to become a wizard in your own life. You are able to consciously create your life. You see clearly how to master reality. You believe good things will come if you create them. You are curious about life, and you approach living as a series of ongoing lessons, so even the so-called "bad" events are perceived as good experiences. You decide how you want to experience life, and you truly *believe* it can happen. Then you eagerly await the imminent arrival of greater things.

You don 't spend time doubting. You believe. You learn and practice to be vigilant with your mind. You manifest what you want, and your life flows with ease and grace. It is a powerful, magical way of life. It is mastery. Not good or bad ultimately—you simply walk in the footsteps that are in front of you. That is called Wu Wei.

Wu Wei is the way of the Alchemist.

In ancient times, some very wise human beings observed the nature of life and the natural human responses to it. Instead of trying to teach humans how to deal with the choppy waters of life without a rudder, sail, or oars, they decided to raise the bar! They wanted more, asked more, needed more—and they sought knowledge, rather than material items. These ancient Alchemists discovered a way to navigate the tumultuous waters in their lives and set sail to a particular destination of their choice. They set out to become what the Chinese called a "realized human being" or what's known as a "Zhen Ren" in Chinese. They were the wizards and magicians who cracked the code on how to transcend the life of an "average human being." We think it is truly a road worth taking.

> *Alchemy is mastery of your own life. It's not easy to achieve, but **anyone** can achieve it.*

The Eight Immortals of antiquity in China are considered to represent all the types of people in the world.

In today's language, the Eight consisted of a healthy young man, an elderly man, a woman, a wealthy man, an under-privileged, gender non-conforming person, a handsome prince, a creative artist, and a man with a disability. The diversity of the group is meant to show us that anyone, at any point in their lives, can start their journey and achieve mastery in their own lives.

> *You can be on your deathbed taking your last breath or recently born and taking your first breath and still discover the meaning of Alchemy.*

You just need the tools, the awareness, and some guidance—though that guidance could certainly come from within you.

Alchemy came to us through the guidance of many teachers and life experiences, but our true inspiration to learn more about Alchemy came from Master Jeffrey Yuen and his vast knowledge of ancient Alchemy.

We think of the *Nine Stages of Alchemy* as a roadmap that can guide us with specific directions that say *Now turn right here. And make a left there.* It's not the only way to get to our destination; in fact, anyone could invent their own Alchemical road map. However, we believe that a group of very wise people created a wonderful map for us a very long time ago—so why not follow the stepping stones they laid out for us to follow? It's just one way to get there. The ancient Alchemists did it, and they surely wanted us to give it a try.

Buddha created his own path. It led him to the Bodhi tree where he sat and found enlightenment. He didn't have a guide or a teacher to walk him through it. Anyone living in our times can theoretically do what Buddha did too!

Maybe those roads are a little less-traveled, but we like knowing a little bit about how to walk ours. We like a little linearity. "First do this. Then next do this. Third, do this." These Nine Stages can actually be done in any order, but in this particular order, everything can go more smoothly.

We will dedicate a chapter to each of the Nine Stages of Alchemy to lay out this roadmap and the set of linear directions developed by the ancient Chinese Alchemists. You could spend a lifetime studying these Nine Stages. We learned them from Master Yuen and have studied and practiced them ourselves and with others in our healing clinic for many years.

The Nine Stages of Alchemy have changed our lives completely. It's hard to explain without describing the whole process, which we are setting out to do in this book, but each stage is a paradigm shift that alters your beliefs. Your perception of the current reality will be adjusted because Alchemy asks you to walk through doors fearlessly —doors that open up new worlds, realities, and perspectives. In fact, because crossing these thresholds is so personally experiential, your way of Alchemy can sometimes feel like a lonely path. And in a way, it is, because you can't necessarily easily share what you're experiencing with others.

Alleviating that loneliness is one of the driving forces that led us to teach and write books. We hope to help you along your journey, and perhaps to feel the comforting presence of kindred spirits or old friends. If you would like to read more about the Daoist classics and companion texts, we have included a reading list at the end of the book for your enjoyment. In this book, though, we are aiming to keep the information as simple as we can, which is not to say it won't be challenging! It could feel easy to understand or may feel like it will take lifetimes to master.

Is Alchemy for You?

As we've been saying, Alchemy is the transformational process of becoming a realized human being—the wizard and creator of your own life. It's the process of finding your own rudder and your own sail and even creating your own breeze to sail on, so that you are no longer a victim of life's randomness.

As such, the Nine Stages of Alchemy may not be a journey you are ready to embark on right now. How can you know? Well, if you want to know whether Alchemy is a good fit for you, ask yourself this simple yet profound question:

Is there more to life than this?

If you think your answer might be yes, or at least you're already asking yourself this question, then you may be an Alchemist.

The typical human life begins with the growing up process. Then perhaps you start studying skills for a particular career. As you mature, you might look for a mate, try to secure some kind of home and material possessions, possibly raise children, and try to provide for them as best you can. Along the way, perhaps you save money for the kids' college, as well as for your eventual retirement in forty or fifty years. Whatever your particular adventure is, the next question is:

Does it feel like enough for you?

Perhaps your life feels like the character in the movie *Groundhog Day*, living the same day over and over, even though on the inside you are desperately wanting your life experience to change or hoping for a different outcome to develop. The cycle of death and rebirth continues over and over in this movie. The Buddhist name for this kind of cycle is called *samsara*. The idea of *samsara* is to be continually subjected to rebirth and suffering.

You may even feel that you have something important to offer to the world—something that only you can uniquely bring—but you just can't get enough momentum on your life's runway to take off. So you wait, and wait, and wait for the right moment to make changes in your life.

If you're curious about what more there can be to life beyond the cycle of the ordinary, if you want more answers, more meaning, more time for experiences, if you want to discover your full potential and actually *fly* in your life, then Alchemy could be for you. Alchemy is a powerful way to transform yourself from someone who is stuck to someone who can metaphorically soar.

Ego-less and humble, but focused and free
—limitless is what you will be.

This may all sound a little out there, a little "woo-woo" and bizarre to you, and it did for us too in the very beginning. But—and this is the biggest but of all time— that's only because you haven't been introduced to the concepts and theories of Alchemy yet—and even more importantly, the *experience* of it. So, let's start at the beginning—IF there truly is one. And is the end really the end?

We humans, according to the ancient Alchemists, are perfect, like gold. We just don't believe it. But in fact, we were born that way. We are born perfect, in so many ways!

–Leta Herman

Born Perfect

Some ancient Chinese Daoists believed that, as human souls, we are like gold—a metal that doesn't ever corrode or break down. You can bury it in the ground, leave it there for years, and when you dig it up and polish it, it hasn't changed a bit. Even if you heat it or freeze it, it doesn't change its *essential* qualities. It's as beautiful as it has always been.

The average person today thinks we're more like silver or worse, lead. We rust, corrode, break down, get holes in our bones, fall apart, and finally, disappear back into the earth. This mentality is how most people live today, in the modern-day world. We *fully expect* to grow old and decrepit. We expect to die, broken down and used up, at a fairly predictable expiration date. And guess what? Most people follow that exact path.

In ancient times, people often lived to be many hundreds of years old because they didn't have such limitations in their minds. The Immortals were believed to have overcome death. They were, at the very least, extremely long-lived and had very powerful life force energy.

We were very fortunate to have joined a group of Chinese Medicine practitioners on several trips to the sacred mountains in China where these venerable Immortals lived, practiced, and studied. In particular we visited the ancient mountainous homes of two famous immortals, Sun Si Miao and Ge Hong. Much of the work in this book stems from these great thought leaders and philosophers of antiquity. As old as their writings are, we believe they are key to our modern-day spiritual evolution. We have studied their works fervently, all the while knowing that it may take a whole lifetime to truly understand their teachings.

We twenty-first century humans are entering a new era—a time when modern science is giving us the means to *believe* that we can live well beyond 100 years. These days the question is not "**CAN** we live to be at least 100 years old?" The real question is: "Do we **WANT** to live to be 100 or 200 or 300 years?" Why would we want to? Or perhaps a better question is:

What is a life worth living?

Do you really want to live beyond a hundred years if you cannot enjoy living during old age currently? What's the point of living to be a hundred years of age if you're not happy today—no matter what age you are today? What's the point of living even fifty years more, for that matter, if you're not happy or healthy? The most important questions to ask yourself right now, today are these:

- *Am I truly living, or am I just going through the motions of life?*

- *Am I seeking internal growth or am I just constantly reacting to what is around me externally?*

Most of us would say that we want to be free, and to feel like there are no limitations or restraints on us. But we have been trained to believe that age is the biggest limitation on life experiences. We may go through our lives feeling alternately that we are too young, too old, or past the appropriate age, to experience a given dream or goal.

In our communal mindset, old age particularly equates to limitations of movement and doing the basic things we enjoy—like having sex, dancing the night away, or simply eating with a full set of teeth. Old age holds such a negative place in our minds that we would do anything to avoid it. Whole industries thrive on our fear of age-related decline. So much of our culture shuns the aging process and misses the actual *value* of old age, which among other things is wisdom.

What if we could live healthy, strong, and vital well into our 100's, 200's, or even 300's? What if growing old just meant more life experiences, but without all the baggage that weighs us down, even to the point where our backs get hunched over from all the weight we're carrying.

Accumulations and Concentrations

In Chinese Medicine, gerontology, which is the study of growing old, is a moot point. Age has nothing to do with whether you're healthy or not. You don't get pain because you're old. You don't get diseases because you're old. You get pain and disease because you aren't taking good care of yourself. Habits like overworking, eating unhealthily, or not exercising can lead to what Chinese Medicine calls *accumulations and concentrations*. These can be accumulations of blood, phlegm, energy, or even stuck emotions. And those lead to disease and to the body breaking down on many levels.

What happens then, when you get accumulations and concentrations in your body? You can get rigid in your habits of life. From a Chinese Medicine viewpoint, accumulations of chronic phlegm, for example, cause cataracts, weight gain, and artery blockages. These are heavy, depressing burdens to carry around in your body. And rigid habits can severely limit your sense of freedom in life. Guess what? Every time you say, "I can't do that because I'm too old," your body is hearing what you are saying, and it listens. Soon enough, it will start to comply. Your body starts believing any story you are telling it.

What if you didn't even think about it, and you just did what you wanted to do despite your age? You could start to be free of the kind of rigid habits and accumulations that are major factors in all of the diseases we think of as "age-related."

Let's look at arthritis. In the US alone, over 40 million Americans suffer from arthritis, or swelling and pain of the joints. Worldwide the number is 350 million. This is an accumulation of what we like to call toxic "gunk" in your body, breaking down your joints, limiting your movement, and forcing you to move and act in a certain slowed-down way. Western Medicine offers few options. Doctors prescribe medications to ameliorate the pain, which in the long run can cause the body to be in an even more toxic state.

In Chinese Medicine, you have more options. First, you could live well—eat well, move your body, move your Qi (energy) regularly, and live a happier life. In other words, you could not accumulate that "gunk" in your joints in the first place. But apparently that's easier said than done for hundreds of millions of people all over the world. We live in such an over-doing society. We over-eat, over-drink, and over-indulge in—just about everything. You name it, and we probably overdo it! Alcohol, tobacco, sugars, grains, wheat, processed foods, and even prescription drugs or street drug use—just to name a few.

We also over-do many kinds of activities, such as scrolling the endless feeds of social media, binge-watching TV and Netflix, work, gambling, and playing video-games. Even though there is nothing wrong with any of these activities in and of themselves, when they are out of control, they become taxing on the body. Even too much exercise and sexual activity, while they can move your Qi, can be taxing as well.

Many of these over-doing life choices actually encourage a sedentary life, where there's little physical movement or real social activity, and that can sometimes lead to depression or worse. This non-doing way of life is rising in epic proportions.

For the last 40 years as a culture in general, we've gravitated towards the "more is better" way of being. The truth is *more is just…more.* You eat more, you gain more weight. You drink more, you tax your organs more. You take more prescription drugs, you prevent your body from doing what it was designed to do, which is to heal itself. More, more, more is not always the way.

The good news is that you can change your lifestyle at any time along your life's journey. Even right before you take your last breath in this lifetime, you can improve your health and change your mind. In any and every moment of your life, you have two secret allies—free will and choice. You can always make the choice to change.

In Chinese Medicine, a practitioner can dredge the gunk out of your body using herbs, acupuncture, acupressure, or even the ancient practice of Stone Medicine. You can sometimes get a second chance at life—another chance to eat well, exercise right, move your Qi, open your heart to love and live a happy life with no stuck emotions. This kind of life doesn't accumulate more of the old blocks. It promotes well-being, movement, growth, and acceptance of change. It gives you more energy and more time in this lifetime to have happy experiences.

Throughout China, if you go to any park, you will see people of all ages doing Tai Chi, Qi Gong, and even square dancing together in the courtyards. The dancing, the music, and the energetic movement helps their Qi flow. They're not thinking about what they can't do. They're out doing what they *can* do. They're cultivating good habits, eating well, moving, laughing, and having fun in their lives. They form groups with other like-minded people, and they get together to move their bodies, their minds, their Qi—it's fun to watch as a spectator!

Let's take a look at chronic diseases, such as diabetes, gout, fibromyalgia, Lyme, ALS, MS, Parkinson's, and many other autoimmune diseases as well as the mental health issues that trouble modern people. Many of these stem from a breakdown of bodily functions over time as a result of more and more rigidity in habits of thinking and doing in life. Strong patterns of rigidity result from more and more stagnation and as a result possibly form a lot of *anger and bitterness*.

We have seen clients who are very ill and very "pissed off" at life, for lack of better words. They hold that anger, regret, and bitterness for the entire day—day after day, month after month, year after year. They simply can't let go of the negative energy. It is the story they tell themselves all the time, practically non-stop.

Stagnation, which is caused by slowed down Qi movement through the body, and stasis, which is caused by no movement of blood or Qi, are huge sources of illness. How can your body possibly get better if that's what's going on (or rather not going on) inside it?

To stay healthy, stagnation and stasis must be constantly challenged and motivated to shift, fueled by a person's desire to be healthy and well. If they are not challenged and shifted, that person is likely to be on the path to more serious disease.

Many societies around the world are moving toward a more sedentary lifestyle due to smartphones, computers, tablets, video games, and of course TV. In fact, today in the US the average person spends over ten hours a day consuming media in some capacity. That is time spent not *doing* anything and *not moving your body*. Sitting on our butts for hours and hours a day, over months and years is not good for our health. We need to move, breathe, and laugh. We need to be social and that means interacting with real people in real time...face to face. This is the human connection that we think is vital to a healthy society.

We often recommend to clients that they add more humor into their lives. If they must watch TV, we have them watch funny TV shows and movies—or even better, go to see live comedy with friends for a social connection—to begin to awaken that laughter and joy inside themselves again. Doing it with others is especially powerful and healing. You may think this corny, but *laughter is a great form of medicine.* It's certainly a way to shift the focus off of anger, bitterness, regret, and frustration, even if it's just for an hour or two. We do not underestimate the power of humor in a balanced life.

Deficiencies

Habits can often prevent you from doing what your heart really wants to do. This can lead to long-term deficiencies. Besides accumulations, deficiencies are the other cause of what we think of as "old-age" symptoms. These symptoms can really appear at any age but are most often associated with the kind of weakness and feebleness often seen in the elderly. Deficiencies can cause you to lose hair, lose tone in your skin, feel tired and weak, and have difficulty with digestion.

Avoidance of change is the number one cause of old age-like symptoms. Old habits take some effort to overcome, but you can in fact teach an old human new tricks! With Chinese Medicine, you can rebuild your vitality. Energy medicine can rebuild what has been drained over time, but only if a person is willing to fully embrace transformation.

> *Willingness to change is the answer. This is the secret to longevity: don't hold onto anything for too long! You need to let it go!*

If you want to be free of limitations, you need to unload all the mental and emotional baggage you're carrying around and clinging to. The Buddhists call this way of being non-attachment. Staying attached means you're unwilling to allow change. We become afraid of things or people going away. If it's too painful for you to imagine your life changing, that's a strong sign that you're either creating stagnation and stasis in your body, or you're literally draining your life force and becoming deficient.

The Secret to Long Life

The ability to change is a secret to long life.
And everyone has the ability to change.

This statement leads us back to our original questions but let's ask them in a more pointed way here.

Why would you want to live a long life if you are not happy today? Why not just die so that you can reincarnate and come back in a fresh new body and start over?

Another question to ask yourself is:

What do you believe happens after death?

Millions of people throughout history have lived and continue to live believing in reincarnation. Others believe that you can go to heaven after life on earth, so you can look forward to getting there instead of focusing on changing while you're alive. Still others believe nothing happens after death. Or in other words, you get to stop all the pain and suffering of being alive once you die. For some, these are valid plans. For others, well—not so much.

Alchemists are seeking more from life in the here and now, as if heaven is here on earth already. They are looking inside themselves to find peace, happiness, and a joyous, kind, and loving way of life.

> Everything you want is because you believe you will feel better in the having of it.

> **—Abraham-Hicks**

What if in this lifetime, you're having a really good life? It feels like you've finally figured everything out, and you're really getting the hang of all the joy, happiness, and magic life has to offer. In that case, what would it be like if you could take all of this and *really* fly in your life, using *all* the potential you have?

> *What if your life could feel like this life is the one? It's happening!*

Why then would you want to start all over when life is just getting *good*? The wisdom you've gained, the freedom you've found—why cut it short? What if you are enjoying living life? Then what if you could actually keep going?

Life doesn't have a ticking time bomb that kills you at some unforeseen moment. What if *you* control your clock? What if you can "transform" into death whenever you want, but on your own timetable. What if you could conceivably be 60 or 160 or 600 years old? If you're having fun, growing, changing, creating, and believing, then why stop?

What would happen if at age 75, 80, or even 90, someone told you, "Hey you are only halfway through your life. What are you going to do next?" What would you do next, if you believed that you had come to the end of your life, and you suddenly got 50, 60, or 100 more years to do whatever you wanted starting in that very moment in time? What would you do with this time?

Most people today cannot wrap their brain around that concept—not just yet anyway. We are here to tell you: We think it is possible. We can look to the ancient Alchemists for some direction to move us forward in the aging department.

The Alchemists

There were Daoist Alchemists in ancient China who believed that a human could become immortal. These Alchemists believed that our spirits are immutable, impermeable, and undeniable. Nothing can ever truly harm us, break us, or damage our spirits. We are *born perfect*.

However, we *think* we are vulnerable. We believe we are damageable. We feel that we can break down and die. Remember we talked about the immutable qualities of gold? What if, like gold, we truly didn't have to break down physically or spiritually? How would we live our lives then?

We have been heavily programmed by our parents, their parents, and their parents before them to believe that we are damageable. Somewhere along the lineage of history, we humans were convinced of our own vulnerability. Here is an important truth:

> *Our beliefs are the most powerful influence on our experience of reality.*

The Daoists would go so far as to say that whatever we think becomes a reality. So whatever we expect is what we get. If we expect decline and death, then that's what becomes real. If we expect health and longevity, even physical or spiritual immortality is within our reach.

Alchemy, then, was the name for the philosophy the Chinese Immortals (and those who wished to be immortal) followed, in which they were attempting to be free of the life and death cycle, to choose their own entry and exit times.

> *You exit into life from Source, and enter out of life back into Source. Ironically, most people think death is the exit when in fact it is just a beginning! Daoists believe death is the start of something new, not the end of something old.*

Many Alchemists believed that we come into this life to play and create, as well as to love. In Source, we are not separate—we are simply part of the whole. So in that dimension, there is no creation. There only *is*. That's it. Just *is-ness*. But what if we have a curiosity, a *wondering*? Then we can ask the question:

What would happen if...?

The exploration of this question *What would happen if*, cannot be done from the vantage point of being a part of "the whole." When we are still in Source before we are born, we can't have a sense of an identity because we are not separate from anything. In order to explore our curiosities, we have to be born—we have to become an individual, separated from the whole with our own individual perspective.

As humans our original impetus for being born was a desire to come to physical life to do something, try something, and to have experiences. We came into a body, with a singular mind and a spirit of our own. We're not just inhabiting the collective spirit of the whole. We can move our individual bodies in time and space. We can think thoughts that are completely our own, separate from the whole. We can have many, many thoughts, feelings, and desires, all of which can often be contradictory. And that's okay—it's all good.

Many Alchemists believed that we continuously reincarnate and get a new "curriculum" for each lifetime. This curriculum needs to play out, so that we can answer our *what would happen if* question, which is the question we asked before we were born into this time/space reality. To answer this question, if you can see this life on earth as a theater production that we are "playing out," you may be able to grasp more of the meaning of why "reality" itself is an illusion.

Think of it as a video game. As Player One, you get a "life," and you try some things, navigate around the levels, have some fun, try some more things out, and suddenly— oops! You make a "wrong" choice and die. You simply hit reset and the video game continues or starts again. No harm in trying that silly move or taking that wrong turn— the video game lets you try again, and again, and again until you get it right. There is truly no wrong choice in this game called life either, because you can simply press a "reset" button, and, like magic, you are reborn and ready to try again. You die, and then you are reincarnated.

This time, you have hopefully figured out some things and you try a whole new tactic in the game. You think, "Now I know how to do this." So this time you get further along in the game of life before dying and being reborn again. We play this game over and over, and each lifetime we learn a little bit more. For this reason and many others, the Daoists are not in a rush to get to the finish line, since there's nothing ahead of us except more and more expanding experiences.

And that's it. Lifetime after lifetime, we come back to this "illusion" of a life, and we try out something new. We have a new curriculum. We say, "Okay, so *this* time, I really want to experience this particular new way of being so that I can learn all about what that will be like."

Your Current Curriculum

You chose your curriculum before you were born, and so far, you have spent a considerable amount of time in your life trying to figure it out. This is where some knowledge of the Nine Palaces, also called the Nine Heart Pains, or The Nine Palaces of the Heart, can be invaluable.

Perhaps your curriculum is all about Love. You came to this lifetime to discover some of the deepest things that can be known about love—true love, deep love, unconditional love, or even unrequited love—your lessons will be about love, love, love. Or perhaps your curriculum is about greatness, expansiveness, or extraordinary experiences, and you spend your whole life pursuing these goals in every facet of what you do in life. Each one of the Nine Palaces or Nine Heart Pains is part of your curriculum of life experiences.

These curricula often correspond to what Chinese philosophy calls the Five Elements theory of energy, which in turn corresponds to our energetic temperaments in Chinese Medicine.

- A Fire person is the one who likely comes in with a curriculum about love and relationships.

- The Wood person comes to pursue greatness.

- The Earth person wants to know about caring and self-understanding.

- The Metal person is here to learn about respect and honor.

- A Water person wants to explore what it means to matter in the greater scheme of things.

In fact, we believe you choose the type of person you will be—your Elemental type—based on what is most likely to help you fulfill your curriculum goal! We also say your curriculum relates to your Nine Palaces. These are indeed the Nine facets that every human has to work on in their lifetime: Career, Relationship, Health, Wealth, Home, Children, Travel, Wisdom, and Prosperity.

If you start to combine a knowledge of the Five Elements, the Nine Palaces, and the Nine Stages of Alchemy, we think you will have the secret recipe for living an amazing and magical life! For this reason, we believe that understanding the Five Elements and the curricula of the Nine Palaces are "pre-Alchemy" courses of study. "Enrolling" in those courses will help you begin to truly know and understand yourself even better. Before you transform, you first need to have a clear picture of where you're coming *from energetically*. Then you can start to see where you're *energetically going to*.

To recap, your particular Five Element *stack-up*— which is the order of your Elemental makeup, such as Fire/Earth/Metal/Water/Wood—determines how you move energetically through the world. The Nine Palaces of the Heart is your curriculum, or what you will work on in this lifetime, and Alchemy is the mystery that allows you to live the most amazing life—the one you truly want to live.

The Chinese Alchemists believed that we need to honor our own curriculum. Each person's curriculum needs fulfillment. So you work something out every time you are in a lifetime. You *learn something* new or *more deeply* or in a *more meaningful way*. Maybe you find the perfect love, or you win the Olympic gold medal, or you discover the deep mysteries of quietude and solitude by living as a monk. There is value in every experience in each of the Nine Palaces of the Heart.

Everyone has a desire to complete their curriculum. It's innate. We all want to move towards a feeling of completion. What happens when you solve that initial question, that first curiosity…What then? When you actually fulfill your quest, do you just lie down and die, so you can come back and play again with a new life lesson to learn?

Once your curriculum has been completed, you *could* die and leave, and go back to the wholeness where everything is bliss. Who wouldn't want that? But, what if you don't want to go back yet?

You don't have to stop just because you learned the lessons you came to learn. You can choose to stay in your current lifetime and live like a Bodhisattva to help others. In Buddhism, a Bodhisattva is a person who lives like a saint to help others reach enlightenment. The purpose of the Bodhisattva role is to help others complete their mission in life and complete their curriculum. In Daoism, they talk about becoming a Zhen Ren—a realized human being, which is the Daoist version of an enlightened being.

Other options you may want to consider as reasons to continue living after you complete your curriculum could be to ask new questions, create new curricula, or indulge new curiosities, new creations, and new experiences, right in the life that you have been living and are still living now.

One of our dear Wood Element clients had come face-to-face with his mortality while recovering from a difficult illness that Western doctors had been unable to help him with, and we asked him why he would want to continue living in this lifetime. He answered:

Because there is still Greater in me.

It was the perfect answer for him. He was truly honoring his authentic Wood energetic self. Perhaps you too have more life to live? Perhaps you wish for something greater this lifetime? More love, more achievements, deeper understandings, more experiences...more joy?

As you grow older, in this lifetime, your wisdom can grow too, as you find your own answers to more and more questions. If wisdom is what you're after, then you'll definitely want to learn more about ancient Alchemy. When the Wisdom Palace is fulfilled, true simplicity in life is achieved. That simplicity leads you to return to the most important of the Nine Palaces, the Home Palace. To live beyond your curriculum of this lifetime requires a certain level of mastery of your own life. Here is one roadmap to this mastery. The next chapter contains one particular roadmap to get you there.

All we have to decide is what to do with the time that is given us.

–Gandalf, *The Lord of the Rings*

Understanding the Nine
Stages of Alchemy

T he Nine Stages of Alchemy are lessons in wizardry—
teaching you how to become a powerful wizard for
your own life. We are not talking Harry Potter kinds
of wizards and witches, although those were powerful too
—no judgments here! But this is a different kind of wizard.
The Nine Stages of Alchemy are a set of treatments,
exercises, and meditations that convey spiritual lessons for
you to learn so that you can master your own life. We like
to think of the wizard Gandalf in the *Lord of the Rings*
stories. He was very powerful, and yet he was on his own
unique journey. He was Gandalf the Gray, and then he fell
into a deep, dark chasm and returned as Gandalf the White.
He was on a path of evolution, transformation, and self-
realization. Even as a wizard, he continued the journey of
self-discovery.

Here is a list of our favorite pop culture legend
wizards: there's Merlin, Gandalf, Dumbledore, Morgan le
Fay, Yoda (who's a Jedi wizard), and let's not forget Glinda
the Good Witch. So many powerful wizards! All have the
ability to control energy all around them, and guess what?
So do you! Bonus, you won't even need a wand or fancy
staff to move forward.

Moving through the Nine Stages of Alchemy, you
become more and more realized, awake, and aware in every
aspect of your life so that you can stop being the little boat

tossed about at sea, and become the captain of that little boat, steering a powerful on-board engine, right towards the life you truly want to live.

The Nine Stages of Alchemy are grouped into three sets of three stages. We call these trinities. We have, over the years of studying and practicing, overlaid the Five Elements and the Nine Palaces on top the Stages of Alchemy and it seems to fit perfectly. While we have never read or heard this theory put forth before, they seem to weave together a more complete picture and understanding for us.

• Stages One through Three clear away what inhibits you from being truly free in your life and relate to the Palaces of Health and Wealth (the Wood Element), Relationships and Prosperity (the Fire Element), and Home (the Earth Element).

• Stages Four through Six take away the blinders that limit your perception of life, open your mind, and allow a truer life experience. They relate to the Palaces of Travel and Creativity/Children (the Metal Element) and the Palaces of Career and Wisdom (the Water Element). After fulfilling the Palaces of all Five Elements, you arrive at Stage Six, and you begin to fly in your life. We sometimes refer to mastering all your Five Elements as Connecting Your Circle. We think to be able to truly fly in your life would be a great reason to study the Five Elements in your own life.

- Stages Seven through Nine defy the limitations of the reality we all tend to believe in—such as the law of gravity, and the dictates of time and space—to allow for the true wizardry of time travel, flying, morphing, and becoming invisible.

We have witnessed many peoples' Alchemical journeys in our clinic. The results for doing Alchemy are often dramatic. It's the kind of magic that instigates deep, amazing transformations. Here are just a few very short stories from the many, many examples of the inspiring metamorphoses that our clients have gone through.

From Under Attack to Peaceful Bliss

John came to us complaining that he was being attacked by everyone in his life. At work he was proverbially stabbed in the back. His industry group all ganged up on him and attacked him publicly. Even his girlfriend was constantly upset with him for not being orderly enough. Over a period of five years, we did Alchemy together and his life completely changed.

Even during the First Stage of Alchemy, which took a whole year, his intense, crazy life completely transformed into a calm and peaceful experience. He stopped working in the industry group that was so contentious and found a new job that was no longer disruptive—he even had success becoming a spokesperson for his industry. He and his girlfriend worked things out and got married. As we continued our collaborative work on his Alchemical journey, the serious health issues, which had brought him to the clinic in the first place, also cleared up. In fact, his teeth, which had been scheduled to be pulled due to serious tooth decay, mysteriously recovered and his dentist could not figure out why. In fact, the dentist urged him to tell him what he had done to reverse the tooth decay. Now, many years later, John continues to pursue his work with Alchemy, and we will return to his story later in the book.

From Misery to Happy on the Way to Happiness

Jade was pretty much incapacitated with chronic Lyme and depression. She struggled with exhaustion, body pains, and a difficult array of baffling symptoms for many years. She had been to every healer she could find, including some who are considered to be the most respected healers in the world, but to no avail. She tried herbs, pills, magnets, divination, emotional therapy—the list is so long that she stops about there when she tells her old story. She was so confused as to what to do that she often struggled to find Divine guidance in the morning to decide what supplements to take from the many dozens that had been prescribed.

When Leta started Alchemy with Jade, it took some time to take hold. Strong patterns of fear and confusion had really taken over during her illness. Even after she began to feel better, the smallest relapse or symptom could frighten her deeply and trigger a cascade of stress that then impacted her health. It was a vicious ongoing cycle. Doubt and fear had her in a stranglehold. Alchemy works from the inside out, so, first, these ongoing fears and beliefs about her ill-health had to change—and slowly, they did. Within two years and only starting to work with the first three stages of Alchemy, she was able to begin living her life again —going to work, doing the things she loved to do that she'd abandoned, and returning to socializing on a much bigger scale. In the process, she was able to release the traumatic memories from her early life and began to change some toxic relationships that had been holding her back for many years. She continues to pursue Alchemy and has had many more big transformations along the way—a poster child for being happy on the way to happiness! We will also return to her story later in the book.

From Fear to Freedom

One of our very first Alchemy clients came to us over 16 years ago. She is a master healer in her own right, and at the time she began the Alchemy work, she had raised two children, one of whom had already gone off to college. She had a beautiful life, except for one horrible fear that was gnawing away at her. Her husband had cheated on her, and he seemed to be cheating on her again. She didn't have the courage to do anything about it at the time and was feeling quite miserable. We started Alchemy, and soon after she gained the strength to confront her husband. As we worked through the Nine Stages, she was able to go through a divorce and set herself free. She still lives in that freedom today.

Why Alchemy?

We often tell folks that we haven't seen anyone levitate off the clinic tables. Yet. However, we're looking forward to that one day. What we have seen is many clients begin to metaphorically fly in their lives. We're open to the idea that someday they'll actually defy gravity and truly fly, but we are satisfied that they can really take off and become wizards, mastering the trajectory of their lives and their destinies. This is what motivates us to do Alchemical Healing.

> The Heart is always seeking a sense of purpose. Experience is the Spirit finding purpose in life.

> **—Master Jeffrey Yuen**

The Nine Stages of Alchemy are helpful for people who fall into one of the following two scenarios:

1. Life is pretty good for me. I'm doing okay. I'm sometimes happy. But isn't there more to life?

2. Life is so, so bad. I don't know if I can go on. I can't remember a happy time in my life. What's the reason to keep going?

The preference is always to begin to do the steps of Alchemy for the number one scenario. We feel that it was really created for that purpose. In the second scenario, we have found that Alchemical Healing can often help a person who is really suffering and needs to deeply shift things. However, in those cases, we typically start with the Thirteen Ghost Points treatment, which is a powerful Alchemical treatment that clears away the things that haunt us from the past. We discuss this treatment at length at the end of this book. After the Ghost Points treatment, and perhaps the Heart Pains (a.k.a. Loving Yourself) treatment, and the passing of some time, it becomes much easier for these people to begin the actual path of Alchemy.

> On the path to self-discovery, there can be
> some dark patches, some forks in the road,
> or just some bumps. Your sincere heart can
> guide you along the way.

Alchemy is a path to self-discovery. You must have a sincere heart to engage in the Alchemy process. Are you willing to forgive and forget, for yourself and others? Can you let go of things from the past in your life? If not, Alchemy might open your personal Pandora's box. We have had many clients who had the desire to do Alchemy but did not yet have a *sincere heart* (we explain this term below). We encouraged them to pursue understanding their Elemental temperament before they began Alchemy. Being patient and kind to yourself is a skill many people need to learn or re-learn. If you feel that you do not yet possess a truly sincere heart or perhaps don't have much access to your heart (or maybe you don't particularly even understand the concept), it just may be that you need more work on the Nine Palaces of the Heart. This means digging deeper into your past, releasing what we call "tentacles" wrapped around your heart that hold you back from living the life you truly want. In this case, we typically start with a

Nine Heart Pains treatment, which invokes self-love and allows the heart to be vulnerable and sincere again. We also discuss this treatment at length at the end of this book.

Since we are here to help people understand as much as they can about the process of living the stages of Alchemy, let's take a look at the answer to what people often ask us:

What is a sincere heart?

The heart wants what the heart wants, right? Yes, and…Well, not always! If we have lived a life filled with fear, mistrust, and insincerity for years and years, it can eventually become difficult to connect to your real heart.

If you have lived your entire life based on lies on top of coping mechanisms on top of inauthentic living, how do you begin to untangle your life? How do you find your true self in the mid-stream of a life that is not serving you?

> *Ask yourself better questions, and keep asking! Keep seeking your truth in your own life.*

Not only do you need to ask yourself better questions, you need to seek better answers. To do this, you need to be honest and open—and yes humble—with your own heart. You need to ask it to be true and honest as you take a closer look at yourself. The gentle path of honest self-reflection is the most beneficial one you can take. It can be scary at times and fraught with obstacles, sometimes big ones, with many tentacles from the past. Perhaps some of those were put there by others, and even in those cases, with some work you can remove them from your heart.

Think of an octopus that has wrapped your heart up tightly in its many long arms. Those tentacles are old, unhealthy beliefs and ways of coping that have hooked into your heart. To free yourself you can't just rip the heart out. You must go deep inside your past, find where those beliefs have been hooked, and then gently but firmly untangle, address, and unhook them, so that you can completely release them from your present-day reality.

These tentacles around your heart are not only caused by pain that others have inflicted on you. They can be ones you've created. Sometimes these can actually be harder to move out of the way, since you have created them to protect yourself and your heart. Regrettable past events and actions that you have been a part of can be painful to remember. But if you're brave enough to keep looking, you will find that you know more than anyone else what is stopping you from moving forward in your life. You will find that the key to loosening the grip of these tentacles is to change your inner story. Sometimes a whole new dialogue created with a different set of language skills needs to be put into place in order to retell your life's story in a healthier and happier way.

Positive affirmations and loving thoughts about yourself can be so useful here. A growing self-awareness will allow you to release any pain, suffering, or lack of self-trust that you encounter as you pull off those tentacles. The *What Do I Really Want* meditation described later in the book can be useful here, along with some soul-searching journaling. We often suggest what we call a Hundred-Day Quest to being this process with a guide or group if possible. Undoing bad habits, rerouting negative thought patterns, and abandoning any harsh language that you use with yourself is key at this pre-Alchemy discovery point. All of this takes time and patience, but it is worth it. You are worth it! Remember this is all about you finding your sincere heart. A giant dose of self-love will work wonders to move you forward in your quest. Creating new habits is key here.

> To embark on the Alchemical journey, you must first acknowledge all the work you've already done.

Where are you in your life at this very moment in time? Where are you as you read this very page of this book? You may be someone who has arrived here after having sat in meditation for years to further your spiritual development. Or you may have been led here because you experienced extreme trials and tribulations that actually catapulted you forward in your self-realization. Or you may be starting out on your journey of self-cultivation. We've learned over our many years of work that there is no hierarchy in the realm of personal spiritual development and growth. It can come after years of hard work or harsh experiences, or it can appear in the blink of an eye. Your progress can be slow and steady or it can play leapfrog. A person who is "enlightened" by all definitions of the word can still be reduced to their most disempowered state by some trigger that they never worked through before. We have seen it happen over and over. It still happens to us from time to time. Setbacks and road bumps are just that— they require a moment of thought and an introspective breath, and then the transformation can begin again. Everyone keeps a different pace in their process of self-cultivation. In this phase, the "no judgment" concept is important to embrace, both of yourself and of others.

We always chuckle when we think of Jack Kornfield's book, *After the Ecstasy, the Laundry*. As he shares in his story, we often come to huge realizations in our lives that give us a sense of having *arrived* at our destination! But then…it's back to the seemingly mundane and, for some, even boring daily grind of life. We all need to do the laundry after our meditations are done! It's as if we rise above the clouds and see clearly far and wide, and then as suddenly as the clarity comes, the clouds reform and we're "Back on Boogie Street," like the title of the old Leonard Cohen song.

> *The present moment is the only moment*
> *that truly matters in life.*

We can try to look at it all as if we are simply going through circles—many, many circles—throughout our lives. We don't really move through life in a linear fashion, as much as our left brains might try to lead us to believe that. We go forward, and then we circle back. We move right, we move left, then come to forward again. We think we've advanced, but then we can retreat back to before the starting point, in the blink of an eye. Just recently, something triggered a memory for Leta of being scolded, and just like that she could hear the words "bad, bad, bad" (for sticking a napkin in a candle flame when she was only three).

We have worked through so much of this lifetime's emotional baggage (Stage Two of Alchemy helps you unload it all), but when Leta was triggered, there she was, suddenly back in that memory—and existing inside that time all over again. Her mind had instantly circled back and it felt real. When we get triggered like that, we have to work through it again and re-experience all the uncomfortable feelings of having been scolded, shamed, and afraid. After doing so much personal growth work, how did we end up there— again? Does the work ever get completed? The past moment interrupts our present moment, and it feels real.

The good news is, we do think it gets easier the second, third, and maybe fourth times around. And certainly, as you progress through the Stages of Alchemy, each stage helps you let go of more and more of the past. What we've learned most through doing the Stages of Alchemy is that it is a constant process!

> *If you are alive, you are evolving. If you are evolving you are growing. If you are growing, you are changing.*

Life is for the living. You cannot fully escape life. Even as you're moving through time awake and aware, something can still jarringly awaken a memory from the past, and then another and another. You can find your bliss and then "shit happens"—or maybe more to the point, you happen—you, as a being with a life history. So what did Leta do when Stage Two popped up again? She worked through it. She sat. She meditated. She did the homework for Stage Two again. She experienced it all over again. And then it was done. She let it go. And she felt so much lighter and freer! It was easier this time around than the last time, but it still was work. Will it pop up again? Maybe. Who knows? But she is releasing it back to the void between heaven and earth, back into a place where it does not scare her and does not affect her life.

Discover Your Authentic Path

At any point in your life, you may have already worked on these stages in other ways. Many of us have experienced some of these Alchemical Stages throughout our lives without consciously setting out to do that. And we've grown and changed accordingly. **You don't really need a book or us or even a wise old Chinese Alchemist to tell you how to do Alchemy. There are infinite ways to transform.**

The difference is that when you do the Nine Stages of Alchemy with conscious intent, you do the steps in order and you stay engaged with them while you're doing them. The emphasis here is on *staying engaged.* We refer to this as keeping the thread going. We have clients who come to us once a year to do their work, and in the interim they are able to stay engaged and connected to their Alchemy journeys on their own. They go home, and they work on the Alchemy stage they are in every day. They may have meditations, visualizations, affirmations, and homework that we have created for them specifically. The time they spend on this work is important to them. It's a priority. They stay connected to it. It may sound serious and it can be—but fun, excitement, love, joy, and thrilling times are also a big part of it. Laughing and being silly is also doing "the work."

On the other hand we have people who come to us once a week to do this work, because a week is how long they can stay engaged before they lose the thread of their practice and slip back into their so-called old life. They are happily working at their pace, being engaged and alive for as long as they can at a stretch. It is a process. It's a journey that is about being joyous, kind, and loving to yourself. Respecting the journey is a wonderful thought here.

One point to pay attention to is the important aspect of Alchemy that asks you to take time to step out of your normal life and *watch yourself* as you're living your life. We often refer to Eckhart Tolle's wonderful idea of becoming "the watcher" and recommend his book, *The Power of Now*, to enhance your Alchemy work. As the watcher, you carefully witness your life, tracking your inner and outer realities as you work through your Alchemical process. You may watch yourself let go of the emotional baggage of this lifetime in Stage Two or from previous lifetimes in Stage Three. You may see yourself opening up your brain to new ways of experiencing the world in Stages Four and Five. You may get to watch yourself truly flying in Stage Six.

When we work with people going through the stages, we are also watchers of those transformations on their behalf. Having an outer witness who can validate your own witnessing of your transformational experience is reassuring and encouraging. One essential component of the Alchemical process we have developed at the clinic is a series of coaching encounters we call our Alchemical Life Strategy sessions. These sessions address the complexities of life, often through the lens of assessing our clients' Five Element stack-up and the state of their Nine Palaces. Focused guidance like this can help them stay connected and strengthen the Alchemy thread, if needed, through observation, honesty, and motivational conversations.

Through this work, we have discovered that the Nine Palaces play a much bigger role in a person's progress than we originally thought. In Chinese philosophy, every human being has nine areas they must address in their lives to feel a sense of balance and completion. As we mentioned before, this system goes by a few different names—the Nine Palaces of the Heart or the Nine Heart Pains. We often simply refer to them as the Nine Palaces. Each individual "palace" may also have multiple names or references. Here are the translations of the names we prefer in numbered order:

1. Career/Knowledge

2. Love/Relationship

3. Health

4. Wealth/Abundance

5. Home

6. Travel/Global

7. Children/Creativity

8. Wisdom

9. Prosperity

Alchemical Life Strategy sessions use this framework of both understanding your particular Five Element nature and assessing the strength of each of your palaces as a way to put your transformation into practical day-to-day terms. This gives you the tools and momentum you need to head down the runway, and begin to take flight in your life.

Understanding each Alchemical Stage is somewhat challenging. If you approach it from the vantage point of the Knowledge Palace, which is about learning and assimilating information, it can feel like jumping into a dark, bottomless chasm. However, if you come at it from the vantage point of your Wisdom Palace, you are simply walking through the stages yourself and experiencing them, and gaining your wisdom from those experiences.

When we do Alchemical treatments with clients, we are working with acupressure points and sometimes moxibustion, which is an ancient technique that involves burning a very small nugget of the herb mugwort or *artemisia vulgaris* on meridian points to slowly warm them. These treatments can help a person activate a particular stage.

However, Alchemy is not just about being coached or about receiving specific treatments for each stage. You can also move through Alchemical Stages by doing Qi-Gong, or deep long-term meditation, or Stone Medicine, or many other specific methods. Chinese Medicine treatments are not the only way. They are part of the method *we* primarily use because we have a Chinese Medicine clinic and have chosen this path.

> *Because Alchemy is a path of self-discovery, each person needs to find the modality that fits them best. There is no one way; there is only your way.*

Once you understand the theories of each stage, you can find what the Chinese masters call the "superior" points for that stage. Or if you're working with another modality, you can find the superior herbs, the superior stones, the superior meditation, or the superior Qi Gong exercise that may help you move through that stage. When you routinely work with a superior point, an herb, a stone, a meditation, or Qi Gong exercises, you establish a connection or communication with your higher self and with the Divine. You want the point to break through your ingrained patterns and create a reaction. Then transformation will occur.

We love to give our clients homework that helps them continue to stay engaged and working through their current stage, wherever they are in their journey, until we see them again. You will find many examples of our "assignments" in this book. However, while we are going to describe, in detail, the process of Alchemy here, we have chosen to resist the urge to get into the finer details about each of the Alchemical treatments. Those are best taught in Alchemical healer trainings because they are based on the fundamentals and ancient theories of Chinese Medicine. Perhaps that will be our next book! What's more important overall is the concepts behind this work rather than the specific points, herbs, meditations, or Qi Gong exercises. What we set out to do was to help you see the possibilities and the challenges so that you will be prepared as you can be to move through the stages.

With that kind of preparation, what you will find as you journey through the Nine Stages is that each stage evolves naturally. Flow is a great word here. The stages will flow from one to the next, overlapping each other. In other words, you can't "force" yourself through a stage any faster or slower than you actually need to go, although many people try! Most people want to rush and hurry along as fast as they can. They may feel like they need to catch up on a part of their life they have missed out on, or have kept buried, hidden, or stagnant for so long. Sometimes it's ego, sometimes it's fear, sometimes it's just impatience. People start to see early results from Alchemy and get excited and want to move very quickly through to the next stage. Neither slow nor fast is better or worse. Again, the pace is highly individual!

We are working now with a lovely woman in her eighties who started Alchemy about a year after her husband died. She was devastated by his loss and had completely shut down with no will to live her life without him. However, with Alchemy she started experiencing a true renaissance in her life—embracing art, writing, photography, and even publishing her creative works. She said to us recently, "In case you haven't noticed, I'm in a bit of a hurry here. I've been waiting my whole life to do this!"

We get it! Everyone loves to begin moving again once the traffic jam begins to clear. It's human nature!

Alchemy requires engagement, but the actual movement through the process happens organically. The changes come from consciously engaging in the work, but your consciousness never forces the change. You just change. Almost effortlessly, magically, easily. You find yourself in a new place, suddenly—realizing that everything is different. It's a new vantage point from which to see your life. You actually feel different. Many longterm issues and struggles simply melt away. Those are the "ah-ha" moments we all are craving and seeking. Suddenly we have new eyes to see a whole different array of choices that are now in front of us.

Since the flow from one Alchemical Stage to another is so organic, how do we know when that transition is occurring? Usually, we know a person is ready to move onto the next stage when they come in already talking about the next stage before receiving the treatment or before we've even talked with them about the next stage. Not only are they ready to move on, they actually *have* moved on to the next stage on their own. The Alchemy treatments we do are just signposts; often the person is already on the road and passing the signpost even as we prepare to do the next treatment. We can only be the gentle guides, giving them an explanation of the next set of steps along their path.

Preparation

Before you launch into the Nine Stages of Alchemy, it's a good idea to begin your own meditation practice.

> *Self cultivation is the attention you give to yourself on a higher level. And yes, it is selfish. But in a good way.*

Alchemy may seem selfish—but you can think of it as centering in the self instead of "self-centered." You may already have a robust meditation practice. If so you can use this section to embrace a visualization meditation based on traditional Daoist meditations. If you have tried to meditate but have found it to be a difficult practice to sustain, many people have told us this type of meditation is much easier to do than other kinds. We strongly encourage you to begin with a simple relaxation meditation, and the one that we are about to introduce you to definitely qualifies as that.

The Alchemical meditations draw you to an inner focus: you could also call it Inner Alchemy. This is a necessary attribute to cultivate, since the consolidation of Qi and the movement of Qi in the body requires practice and patience. Inner Alchemy builds Qi in your stomach, or what we call your Alchemical cauldron, and the proper "firing" times of this cauldron, which we will explain later in the book, are very important to your progress. Alchemical meditation is a good place to start your practice, and a good place to come back to as a touchstone if you wander off your path. In fact, we feel that this first meditation is also the best way to begin every other meditation in this book.

In the beginning, we recommend doing this meditation for about 15-20 minutes every day. It is an especially good one to do at the beginning of the day. Once you become very familiar with this type of relaxation meditation, you can get into this state of relaxation very easily in other meditations, sometimes only taking a couple of minutes.

You may listen to this recorded meditation as a companion to this book at the Alchemy Learning Center website: AlchemyLearningCenter.com.

Relax Your Body, Clear Your Mind, Open Your Doors Meditation

The goal of this meditation is to let go of your resistance by relaxing your body and clearing your mind, so that you may open all the doors of possibilities in life. In order to attain the inner focus common to all Alchemical meditations, you must begin to lessen your focus on your outer experience of the world. Once your body and mind are in a calm and clear state, it will be easier to open up to each type of meditation.

This meditation is often done from the top down, though can also be done from the feet up to the head, which is more energizing. We recommend you begin with the top down approach because it has a more calming effect, starting with your head, then moving through your torso, and finally ending with your legs and feet.

Sit comfortably in a chair with your feet on the floor and your hands resting on your thighs near your knees. If you wish to sit cross-legged on the floor, let you hands rest in your lap in this simple hand mudra (hand formation). Create a small bowl with the palm of one hand, and put the back of your other hand inside it, as if you're ready to accept heaven's gifts. Rain is traditionally considered a gift from heaven, so you can imagine rain resting inside your cupped hands.

Traditionally for males (or those who have yang-dominant energy), the left (or yang) hand rests in the right hand, and for females (or those who have yin-dominant energy) the right (or yin) hand rests in the left hand. We explain yin and yang dominance as it traditionally relates to gender in the Stage Four chapter.

Close your eyes and breathe in slowly with your tongue touching the roof of your mouth. Now focus on the area around your eyes. Gently ask yourself, "How does the area around my eyes and temples feel?" Does it feel like it can relax easily? Or do you feel an area of resistance and tightness?

As you exhale, you allow the area that you feel might be tight and tense around the eyes to relax. Imagine a gentle wave of water or smooth and calm energy slowly flowing down over your eyes and cheeks, washing away all the tension you may feel.

As you breathe in again, focus on the area around the jaw. This is the area where we often hold our determination to make things happen, which is a form of resistance. If your jaw is clenched or you feel any tension in the area, slowly breathe out and relax that area. If you feel like you're pushing to make things happen in your life, let that pushing go while you relax that area, allowing yourself to *trust* that it will happen because you are creating it.

Breathe in again and notice if there are any other areas in your body tensing up, especially in your legs. They might be tensing up as you try to relax those areas of the jaw. If you feel any tension in the legs when you relax above, exhale and relax the areas that are tensing up below, which helps you relax the jaw area.

Next slowly breathe in and relax the area around your throat, down your neck, and into your shoulders, while mindfully allowing your lower body to stay relaxed as well as you exhale.

On your next inhale, breathe into your shoulders and chest and on the exhale imagine water or energy moving down your chest and into your belly.

Now breathe deeply into your belly. Scan your abdomen to see if there is any tension, resistance, or fear there. If you feel an area of tightness, ask yourself what you're determined to prevent from happening or what you're afraid will happen. On your exhale, release that tension, knowing that everything is going to be fine. You do not need to prevent something from happening. Think about what you want to happen instead while you release this tension.

Breathe in again and focus on your limbs. If there's any tightness or resistance in your arms or legs, give yourself a moment to allow them to relax with your exhale.

Take a few minutes to scan your entire body again. Is there any tension in your body? If so, what is this resistance about? Focus on that tightness and ask yourself what it's about. Then breathe in and let it go with the exhale.

Now that your body is relaxed, imagine your entire body is covered with tiny little doors. These are the doors that allow you to receive cosmic energy from the universe when they are open. They tend to close up whenever you are tense, stressed, or in a fearful state.

Take a moment to check for any closed doors. What areas of your body feel closed down to the cosmic energy of the universe? Where is the resistance? These might be the same areas where you were holding tension and resistance in your body. These places are where those tiny doors are closed up tight.

Now imagine slowly opening these doors back up. Allow the cosmic energy of the universe to flow through these doors into your body. This is the energy that will empower you throughout the day.

You can imagine this energy flowing in a few different ways:

- If you are a *visual person*, you can imagine a lovely yellow or white light shining in through the doors and filling you up with light.

- If you are an *auditory person*, you can imagine the most beautiful music coming in through these open doors and filling your body with sound.

- If you are a *sensory person*, you can imagine energy flowing in through the doors and filling your whole being with warmth.

Breathe in and allow this energy to fill you up entirely and strengthen your ability to do whatever you want to do and have to do today.

Now focus on your intention for the day. In this moment, imagine you already have whatever it is that you desire. What thoughts arise in your imagination? What are you doing? How does it feel? What kind of person are you now that you already have what you want? How does it change your identity to be that person doing whatever has arisen? Take a few moments to visualize yourself receiving all that you want.

When you are finished, slowly open your eyes and see the present *now* moment around you. Breathe slowly. You may want to smile. You are right where you need to be in this very moment.

The Five Elements and the Nine Palaces of The Heart

Before we go any further explaining the Alchemy journey, we first want to be sure that you're familiar with the three major Chinese philosophical concepts we've been referencing so far. We have laid out a brief overview of these important concepts in this section. Please feel free to refer to this section as you're reading through the book, as we will mention these ideas numerous times.

If you would like more information about these concepts, we suggest you read our previous two books on the Five Elements: Connecting Your Circle and The Energy of Love.

We are also currently finishing up another book on the Nine Palaces of the Heart, from the point of view of the Alchemical Strategist. In addition we've created two online classes to further familiarize you with the Five Elements and Nine Palaces in theory and practice. You can find these classes at the Alchemy Learning Center website: AlchemyLearningCenter.com.

- **The Five Elements**: This is the way we describe the five essential types of energetic movement in the universe.

- **The Nine Palaces of The Heart**: These are the nine essential lessons in life that must be attended to in order to live a balanced life and attain peace.

- **The Magic Square**: This is the story of Yu the Great

and the paradoxical order of the Nine Palaces. This explains why Home, although it's technically the fifth palace, is also the last palace we complete.

The Five Elements

The Five Elements are based on the concepts of Yin and Yang. *Yang Energy* is energy that travels upward and outward. *Yin Energy* is energy that travels downward and condenses inward. Because Yang and Yin are in constant motion and flux, the Five Elements are five different ways the Yang and Yin energy play out in the world.

- **Wood**: When Yang energy rises out of Yin, it has an upward strong energy that can break through barriers. However, like a sprout in the Spring, it is ultimately a little fragile. Wood is out front, a leader with strong opinions, who likes to spearhead new projects.

- **Fire**: When the Yang energy reaches its pinnacle, it begins to branch out and start to tip downward into Yin, like a flower opening and blooming in mid-summer. Social, energized, optimistic, needing to be admired and loved, focused on beauty and harmony, Fire wants to be the lover in the world.

- **Earth**: When the Yin and Yang energy are balanced, we have the Earth element. Social, community-oriented, care-taking, and hospitable, Earth is at the center of everything and is the glue that holds us all together.

- **Metal**: When Yin Energy begins descending out of Yang Energy, it has a withdrawn aspect but is still a force to be reckoned with. Observant, conscientious, exacting, conserving, and deserving of respect, Metal wants to connect in whole-hearted sincerity or not at all.

- **Water**: When Yin energy condenses to its furthest downward point, it gathers power to shoot up into Yang again. Water alternates between quiet and resting for long periods followed by periods of intensity. Water wants to matter to others and ultimately, to themselves as well.

Now as we introduce you to each stage of the Nine Stages of Alchemy, you'll see that each stage has a resonance with one of the Five Elements.

The Nine Palaces of the Heart

The Nine Palaces are the nine areas of a human's life that must be attended to for a sense of fulfillment and completion in life, which is sometimes what we call your *curriculum*. This may explain why sometimes they're referred to as the Nine Heart Pains, because being unable to achieve fulfillment in any of them causes much heart pain. Here's a short description of each palace.

- **Career/Knowledge**: The knowledge you gather is put together into skills that then become your career, which is the way you offer yourself to the world. It's a Water Element palace.

- **Love/Relationship**: We begin life with the relationships we are given through our birth circumstances. However, as we become independent, we have choices about who we choose for our relationships. Love and unconditional love experiences belong here. It's a Fire Element palace.

- **Health**: The most basic and fundamental of all the palaces, our Health is paramount to our survival. We may choose to protect our health or perhaps endanger it or simply ignore it. This palace is an important starting point for everyone. The strength of our health palace is key to our ability to acquire good experiences in all other palaces. It's a Wood Element palace.

- **Wealth/Abundance**: Having a sense of abundance, no matter how much money or how many material objects you have accumulated is the core issue here. Being able to allow abundance to flow to you is the focus of this palace. It can be challenging to unravel the ultimate truth of our Wealth Palace because our modern society is so materialistic. It's a Wood Element palace.

- **Home**: Having a sense of belonging and peace in your life is what the Home Palace is all about. We like to call it, "Home with a capital H." This is the last palace before your life's journey transitions towards completion. It's an Earth Element palace.

- **Travel/Global**: A sense of adventure and knowing somehow that people all around the world are fundamentally the same—that's the spirit of the Travel Palace. The global perspective is a human existential theory that we are all sharing the same experience, but just coming to it from our individual perspectives. The commonness of human experience is key here. It's a Metal Element palace.

- **Children/Creativity**: This palace concerns our ability to create new life as humans, as well as the ways we relate to our creations of every kind. How will your creations be viewed by others in future generations? What will your legacy be? Think of it as your cosmic ripple in the universal pool of time and space. There's a sense here of *either it's meant to be, or it's not.* It's a Metal Element palace.

- **Wisdom**: We gather knowledge through studies and experiences, but we don't achieve wisdom until it coalesces into a deeper knowing. This palace differs from the Career/Knowledge Palace in the sense that Wisdom flows from living and having experiences, not necessarily from book learning or the acquisition of skills. It's a Water Element palace.

- **Prosperity**: From our sense of abundance, a deep desire to give back to the world is born, a sense of generosity and a desire for creating a legacy for future generations. This palace is a challenge for many people, yet it is foundational for human existence. Think of acquiring wealth or resources like time, money, fuel, or land and freely giving this bounty to those who may be in need, without any strings attached. Can you detach freely and willingly from what you have in order for someone who has less than you to receive? It's a Fire Element palace.

The Magic Square

The ancient legend of the heroic king, Yu the Great begins with a great flood. Yu the Great climbed into the mountains and drilled holes into the rocks to drain the water away.

As the story goes, he conquers the flood, and soon afterwards a mystical tortoise appears on the banks of the river Lo. On the tortoise's back are the strange markings in the formation of the mystical magic square.

The markings aren't just an interesting design. The magic square is really magic because of the numbering system in it. Each row and column of the square adds up to the number fifteen.

The part we're interested in here is that the order of the Nine Palaces corresponds to the Magic Square. If you would like, you can think of it as a game board where the objective of the game is to get to the center square, but you first have to journey around the outside and complete your assigned tasks at each square.

MAGIC SQUARE

4. WEALTH/ABUNDANCE	9. PROSPERITY	2. LOVE
Wood	Fire	Fire
3. HEALTH	5. HOME	7. CHILDREN/CREATIVITY
Wood	Earth	Metal
8. WISDOM	1. CAREER/KNOWLEDGE	6. TRAVEL/GLOBAL
Water	Water	Metal

You start at the bottom center with the first palace, the Career/Knowledge Palace, and proceed in numerical order through each palace. Once you finish your eighth square, you're allowed to receive access to the final square in the center, which was given the number five, exactly halfway between the number one and the number nine. Therefore, the Home Palace, number five—the one that's in the center of all the others—is the last palace in your Nine Palace curriculum.

As we said earlier, we wanted you to have some understanding of the basic principles of Alchemy before we dove into the actual Nine Stages. We can't think of a better place to dive in than from the doorway of the Home Palace. So please take a breath, get yourself a glass of water or a cup of tea, and be ready for just about anything!

I'm recognizing
that there's more
to my life than
what I'm
experiencing right
now.

—Master Jeffrey Yuen

Stage One: Initiation

In this book, we are not actually standing by your side doing physical treatments with you, but we want to share with you how you can do this work yourself–by watching your own thoughts, being vigilant with your mind, and practicing Alchemical meditations. Perhaps you can imagine that we time-travelled to you and showed you personally if you like; we don't mind at all. But for this book, we want to make clear that you actually have the ability to work on the many facets of Alchemy on your own. We will explain each of the Nine Stages of Alchemy in turn for you to understand and contemplate. As we go through each of the stages, we will give you some exercises and several theories to consider that can help you move through each state of being. You can then work through the exercises and meditations on your own time and at your own pace. Even if you finish reading this book in one sitting, we suggest you take your time working with the content on your own schedule, which may be years or lifetimes! You can always seek out an Alchemical practitioner too.

Stage One is quite complex. It may be one of the most intricate and challenging stages for most people. Due to that fact, we want to underscore what we said above about taking your time with this stage in particular and working through it as thoroughly as possible. We see a fair number of people who have done a lot of this work already using other modalities, but many haven't and are, instead, eager beginners. So it's important to be honest with yourself as you go through this process of dipping into self-awareness practices and self-cultivation. *Honesty is the best medicine* is the operative phrase here. Always keep in mind that we are preparing the mind, body, Qi, and spirit to move through the stages of Alchemy, and there is never a need for speed in the voyage to find your authentic self.

> *You enter with sincerity and a willingness to change your life.*

–Master Jeffrey Yuen

The Elemental Theme for Stage One—Wood

Each of the first Five Stages of the Nine Stages of Alchemy has an Elemental Theme. The overall theme of Stage One is that life *can* be easy. This is the very essence of Wood energy, and the themes in this stage require that your Wood energy be allowed to feel flowing and free inside you. Everyone has access to all Five Elements within. Wherever Wood falls in our personal stack-up, our aim is to feel "free and easy" when we access the Wood Element inside us. We can easily overcome obstacles in our way and allow for greater ease in our life. This doesn't mean we have to give up on any of our dreams. In fact, quite the opposite. We must embrace what we truly desire and believe anything can be possible. This is the Wood process of removing obstacles, like a young sprout that must find its way up through the obstructing dirt and rocks as it starts to grows. The Wood Element is the Element of hope. We must have hope in our lives to begin Stage One of Alchemy.

The Five Steps of Stage One

There are five steps contained within Stage One:

1. **Entering the Mystery Gate**–This is the entranceway into Alchemy.

2. **Asking Yourself the What Do I Really Want Question**–Finding clarity in the newfound light at the end of the dark tunnel.

3. **Aligning Your Heart with What You Really Want**–Knowing what you really want, and being brave enough to allow yourself to truly want it.

4. **Releasing Rebellious Qi**–Resistance, or what we call Rebellious Qi, comes up as a result of knowing what you want. In this step, you now release that resistance so that everything can come to you easily. There is no need to fight for what you want.

5. **Journeying to Your Higher Self**–Once you've stopped all fighting, you can connect and commune with your own higher self, face-to-face.

Step One: Entering The Mystery Gate

The very first step in Alchemy is the willingness to embark on this journey–your initiation. It's marked with a point in Chinese Medicine called *The Mystery Gate* or *The*

Dark Gate. You must have the willingness to enter through the dark gate—and *enter into the Mystery, with a capital* M.

There is often an aspect of existence that we don't understand. Some people describe it as the veil. To embark on the road of Alchemy, we have to want to peek behind the veil. You could think of this as the willingness to walk into a dark tunnel with *the belief* that there will be light at the end of the tunnel, even though you don't see any light and you're forced to feel along the unknown sides of the tunnel in the dark, to find your way. For a lot of people, that is tremendously scary. Someone might encounter frightening things in the dark tunnel or, worse—inside the darkness of us! What if, in the tunnel, we run into bats, slimy things, biting things, dangerous things, who-knows-what things! We might put our hand out and touch something that feels unnerving and not have any clue what it is.

The Mystery inside each one of us and the Great Mystery of the Universe are similar. If you can overcome your fear, and embark on this journey with some *Trust* that you are safe and will always be safe, then you will be able to enter into Stage One of Alchemy. Some of us aren't ready. We haven't yet mastered a sense of safety and, what we call, *Trust with a capital* T, the kind of Trust that comes from deep inside us. When you do enter the Mystery Gate, you're walking through the dark to the light. This light is what allows you to enter into a state of *divinity*.

We suggest engaging this step of Stage One by doing a meditation where you visualize walking through this mysterious gate and into the dark tunnel. It may take a few times or many times to really become engaged in this meditation.

We explain this meditation in detail later in this chapter. We have also recorded a guided meditation called Entering the Mystery Gate, which you may listen to as a companion to this book. You can find it on the Alchemy Learning Center website: AlchemyLearningCenter.com.

Facing the Fear of the Unknown

As you visualize walking through the tunnel, it's completely fine and normal to feel fear arise. Even if you have a general sense of safety inside yourself, you may still feel it. Am I safe? Who am I really? Am I good inside? Am I okay? Can I really do it? Why am I here?

> *All fear comes from the fear of dying. What we are afraid of is the unknown. We want certainty in life.*

–Master Jeffrey Yuen

Paradoxically, fear is nothing to be afraid of. Fear can even be your friend. It can sometimes be saying to you, "Hey, let's be a little cautious here. Let's use caution while entering into something new." What should I look out for? What should I put my attention on? What is this all about? All of these thoughts are natural and should not cause stress or lead you to even more fear!

One of the things we do in the clinic during Stage One treatments is to acknowledge the fear if it comes, and add moxibustion, which is the burning of a little bit of mugwort herb, on a specific acu-point. The moxibustion symbolizes warmth and safety. It's like a kind and loving mother suddenly showed up in the tunnel with you, and now she's holding your hand and leading you on your way to safety. Suddenly you are able to relax more, because she's looking out for the both of you, and protecting you, and you no longer have to worry. Fear melts away and you feel safer. Moxibustion has helped many people feel like they have the ability to go deeper and look more closely at their lives.

> NOTE: Moxibustion is best done by a Chinese Medicine practitioner due to possible contraindications.

If you feel generally unsafe in most areas of your life, which we both often did a lot before we started Alchemy, we recommend you spend some time cultivating a full sense of safety and trust inside yourself. This, again, takes time. This is a process of simply focusing on releasing your fears. The foundation you build in Stage One will support you through all of the Nine Stages of Alchemy, and everyone's timetable is different. Again, there is no rush here! Consider any time that you take to work through all of your unsafe feelings as being part of the stage itself. Doing any necessary work on yourself to get you to the starting line is a very important part of any of the stages of Alchemy.

So where do you begin to face the fear of the unknown? A helpful starting place is to first accept your fear. It's okay to be afraid! In fact, it's pretty normal. Some people have been told that fear is not acceptable and is something to deny or run away from in life. Having fearful thoughts is almost shameful in our modern media-saturated culture. Many people have had the experience of being shamed by others because they felt fear and let themselves show it. Many have lived their entire life trying to avoid fear at all costs. If you've had a difficult relationship with feeling fear or believing it's not okay to feel it, the first step is acceptance.

Homework: It's Okay to Be Afraid

The desired outcome of this exercise isn't to change anything *yet*. You are simply observing. You are watching your own life unfold in real time, as it happens. It's an old adage that you must first know yourself before you can change yourself. Before you can enter the Mystery, you must first understand your fear. **Observing, accepting, and recognizing your fear comes first**.

Before continuing further along in Stage One of your Alchemy path, spend a few weeks watching where and when fear appears in your life and try writing answers to the following questions in your journal every day.

When and where does fear come up?

Do you squash it or push it away and if so, how?

Does it overtake you and incapacitate you in some way?

What other emotions does it bring to the surface?

Is it a catalyst for other actions or emotions?

What does it feel like when you are in fear mode?

What is triggering fear to arise in your life?

Who is triggering fear in your life?

If this is a person or situation, is it in your "real" everyday life or is it from social media or news outlets?

Mothering Yourself

Once you accept that fear is normal, *you can then let safety into your life*. What do mothers do? They make their children feel safe when they are scared. They say, "It's all right if you're afraid. I'm here to protect you."

I Am Safe, I Am Safe, I Am Safe Exercise

Spend some time mothering yourself. Nurture yourself. Take your own hand in the dark. Wrap your arms around yourself. Meditate on feeling safe. What does safety feel like for you? Can you recall a time in your life when you felt completely safe?

One of the simplest techniques is using affirmations to combat fear and anxiety when they pop up. We are also big fans of journaling as a way to work with creating a safe container for yourself.

- When you feel frightened, recite in your head over and over again like a mantra: *I am safe. I am safe. I am safe. I am safe.* Don't stop until you start to *feel* safety flowing into you or through you. It should feel like something inside is starting to shift, and your body is filling up with a new calmer sensation.

- If you don't feel a shift because you are in an actual scary situation, you can start with *I want to feel safe, I want to feel safe, I want to feel safe.* Repeat that until you start to feel safer. Then switch to *I am safe.* Keep going until you can breathe more freely, walk with your head held high, and feel that you really *are* safe. Believing that you are safe, causes it to be so. You create your own safety! This is your reality. If you believe you are safe, then you can walk your walk.

- If you have difficulty finding safety in yourself and have a constant level of anxiety, you may have what we call Chaotic Energy. Chaotic Energy is like having the energy inside you scrambled. It's a condition that is very common in the modern world due to our high levels of stress. We recommend that you see a Chinese Medicine practitioner or learn how to release Chaotic Energy for yourself. If you feel chaotic inside and can't find a safe, restful place to resolve it yourself, Five Element Acupuncturists can release this Chaotic Energy. J.R. Worsley, the founder of Five Element Chinese Medicine, also called it "Aggressive Energy." You can learn to recognize it in yourself when it may have taken you over, and you can learn to release it yourself with a series of acu-points. We have created an online class called *Releasing Chaotic Energy* that's available on the Alchemy Learning Center Website: AlchemyLearningCenter.com.

Walking in the Dark

Once your sense of safety begins to take form and you are more confident in yourself, you can begin to metaphorically walk through the tunnel. This means you've found the bravery to enter the Mystery Gate. Bravo! You're on your way!

As you walk through the dark tunnel in meditation, allow yourself to engage any fears that arise. What are the true fears of your lifetime? What are the creepy crawly monsters hiding in your darkest unexamined realms? Who gave you these fears? Instead of running from them, it's time to face them and find out what they are and where they came from.

As you are getting answers to these questions, or if you are still too fearful to pursue them, this is a great time to consciously examine and assess why you would want to do something like this in your life. Why would you want to enter the Mystery and keep going even when you can't see the clear way out of the tunnel? Why would you want to face your fears when you could keep the status quo in your life? Facing your own monsters is never fun for anyone, but how will they ever dissipate, disappear, or lose their power over you if you don't ultimately conquer them and remove them from your heart?

The Entering the Mystery Gate Meditation

The intention of this meditation is to enter the Mystery Gate, and thereby begin your Alchemy journey. You must be willing to enter the dark gate and face the utter unknown, like parting the veil of mystery. You don't know what lies behind the gate, but you are willing to put your spiritual self first and brave the darkness, knowing that beyond the gate is the tunnel, and there *will be light at the end of the tunnel.*

You can begin by finding a quiet space and having your journal or notebook next to you for recording your reflections after the meditation. Then follow the Relax Your Body, Clear Your Mind, Open Your Doors Meditation on page 79 of this book.

Once you are relaxed, take a few moments to clear your mind of any thoughts that arise. Now you are ready to start the Mystery Gate meditation.

Begin by imagining a large gate in front of you. You can imagine it any way you want. It could be an ancient wrought iron gate, of bent steel, darkened from a millennium of time passing, or it might be a stone gate covered with old vines that no one has touched in years. Everyone imagines a different gate—their own particular gate. Reach out your hand and open the gate, your Mystery Gate. You can now enter the dark tunnel that lies beyond it. Walk forward into the darkness and feel it envelop you. Use your hands to feel along the sides of the walls as you walk farther along the tunnel. It's okay to feel a little fear. What might you encounter along the way? Are the walls slimy or bumpy? Will you meet a bug or critter in the darkness? Is it safe to walk in complete darkness?

If you are experiencing fear, breathe in and imagine there is a comforting warm light inside you, softly glowing. As this light penetrates throughout your body, see if the fear dissipates. Your inner light glows and warms you.

Continue to walk forward through the tunnel. If the fear is overwhelming, you can turn around and end the meditation at any time. It is totally acceptable if that is as far as you choose to walk today. Judgments or negative self-talk are not helpful here. No matter what, you are doing great. You can return to the meditation tomorrow.

If you are still feeling safe and confident, continue on to the end of the tunnel. Walk in the complete darkness and see if any feelings come up for you. Imagine the light that *must be at the end of the tunnel.* This is what makes you want to keep going. Maintain the hope and belief that your destination is ahead of you, and that you don't need to doubt your imminent arrival. *The light will be there, and you will see it when you get there*

As the bright light gets closer, you begin to hear the hustle and bustle of big city sounds coming from up ahead. You feel the air in the tunnel begin to stir and change as a warm breeze caresses your face. You have reached the point where there is light coming from outside the tunnel. You step out of the tunnel, squinting, as your eyes adjust to the bright light.

When you are ready, open your eyes and in your journal write how you felt going through the Mystery Gate.

If you experienced any fears, what was stirred up inside of you?

When we embrace the belief that there will be light at the end of the tunnel, the fear often magically dissipates. Then the light at the end of the tunnel seems to appear immediately. In other words, it's almost as if the darkness of the tunnel is only really there because you have to meet some of your fears face-to-face. If you don't have any issues with fear or the uncertainties of life, the tunnel is really just a gate that simply opens quickly to the light, and it might not seem scary at all. But if you have many fears, the tunnel may seem long and impossible to walk through. That's okay! You can take small steps and remember to speak gentle and kind words to yourself. Soon, the light will begin to appear and get brighter and brighter as you move towards it.

If you felt more fear than you wanted to inside the dark tunnel, repeat the meditation as many times as needed until the fear dissipates. This meditation will help you connect with your sense of safety and feel comfortable in the darkness.

You can even practice sitting in actual darkness or walking in the darkness where it's physically safe to do so. This is a practice that many people find extremely challenging. Even if fears don't pop up right away in the tunnel meditation, they are likely to arise when you try walking in total darkness, again of course, only where it is physically safe to do so. Hearing unidentifiable noises and the experience of being cut off from your sense of sight can start to trigger fear-based reactions.

You can also safely sit in a place of total darkness. Keep your eyes open and observe all the noises, feelings, sounds, and smells. Notice how your eyes begin to adjust to the darkness. You may even see shapes in the darkness. Is your heart racing? Or is your mind quiet? Begin with five minutes and then work up to as long as twenty minutes.

Step Two: Asking Yourself the What Do I Really Want Question

After you emerge from the darkness and exit the tunnel of your fears, imagine that you have arrived in a big, unknown city. Let's call it The Mystery City. It's glorious and exciting to come out of the darkness and into the light, but it might feel a little overwhelming as well—like it's too much too soon. Then you realize that you need to move around the city—but how? What is all this big city hustle and bustle about? You can feel paralyzed at this juncture. Relax. All will be well soon.

In Step Two of Stage One of Alchemy, you need to find a quiet place to reflect despite all the noise and chaos in your new city, which metaphorically represents your life. You will need to find a place to go "on retreat" to meditate.

Allowing yourself to be on retreat is the beginning of your Alchemical self-cultivation process and is an important factor in moving forward with Alchemy. We like to say that you are like a wild land that is beautiful exactly as it is. However, if you choose, with a little cultivation and gentle taming of that wildness, it—and you—can become a beautiful garden. This is the force behind Alchemy. It's about directing your energy and coaxing it into something more powerful than it would be if left completely wild. It's all about transmutation and transformation!

This "retreat" phase happens because you have a little homework to do before you can progress any further. As humans, we need to think. We need to process. We need to reflect. We need to ask ourselves questions. We have to leave the excitement and distractions of the big city and our busy daily lives aside to find a quiet place, outside of these things. We need to go somewhere apart to meditate, think, process, and reflect. So we go on retreat to a place of our choosing, and we quiet ourselves and calm our minds so that something new will have the ability to arise within us. This is your safe place. You get to create it anyway you like.

Once you create a quiet place inside of yourself, you can ask this question:

What do I really want?

It seems like such a simple question, and in some ways it is! However, as we said before, it can also be one of the most profound question of our lives. Most people are only asking themselves what they want *in relation to something that is happening in their lives*. For instance, let's follow the trail of the question "what do I want to eat for dinner tonight?" Can you ask this one simple question without any other factors or nuanced meanings being taken into account, such as feeling too tired to cook, or wanting to eat whatever someone else wants to cook?

How about: "I don't have enough money to go buy what I really want," or, "The grocery store is too far away," or, "It's probably going to be closed by the time I get there." There are any number of reasons why you do not actually eat what you really want for dinner. What story or stories are you telling yourself? What are your feelings toward food? What are you willing to do to take care of yourself?

By the time your mind runs through all those scenarios and questions, you might feel like saying, "Just forget about it. Whatever is in the fridge will be good enough." What if we could rephrase the question to: "What do I really want to eat for dinner tonight if I could eat anything I truly want?" Now, that feels like a totally different way of asking the question. Yet "good enough" can come up in most cases for many people.

That's just a single example about dinner tonight! What about other more far-reaching and important questions, like:

What do I want to study at school?

What kind of job will fulfill me?

What kind of person do I want to be with in a primary relationship?

What kind of spiritual life am I leading?

The list of questions is limitless; we imagine that you can come up with lots more right now. But to be quiet and brave enough to meaningfully ask them...that's the challenge—because hidden within each one of these kinds of questions is the real question:

> *What do I really want without putting **any stipulations or limitations on the answer?***

Now that is a very profound question!

Consider this moment of quiet and peaceful reflection on any form of "what do I really want" as a completely open-ended query, with no stipulations, no guidelines, no rules, and no strings attached.

There is one other aspect of this exercise that we want you to keep in mind when you begin to explore the deeper answers. The culture we live in currently has such a strong, subconscious effect on any answer we come up with. We live in a career-driven society that is monetarily based and materialistic. Your very identity is often wrapped up in what you do for a living, or what you have or have not acquired in your lifetime. In fact, for many people it's one of the first questions asked when they meet someone new. Please go beyond those culturally imposed limitations when you are on the quest for your truths.

Sarah's Super Simple Answer to the Question

Sarah once worked for herself, but after fighting a tough, long-term illness, she decided to quit and support her spouse around the home. This was a very conscious decision on her part, and she felt good about it for herself and her partner. However, she was constantly given grief about it from her family and friends. She felt such pressure as she was asked over and over again *when* was she going to get a job or go back to work, and it was difficult for her to explain to people that she was happy *not* working for herself or anyone else.

So when Sarah started doing her Stage One of Alchemy in a treatment with Leta, the question: "What do I really want?" was an essential one. Sarah's initial response was to bristle and frown—it clearly agitated her right from the start. Leta gently talked her through it and explained that the answer to this question need not be some kind of job-oriented goal at all. Sarah really prided herself on her deep spiritual beliefs, and her constant study of the mystical realm through books and teachings. She was a lifelong learner and very intelligent. Leta explained that the answer to this question could be as simple as *to live a life in Wu Wei.*

When Sarah looked puzzled at this, Leta explained that Wu Wei was the Chinese concept of living a life in the now moment, doing whatever Spirit guides you to do. Sarah responded to this with a big smile and an "Oh yes, please!"

Leta went on to explain that Wu Wei is often translated as "non-doing," which is doing without too much effort or involvement of the mind. A better translation might be, "Inspired Action," which is any action that is supported by Divine guidance or higher inspiration and therefore does not involve any struggle.

Sarah wanted to know more; in fact she needed to know more. It turns out that Wu Wei was how she wanted her life to unfold more than anything else. Her simple "Oh yes, please," began the process of opening the door to getting exactly what she really wanted.

The What-Do-I-Really-Want Process

The What-Do-I-Really-Want process, not surprisingly, involves actually asking yourself the question, "*What do I really want?*" This could be the first time you've ever done this sort of deep reflection in a completely open-ended way. Just giving yourself permission to ask this of yourself can be scary.

Perhaps you don't really want to know the answer. What if it is totally the opposite of everything you are right now? What if it flies in the face of all you've done in your life? What if you're an accountant for a big firm, and the answer to your question is that you want to live in a treehouse in the forest and grow and eat berries all day?

Maybe you really, really don't want to know the answer to this question because, then what? Would your life start to unravel? Would you start seriously questioning every choice you've made? Do you really want to know where you took that turn in a direction your heart did not want to go?

And what if the answer is that you want to be president of your country, or an Olympic athlete, or the winner of American Idol or Britain's Got Talent? Is that delusional and crazy? What if you don't think you have what it takes to do any of those things? What if you're pretty sure all you'll get is disappointment? Would people laugh at you or judge you harshly? Will you be let down if you let yourself want something that you honestly believe can't be achieved, so that you have to settle for less? Are you already settling for less now?

Maybe you will be miserable just because you asked that "stupid" question! What a dumb idea, huh? What will your partner, your mother, your father, or your kids think if you tell them what you **REALLY** want to do in your life?

Perhaps you're afraid of the answer because for your whole life everyone has been telling you to be and do something that you don't want to be and do. Maybe they've been complaining about how you're living your life—and questioning your choices—because they actually *want* you to be different than you are, which might mean that they want you to be more like them.

We all deeply want love and acceptance from those close to us. In that respect, it might be frightening to allow yourself to face some radical truth about your true path. Sometimes people have very consciously chosen a path they think their partner wants them to be on. They love this person so much that they're willing to do what the other person wants instead of what they *really* want to do. They don't dare ask themselves what they truly want for fear of losing this person and their love.

You might not want to change your path and risk disrupting the status quo. Yet the answer to this big risky question could validate who you really are and guide you to be more authentic in a way you've been fighting all your life. Maybe you are truly an artist and not an accountant. A singer, not a lawyer. Gay, not straight. Female instead of male. Happy instead of sad all the time. Or maybe it's as simple as: I want to live in a warm climate not a cold one. This list could go on and on. These are all things we have heard from people over the years of doing this work. Remember, when you make choices based on your truth, you can be who you are supposed to be, no matter what that is.

So in light of all that we have discussed here, the supporting questions to ask yourself are these:

Can I be 100% honest with myself?

Am I willing to ask this question and allow the real answer to arise?

Am I willing to be 100% authentic and let my authenticity have its voice?

Please give yourself many opportunities to sit quietly and receive the answers to these questions. Be patient. It may not happen the first time or the second time, or even the third. This is a process of receiving. You can think of it as something that bubbles up from within you. Or think of it as a gift bestowed upon you from heaven. The ancient Chinese describe this process as something that descends from heaven into your thoughts. Here is a meditation to help you along.

The What-Do-I-Really-Want Meditation

Start with the basic Relax Your Body, Clear Your Mind, Open Your Doors meditation as described on page 79 of this book. Once you are relaxed, take a few moments to let any thoughts that arise slow down and pass through. When you are ready, begin the meditation.

Imagine yourself sitting in a quiet place in nature where you can be all alone and retreat from the world. After you emerged from the Mystery Gate tunnel, there was a lot of noise and hustle and bustle that may have been overwhelming. Now you can retreat from the big city into the countryside to find your quiet place. Imagine yourself there. It could be somewhere you've been before or an imaginary place where you feel safe and happy.

Now imagine yourself as a receiver with a giant antenna on top of your head. Think about what your antenna would look like, and then relax your mind's eye.

Now turn on the receiver, extend your antenna, and then wait for the signal to come in. You tune yourself to it through your quietness, through your stillness. Ask yourself slowly, **what do I REALLY want?** Take your time, asking the question over and over until you start to feel like your higher self is connecting, listening, and starting to receive the signal from a place outside your mind. This is a Spirit exercise so don't try to "will" an answer. Release any need to search your mind. The answer will come to you.

When the answer does come, it could feel very different than the ones you get when your mind tries to *figure out* something through logic or reason. It's more relaxed than that. It flows more softly. It could feel like something that speaks to you in a whisper from the space that is beyond your mind. Yet it feels real. Or it may come to you feeling like a gentle nudge or a giant push towards a new direction. If you feel surprised by what it says, the guidance is probably coming from heaven, which is to say, coming to you from your spirit, or your higher self. If it's what you've been thinking you "should" be doing all along, take your time to make sure it's not just your mind interfering.

Everyone is different. There is no right and no wrong in this arena. Stay in the meditation until you feel ready to slowly open your eyes. Then take a moment to adjust to this new thought pattern before writing down in your journal whatever information you received. Repeat this meditation daily until you begin to feel confident that you know the answer to the big question you are asking.

Step Three: Aligning Your Heart with the Answers to What You Really Want

Pondering and reflecting on new thoughts that arise so that you can gain insight into your life takes time and focus. Your answers could be bubbling up slowly as you're gathering and receiving information from your higher self. Time and your curiosity will allow it to gel and take shape.

Rather than just accepting the answer, put it to the test. Ask yourself:

Does it really resonate with me?

Is this really me?

Do I really want this?

Am I interested in this?

Could I invest my time and energy in this new idea?

Could I become passionate about it?

Just let this part of the process flow right now. Let things come and go—there is no need to make big decisions right away. On the other hand, perhaps you are strongly moved to make big decisions. Pay attention to that too. You will know when it is right. You will feel within your soul when you are developing a passionate direction. The ability to gauge the truth of your answers based on how you feel will develop as you take part in this Alchemical process.

The next phase of the work is to take this idea of what you want, and plant it deeply into your heart. Your heart needs to accept it, nourish it, and feed it.

In fact the heart must not only just accept it, but really, really want it—whatever that wanting is for you. You are developing your passion, and that passion—that excitement and drive—comes from within your heart. You want to allow your heart to feel the desire. You want to let yourself *really* want it. And this takes time. Have you ever heard the expression, *their heart is just not in it?* That's what we say when someone is simply going through the motions. We want you to find out what it means to feel the opposite of that. When your heart is truly filled with desire, passion arises.

Give your heart the time to "apply itself" as the Chinese say in the ancient classic texts. When the heart applies itself, it becomes constant and fixed on its purpose. If we acted right away on every good idea we ever had, we'd be doing an impossible amount of things! Luckily, we don't have to do everything. We can wait and do the things that really matter to us, which in truth is like saying what really matters to our hearts.

So now ask yourself, *does this new idea really matter to me?* Do you feel some excitement—that spark from your heart that leads you down the path of discovery? If your heart really takes that on, then you will fulfill your desire. You will not only want to fulfill it, but you will *have* to fulfill it. Your heart will stop at nothing to make it happen.

The heart wants what the heart wants.
The heart has a "mind" of its own.
Listen to what your heart is telling your mind.

Heart Blocks

So why doesn't everyone do this easily? Why is it such a struggle for some of us? For most of us?

The most common energetic emotional block to figuring out what we want is that many people have what is called *heart pain*. How can the heart truly embrace something exciting with such passion and drive if past experiences have resulted in pain? If living passionately has resulted in getting hurt in the past, the memory of that pain is going to hold you back. Living freely and then experiencing trauma may certainly cause heart pain. In some cases, a heart is so hurt that the person has pretty much wrapped it in emotional cellophane to protect it, and as a result everything feels damped down and dispassionate.

When the heart hurts that much, it blocks everything. If you think you have a heart block, or if you know you have a heart block, you can pause and take time to work on releasing your heart's pain. There are several ways to do this. In Chinese Medicine we see people with situational heart blocks that result from a recent, more temporary problem, such as a breakup or a fight. Your heart hurts, but in a relatively short time, you'll recover. However, an early trauma, particularly one from childhood, or one of bigger proportions, can cause what we call a "Major Emotional Heart Block," which is a long-term, entrenched kind of block. These blocks do not go away easily and can last a lifetime. Do you remember Leta's story about being told that she was "bad, bad, bad"? That is an example of how strong and tenacious these blocks can be. Often you need outside help–some kind of therapy–to help you release this type of block.

We have all experienced heart pain, but a heart that retains this pain and is blocked off from the higher self, cannot complete this step of Alchemy. In order to align your heart with what you really want, your heart has to be fully accessible to you. It has to be allowed to feel the passion and excitement for life that only the heart can bring.

If you have such heart pain, you must spend the necessary time to work on releasing it. There are treatments in Alchemy to do this. We discuss the treatment for Heart Pains at the end of this book. You can also do this on your own. It takes time—sometimes up to a year or more—but there are ways to help yourself really let go of these heart pains, one by one, and begin to love yourself. Earlier, we described heart pains as tentacles that have wrapped themselves around your heart. Unwrapping and untangling these heart-entrapping tentacles takes time, self-love, and a vigilant mind. This self-love can be rejuvenated and re-awakened in you, or it can be developed for the first time in your life. Can you forgive yourself? Can you forgive those who have hurt you? These things often go hand in hand. Can you rectify or rewrite the story of your past? We offer you some help in doing this.

The Aligning Your Heart with the What-Do-I-Really-Want Meditation

When you receive the answer to what you really want, we suggest that you practice the Aligning Your Heart with the What-Do-I-Really-Want Meditation. The goal of this meditation is to give yourself some time to align your heart with the answer to your *what do I really want* question. You can find recorded versions of all our guided meditations at the Alchemy Learning Center website: AlchemyLearningCenter.com.

Begin with the Relax Your Body, Clear Your Mind, Open Your Doors meditation. Refer to page 79 of this book to find instructions, or you can listen to the guided meditation recording.

When you are ready, begin the meditation. Imagine yourself sitting in a quiet place in nature where you can be all alone, in complete retreat from the world. Take a moment to visualize sitting comfortably in this quiet retreat space. Pause, breathe, and clear your mind.

Now focus on the answer that came to you through your earlier meditations, the answer that will guide you towards what you really want out of life. If you had more than one answer to your question, select just one of the answers to focus on today—the one you're most excited about.

Visualize whatever it is that you want as if it already existed in your life, as if it already *were* your life! Imagine what it would be like to already be, do, feel, or have the thing you really want—as if it was actually happening now. Let your imagination take off and explore any additional details that come to you. Take your time. Give yourself all the time that you need as you fully experience all the sensations that arise.

Now focus on your physical heart in your chest. Inside your heart is a void. This is the space where the blood flows through. Your spirit lives in that void. In Chinese Medicine we call it the house of your spirit. There is actually an acupuncture point behind your heart named Shen Tang or Spirit Hall that represents the place that your spirit calls home.

Imagine going into that void inside your heart. If you have difficulty imagining this, don't push it. Give yourself some time. There may be some heart pain interference.

Once you can feel that you are inside the void of your heart, spend some time there. Find the quiet stillness within. Ask your heart, do I really want this thing enough that I will have the willpower to do it? Do I really, really want it with my full heart?

As you contemplate this, does your passion for the idea arise and grow? Is your heart aligning with this idea? Take the time that you want to contemplate being, doing, feeling, or having the thing you really want from this vantage point.

When you are finished, slowly open your eyes and write about how your heart felt during the meditation.

If at any point you felt some resistance arise while contemplating your answer, this does not necessarily mean it's the wrong idea. In fact, you may be certain that your heart can be aligned with this idea and that you may still feel resistance. This is normal. In fact the next step in this Alchemical stage has to do with the resistance that may arise *because* your heart is passionate about the idea.

If you did not have a passionate response in your heart for the answer you were contemplating, take some time and sit with it longer. Return to this meditation tomorrow and continue to open to it and all that arises from it. It's normal to have many ideas and answers to the question of what you really want that your heart may not align with. You can return to the What-Do-I Really-Want meditation if your heart is not in alignment with the first answers you received, and see what else arises for you. This is a tender experience for you and your heart, so your patience and kindness will serve you well.

If you are sure that your heart is aligned and you feel a strong passion or desire for what you really want, you can continue on to the next step, which we call Releasing Rebellious Qi.

Step 4: Releasing Rebellious Qi

Once your heart has accepted what you want and embraces it with passion, and you can say, "I really, really want this, and I'm not going to let anything stop me," the next thing that naturally happens to every human being is: every single thing suddenly seems to be conspiring to stop you!

You start to think, "In order to be, do, or have this thing I want, I need my kids to do this, and my spouse to do that, and I need a break from my job, more time, and more money..." and the list goes on and on. Really, it sometimes can seem like the world is against us! Everyone is in cahoots to stop us from getting what we want. You tell yourself "It's clearly going to be a struggle to get what I have finally figured out that I want! I'll have to fight with all my energy, all my weapons, and all of my strategy to get it!" You just know that it's supposed to be and is going to be hard—very hard. Right?

WRONG!

It's the human condition to feel like we have to fight to get what we want. This Alchemical step takes us on a fact-finding mission with what we call in Chinese Medicine, "Rebellious Qi," or fighting energy. This step is about releasing all your Rebellious Qi energy and embracing the idea that, "WHOO HOO! IT'S GOING TO BE EASY." You can have everything you want without the fight!

Really?

YES!

You just have to stop fighting and start ALLOWING it to happen. Actually the whole purpose of Stage One of Alchemy is this step—to get to the point of really wanting something authentically and then ALLOWING it to happen without any fight. There is a component of *Trust with a capital* T that has to be "inserted" here. You have to learn how to trust so that what you want can happen without immense effort and without any need to fight for it.

Allowing

This is the point in the process where we sometimes suggest you can bring in the teachings of Abraham to help you do this work. Esther Hicks communicates to us for a group of beings that call themselves "Abraham." You can explore the Abraham-Hicks material through free YouTube videos of Esther speaking for this "infinite intelligence," or through their many books and workshops.

Abraham's teachings are all about how to flow through life and receive what you want without struggling or expending a lot of effort to get it. If you have a strong belief that everything you do successfully is only due to your hard work and efforting, then you might need to spend a very long time on this step learning how to allow. Take your time. Entering into this world of it's *actually easy* and, *I get to have what I want* is a huge step that's necessary in order to keep going on your Alchemical journey. If you aren't there, that's fine. You can learn how to be a creator of your own life with ease and flow.

One of the exercises we are about to suggest that you try is a meditation where you imagine you are in a little raft on a flowing stream. And instead of paddling up the stream, you imagine yourself turning your raft around and floating downstream. All the good stuff you want is downstream, and you're on your way there. It's as if all the things you want are hanging down from the trees within your reach— and you can just easily pick them as you float by with no paddling and no struggle at all. Effortlessly. You allow it all to just come to you. It's easy!

The Releasing Rebellious Qi Meditation

When your heart is aligned with the answer to your What Do I Really Want question, it's time to move onto the Releasing Rebellious Qi Meditation. The goal of this meditation is to release the belief that you *have* to struggle to get this thing you really want. That feeling is what we call Rebellious Qi.

Begin with the Relax Your Body, Clear Your Mind, Open Your Doors meditation as described on page 79 of this book.

When you are ready, begin the meditation. Imagine yourself lying on a raft that is slowly moving down a quiet, serene river. Allow yourself to completely relax on the raft. Imagine the gentle movement of the water slightly rocking the raft below you, lulling you into further relaxation.

Now begin to think about the answer to your What Do I Really Want question. As you float down the river, look to either side and notice the many trees bending their long, arching branches over the sides of the river. See the trees bearing fruit. Notice the abundance of lush fruit on these branches. These fruits come in all shapes and sizes. They represent the very things you want and they're just hanging there, ready for you to reach out and easily pick them.

As you breathe in, focus on the thing you really want that your heart is in alignment with. This is the thing you want passionately. It could be a favor from a friend, it could be a new skill you'd like to acquire, it could be an object you want to possess, or just a sense of peace in your life. Whatever it is, as you breathe out, the trees appear to be full of what you want, and as you slowly drift by, you can casually reach out and pluck what you want off the trees, all the while continuing downstream, knowing that there will be more all along the way.

Imagine the joy you feel now that you've received exactly what you were wanting! You have it in your hands, right now, on your little raft, and it was easy. So easy. Give yourself a moment to feel that joy.

As you float downstream, continue to breathe in and receive more of the great things you've been wanting. Give yourself some time to receive a good number of them. It's so easy. Just relax and float downstream. Allow these things to come to you without fighting for them! Receive what you want as it comes to you without any effort. You are just floating along, relaxed and peaceful, and expecting what you want to come easily.

When you are finished, slowly open your eyes and write in your journal how it felt to have exactly what you've been wanting. Did you feel happy? Did you feel relaxed? Take this feeling into your day with you or into your night as you prepare for sleep. If you still have a feeling of tension and difficulty about receiving what you really want, continue to do this meditation daily until this sense of ease begins to arise in your life and fills your being.

Step 5: Journeying to Your Higher Self

The final step in Stage One is to meet your spirit face to face. After you've allowed yourself to release your Rebellious Qi, life should begin to truly feel easier. You've stopped fighting for what you want, and you're allowing yourself to get what you want without effort. Now it's time to commune with your truest self.

You can't really commune with your higher self until the fight in you is really gone. Your spirit is all about ease. Rebellious Qi is not the true nature of your spirit. That's more the feeling you get from your mind trying to *figure out* how to get what you want. Your spirit knows that what you want is coming to you if you can relax and *allow* it. According to your spirit, you have limitless possibilities. You can be, do, or have anything you want. It's only your mind that is invested in the confines of physical reality and believes that there are limits to what can be done.

Once you release the need to fight, as you have done on that raft ride downstream, you can relax and spend some time just being present with yourself in a whole new way, with no agenda. You can now open a conversation with your higher self, your spirit.

Journeying to Your Higher Self Meditation

The goal of this meditation is to connect with your higher self, or in the Shamanic tradition, what we would call your teacher in the upper world.

Begin with the Relax Your Body, Clear Your Mind, Open Your Doors meditation. You can refer to the written version of that meditation on page 79 of this book for instructions. Or you can find recordings of all our guided meditations at the Alchemy Learning Center Website: AlchemyLearningCenter.com.

When you are ready, begin the meditation.

Imagine you are taking a trip to the clouds high above you to the upper world. You're floating up through the sky to the clouds, where you can walk on their puffy softness. Just as a shaman might, you can imagine flying up to the sky like a bird or on the back of a bird.

Once in the upper world, arrive and settle yourself, and wait for your teacher to appear. This is a being that comes to you to answer your questions. This teacher may take any imaginable form.

Sit down with your teacher and ask your question. Be respectful and patient. Take your time. Listen to what your teacher has to say.

When you've finished your conversation, imagine returning back down to Earth and slowly return your awareness to your body in the here and now. When you're ready, open your eyes and write in your journal what you have discovered, and what your teacher shared with you.

You might be surprised when you discover who your teacher is. For Leta, it was her grandmother. Leta could ask her questions, and she would gently answer. And these aren't necessarily questions like "How do I make more money?" or "How can I make my relationship work?" Because this teacher is a personification of your higher self, this must be a conversation about what's most important to you in life. For example, you can ask what is your purpose in this lifetime or how you can find better alignment with the choices you've made in your life.

This meditation can be repeated as often as you like when you're in Stage One and even for years to come. Communing with your higher self is a self-cultivation skill that, once developed, will be an invaluable tool that you can use for the rest of your life.

Stage One Homework: Letting Go

The homework for Stage One is to let go of the things you obsessively think about every day. These obsessive thoughts can be related to just about anything.

You may be remembering something amazing or wonderful that happened to you in the past that you wish would happen again, like a really great vacation that you loved. Now you're hanging onto it, and trying to arrange your life to do it again, and wishing you were back there. You dream about it all the time. This could feel like happy musings, or it may feel sad because you feel like you're prevented from getting back to it. Either way you're clinging to the memories. And in either case, it's obsessive thinking. And Stage One is about letting it go.

Sometimes an obsession can be something really negative that disturbed you, and now you can't stop remembering it because it affects you emotionally. Or a traumatic event, like an accident, might replay itself in your thoughts and leave you frightened about it happening again. It could be something mean that someone said to you, that you obsessively review, thinking about how hurt you are. It could be something you witnessed, like an act of violence. Whatever it was, your mind keeps focusing on it. Stage One is about truly letting go of these kinds of obsessive connections with past events. The Daoists even call this exercise Sitting and Forgetting. The goal is to truly forget.

The mind also tends to latch on to things you're planning for the future that are a bit daunting or even frightening for you. Maybe you can't stop thinking about something you want to say to someone, or how to ask for a raise from your boss or a question for your partner that is haunting you. You go over and over it in your mind, reviewing different scenarios of what you'll say and what the other person will say. It's a very common type of obsessive thinking to plan for a future event, and in Stage One you can work on letting that go as well.

We have a choice. We can let things go, or we can be very sentimental and hold onto things until the day we die. We often try to remember the emotions and feelings we felt in reaction to specific events. Sentimental and nostalgic memories and emotions make us feel really alive. But those emotions are the same things that very often keep us too earthbound because they always pull us down into the physical manifestation that makes up the past. If you become too pulled down to earth, it's hard to let heaven pull you back up, and that can lead to various forms of depression or anxiety.

We also often hang onto regrets. We may regret that we can't return to good times in our lives, or that we can't erase something bad that happened, or that we never got to do something we were planning to do. With long-held regrets, we can end up actually dying with unfinished business and come back to finish that business in another lifetime.

In most cases, these things we're holding onto define our very identity. We resist letting them go because it would mean that we're letting go of some piece of ourselves and how we think about who we are in the world.

You might think, "I'm the way I am because that event happened to me." If you believe that, then you're going to be very resistant to letting go of the memory of that event. Forgetting that memory then would feel like losing a piece of your identity. But is what happened in the past really *who you are today in this very moment in time?*

You may also identify yourself with who you plan to be in the future. "I'm going to be a lawyer because I'm in law school and I'm going to work hard and sacrifice until I graduate." If you're very invested in this plan, you're going to be very resistant to letting go of the idea of being a lawyer, even if it turns out to be an unhappy path. If you let go of the idea of being a lawyer, who are you then?

In either case, does this identity really give you joy? Does it make your life feel more fulfilled? If you can let go of obsessive thoughts about memories or future plans, then the Daoists believe you become free, and heaven can exist on earth. The practice of letting go in Daoism means letting go of earthly concerns so you can be free and easy in your present day life.

The practice of "Letting Go" is best done at night, so you can let go of whatever happened that day, but it can be done any time of the day or night.

To practice letting go, you traditionally sit in meditation and go over all the memorable events of the day one by one. Or you can address weeks or months, or even your entire lifetime in a sitting session. As each memory arises, you attempt to release it so it cannot continue to haunt your mind on a daily basis.

The Letting Go Meditation method begins with this kind of simple letting go, and then has several additional approaches for practitioners who do it on a regular basis. In Stage One, we begin with the first level of letting go, which is simply remembering and releasing those memories of the day.

The Letting Go Meditation

This meditation is best done at the end of the day before you fall asleep, but it can be done at any time in your day. The goal of this meditation is to release your attachment to your memories of the day you have just lived through. You review each moment of your day, step-by-step, as if you're writing a mental journal, and let each memory go.

Begin with the Relax Your Body, Clear Your Mind, Open Your Doors Meditation. You can refer to page 79 of this book for instructions, or try using our recorded guided meditations at The Alchemy Learning Center Website: AlchemyLearningCenter.com.

When you are ready, begin the meditation.

Focus first on the crown of your head. This represents heaven, because it is the part of your body nearest to the sky. As you focus on the top of your head, imagine energy pulling you upward. While focusing on that part, you may feel a sense of ease and freedom—a sense of lightness, like you might levitate. Take a few moments and breathe into this area of the body and allow yourself to feel the pull of your energy upward toward heaven.

Next focus on your tailbone sitting in your chair or on the floor. This is the part of you that keeps you on the earth, grounding you and pulling you downward. As you focus on your tailbone, you may feel the weightiness of your body sinking into the earth. You may feel a sense of comfort and safety. Take a few moments and breathe into this area of the body and allow yourself to feel the pull of your energy downward toward the earth.

Next focus on your posture. Imagine a string tied to the crown of your head, pulling you upward, and a string tied to your tailbone, pulling you downward. Imagine now a bridge or tunnel of energy inside your body running from the crown of your head to the tip of your tailbone. This bridge is the space along your spine between those two points. You can envision it as a tunnel of energy or light where things can move freely upward or downward.

Breathe into that tunnel, feeling the strings on the top and bottom gently pulling and elongating your posture.

If you notice any part of your body feeling like it's sagging or flaccid, try to imagine the string on the top of your head gently pulling you upward so your posture elongates.

If you perceive any part of your posture feeling too tight, try to imagine the string on your tailbone pulling down and getting you to relax a bit.

Pay attention to your heightened awareness of this tunnel or passageway through your body. Can you let your breath move easily up or down through that tunnel?

This tunnel is what we call the bridge between Heaven and Earth. With the bridge between the top of your head and your tailbone created, now focus on your center—your chest. This is the center of your humanity, and the third space we're focusing on in this treatment. In Chinese Medicine we call these three spaces:

- *heaven*: your head

- *earth*: your lower torso and tailbone area

- *man*: your chest

Take a moment to breathe into your chest and relax while maintaining the awareness of the bridge you created and the energy flowing through it.

Next breathe in and start to gently replay your day. What did you do when you first opened your eyes in bed this morning? What did you see? What did you do when you got out of bed? Slowly walk through the events of your morning step-by-step.

As you review the moments of your day in order, notice if your mind gets stuck on a specific event that captured your memory. This will be one that stopped or altered your breath in some way, due to some emotional reaction you had, good or bad, big or little. Notice any memory that stands out to you either because it was very good or because it was unpleasant in some way. As a significant memory comes to you, take a moment to ponder it.

Breathe deeply into the center of your chest as you hold the memory of the event in your mind, then as you breathe out, let the memory travel outward through your tunnel to the top of your head and the bottom of your tailbone. Let it go to heaven and earth, so it can vanish from your memory. Give it to heaven for safekeeping or let it be buried in the earth. It can dissipate in the same way the tension left your body when you relaxed.

This may take some practice. You can do it visually in your imagination or you can feel it leave your body through the sensation of your breath expelling.

Now continue to walk mentally step-by-step through your day, finding other significant memories that happened. For each memory that caught your breath and had an emotional impact, good or bad, hold that memory in your chest, breathe in, and on the exhale, let it go through your bridge upward to Heaven and downward to Earth.

Continue until you reach the end of your day. When you are finished, slowly open your eyes and see the present moment around you. There is no need to write in your journal. You don't need to remember this experience either. The past is gone and the present has arrived.

In Stage One it's not about how much detail you can remember of your day, but how much detail you can forget. The more you can remember, the more attached you become to your life. And the more you can forget, the more detached you become. You're not losing your mind; you're losing your attachment to your mind.

> **NOTE**: If you use the bridge visualization between Heaven and Earth to let go of your thoughts, this meditation is best done sitting with your body positioned vertically between Heaven and Earth. You can still do a similar meditation of letting go while lying down, without using the bridge to Heaven and Earth. But keep in mind that finding your own way of letting go, while lying down, often results in falling asleep!

We believe the Letting Go Meditation is simple and easy to learn—yet takes a lifetime to master—as do many of the lessons in this book.

A Few More General Notes

Now that you are starting to get the hang of this Alchemy thing, let's take a bit of a break before we go on to explore Stage Two and all the rest of the stages. There are some points that we would like to share with you that apply to all of them and make them easier and hopefully a little clearer to understand and to undertake.

The Importance of Self-Cultivation

We like to think of the path to Alchemy being paved with an understanding of the Five Elements and Nine Palaces, which is why we require students to start their Alchemy journey by learning about them. Through a growing understanding of your particular blend of them, you begin to examine your life and begin to see the world in a different way—energetically. They also help open the door to the idea of self-cultivation. However, there is so much more to learn than simply studying the Five Elements *in theory*. We want you to really understand how you move through the world with your own energetic Five Elements. What is your Wood energy like? What is your Fire energy like? What is your Earth energy like? What is your Metal energy like? What is your Water energy like? What does it feel like to be authentically in your first Element, your second Element, or your third Element?

Then you can apply that knowledge to how you actually live the life that you're living. You can begin to understand your own curriculum for this lifetime, and grasp the unfolding story of your unique existence, through the lens of your Nine Palaces. This can be a beautiful, humbling, and powerful experience. Understanding how you move through the world energetically and elementally will really guide you as you move through the Stages of Alchemy.

Earlier in Stage One, we talked about the idea of you being a wild untamed land, and about embracing the idea of you cultivating this land into a beautiful garden. The idea is to embrace it without any sense of right and wrong, or any *judgment* about being either a wild or a cultivated garden.

Both are wonderful, but Alchemy *does* require you to begin self-cultivation. Cultivating takes some work. Gardeners put effort into making their plot of land beautiful. It doesn't happen without a little sweat and tears. The same is true for your Alchemy practice. Before you continue on, you need to come to terms with the sincerity of your desire to cultivate yourself. As we move onto the subsequent Stages, you really must decide that you want to make the effort to do this work. It is a practice that requires self-discipline and a vigilant mind. You can certainly read on and learn all about it, but to *do* Alchemy for yourself, you will have to fully embrace your self-cultivation. You will have to commit to continually asking yourself better questions. You will have to commit to a better understanding of you.

Completing a Stage of Alchemy

When you're working through the Alchemical Stages, there is no specific timeline for transitioning from one stage to another. The most important rule is that you pay attention to where you are. We find that it's a good idea to have a little preview of what the next stage is so that you can notice the cues that come up when you're ready to shift. When we're working with a client practicing Alchemy, we often find they come in talking about the next stage when it's time to move on. They don't even realize it. This could be as soon as a month later (which is very rare), many months later (which is more normal), or as much as a year or more later. We even say that a single stage could take a lifetime in some cases and that's totally wonderful and beautiful too.

One of the things we've noticed over the years is that in order to progress or keep the momentum moving through the stages, it's important to keep the thread of the work going, like you're following breadcrumbs on a path. You don't want to lose sight of that trail of breadcrumbs, because if you do, you'll have to go back and find the point at which you and the trail parted company. While it may be frustrating to have this happen, in fact many, many times people intentionally go back to Stage One and get to a deeper experience of ease in their lives.

We ask people to come in for an Alchemy session about once a month or more often if someone needs a frequent reminder of Alchemy in order to not lose that thread. Even if we're working on the same stage for a year or more, reconnecting every month is a good chance to stay focused and to see how that stage is going.

Some people may find a particular stage very easy. It just flows quickly and effortlessly. We think this happens because they've already completed much of that stage's work in their life. For example, maybe they've already asked what their heart really wants, and lined up with it, and then released their rebellious Qi. They've had the deep conversations with their higher self. Then when we start Stage One, it just reinforces all that work they've already done. They more easily remove any remaining obstacles in their life. They move on to Stage Two with grace and eagerness. Then that same person might hit Stage Three and find that it takes many months or years to work through it because that's the stage where all their current challenges are, especially if they haven't done a lot of work on it previously. So how do you know when to move on the next stage in Alchemy?

Proper Firing Time: You are the Cauldron

Each stage has its own timing. You can never predict whether it will be days, months, years, or lifetimes.

If you're working on one of the stages and you're able to keep the thread of that work going, your dialogue and what you're talking about will organically change. Suddenly you may just begin talking about the themes of the next stage.

For example, a Stage One dialogue is all about what's hard in your life and all the obstacles you see in your way. It's all about finding the path of greatest ease in your life and navigating the tumultuous waters around you. At this stage, you are discovering what you truly want in life, and letting go of the fears of not knowing where you're headed.

If you find that you're switching from talking about what's hard in your daily life, to suddenly telling others how life seems so much easier, with all the things that are flowing and happening, then you may be ready to start do some Stage Two work. Generally speaking, at this point, you may begin to think and talk about the past, reviewing old grievances or past regrets. Your Letting Go meditations might become more focused on memories older than today or yesterday. This is another sign that you may be moving on to Stage Two, which is about releasing the baggage of this lifetime.

The phrase *proper firing time* refers to when Alchemists of antiquity used Stone Medicine, to achieve Alchemical progress by actually ingesting the minerals in the stones. They cooked these concoctions in cauldrons and only when they got to the exact temperature could their elixirs be taken without poisoning themselves. With the proper firing time, the elixir would work. Without it, they couldn't achieve the results they wanted. In some cases, they might even be sickened or poisoned, or even die. And although practicing Alchemy as we do will not create situations of poisoning or death, we still honor the fact that we need to wait for the "proper firing time" of each stage before we can move on to the next one.

We have found that Alchemical work is greatly benefited by having a strong foundation of Qi Gong or Tai Chi, or some form of daily Qi moving practice, as well as a consistent meditation practice. In Stage One, this will allow you to feel a sense of ease in life—that everything you want is coming to you effortlessly. You begin to feel that you are just floating through life without obstacles. You simply step around anything in your way and keep going. You barely even miss a step! You also have a strong sense that your higher self is present in your life and constantly communing with you. You are in trusting partnership with your higher self. This is partly why that sense of ease comes. You are happy and healthy and full of abundance.

If you're reading this book and doing the exercises without a practitioner, it's important to be honest with yourself about where you are in your process. For example if instead of a practitioner, you have a close friend who can do this work with you, you will have someone who can offer you their non-biased opinion about this question and a lot of others. This feedback is very helpful. You may feel more ease in your life, but at the same time be talking a lot about what's difficult. Your language could still be negative. New positive language skills internally and externally in your life are imperative. In fact, as you work through this stage, you learn how to be stricter with your mind—to develop what we call a *vigilant mind*. Being vigilant with your thinking means monitoring the negative talk and beginning to replace it with positive self talk. When Stage One starts taking hold and working, this process becomes simpler and rather effortless.

In a sense, the process of Alchemy breaks old habits. Many of us have deeply entrenched ones that we are attached to. That's why each stage takes some time and ongoing daily attention. It's why you need to constantly look for those signs along the way to gauge how you're progressing. Old habits will resurface and try to pull you back onto the old, "safer" path, which is the much more commonly travelled path. So it's imperative to practice being honest with yourself about what's really happening. Alchemy is the path less travelled but the rewards are nothing short of spectacular.

No Room for Ego in Alchemy

Is there danger in trying to force or speed up the Stages of Alchemy? Would it be a mistake to move on too soon? Yes, and also no. Remember there are no mistakes, no good or bad, no right or wrong, when you transcend the illusion of duality. In the early Stages of Alchemy, it's not such a huge deal to move forward and then later find you need to go back to an earlier stage. We call this *peeling the onion skins*. We can have many layers of Rebellious Qi. So even when we're fairly certain we can move forward, as we make progress, we may have to return to Stage One work as new obstacles surface.

This requires the releasing of the ego on a big scale! The path can be humbling. Our steps are often slow, and we may hit an emotional landmine or two, that blows things up —and that's alright. We are more vulnerable, but also stronger. We're on a path to discover ourselves. It takes turns—both bright and dark, smooth and bumpy. The path is all things, and it is nothing. When you move through the Stages of Alchemy, you don't ever stop practicing what you learned in Stage One. It is carried with you through all the stages. When you complete Stage Two, you don't just cease to know all that you've learned about yourself—it stays with you. You are building and strengthening the Alchemical Cauldron—which is inside of you.

As you move into the upper Stages of Alchemy, it becomes more important to wait until a stage is *truly* completed due to the fact that the upper stages require a lot of energy that you begin to build in the early ones. Your self-cultivation practice will be deepening, and your life experiences will be more profound. This requires patience and self-love. If you do try to rush them too quickly, for any reason, you may end up exhausted and drained physically, mentally, and emotionally, and that can be detrimental overall to your health and well being.

When you're practicing Alchemy, we like to say that transformation *comes to you* organically, meaning you really can't *make* it happen no matter how hard you try. Changes happen to you because you're seeking them, not because your mind simply decides to make a shift. In fact, your mind will never win at that game. Practicing Alchemy strips away every untruth we ever told ourselves for any reason, whether it was denial, an escape from pain, or a survival tactic.

In our example of moving from Stage One to Stage Two, once you are ready to move on, you start to shift your focus from the present day challenges that were constantly consuming your day-to-day thoughts, to events that happened in the past. You may find yourself reviewing events from childhood, such as wrongs that were done to you by others, old hurts, and traumas. You might find these things surfacing in your nightly Letting Go Meditation or in your morning meditations.

Instead of thinking about your day, these thoughts of the more distant past are intruding into your meditation. You find you're working on letting go and releasing the bigger stories. When and if this has happened, whatever the timeline is—congratulations! You've moved onto Stage Two: Talisman.

John's "Kick Me Please" Sign

Remember John? We introduced you to John earlier in the book. When he first came to the clinic, he was under constant attack. Despite his affable demeanor, his friendly and smiling appearance, his great social skills and his history of success in the sales world, John was constantly being stabbed in the back by his colleagues at work. He was so successful in his business that he was elected president of his trade group. However, some of the group members openly hated him and fought him at every turn. He was stressed out, and even his wife was angry with him about how messy and unorganized he was at home. It seemed like wherever he went, he was being attacked, as if he had a "kick me please" sign on his back and everyone was taking him up on the invitation.

From a Chinese Medicine point of view, John also had some strong indications that the stress was taking a toll on him. His tongue was very yellow—a sign of heat in the body, which is a symptom of an excess of Rebellious Qi. This heat was causing a variety of symptoms, the most severe of which was that he was in danger of losing all his teeth, which can be the result of long-term excess heat.

We worked with John for a long time to reduce the heat in his body. His teeth started to improve, but his life continued to be fraught with arguments and difficulties. We told John about Alchemy and how it might be able to bring more ease into his life. He enthusiastically decided to try it.

We started Stage One, and not much changed at first in his life. In fact, things even seemed to intensify the first month or two. But then slowly, the tides began to change. He switched jobs and started working for a company with a friendlier corporate culture. He resigned from his trade group leadership position. He and his wife gradually worked out a lot of the troublesome kinks in their relationship.

It took a whole year for these very small changes to accumulate and add up to bigger changes until he was finally ready for Stage Two. But if you compared the John that first walked into our office with the John at the end of Stage One, he was a completely different person! He was, maybe for the first time in his life, living a stress-free existence.

The Best Protection
is No Protection.

—Leta Herman

Stage Two: Talisman

A talisman is an amulet a person might wear as a necklace to ward off evil. As a metaphor, we all want some kind of protection against the things we've experienced in the past that were very painful. We've all had negative experiences—and at the end of those experiences, when all is said and done, some of us swear that *we never, ever want to have that experience again.* Whether it's a lost love, a betrayal, a physical accident or attack, emotional abuse, or any other awful event that happened, we are determined to make sure it never happens again. It doesn't matter what *it* was. That story will be different for each person.

The idea behind Stage Two is that when one of these negative or traumatic events happens in our lives, we build a little fortress to protect our chest—like an amulet of sorts. The purpose is to try and stop it from ever happening again. We may create a complete fortress of protection over the course of a lifetime.

This fortress needs a lookout tower. We try to be on a constant and vigilant watch to make sure we detect any early signs of this bad thing coming at us again. As time goes on, we also try to beef up and strengthen that fortress of ours. We think it will definitely need to be stronger next time. We think *if only I'd been stronger or done such-and-such, I could have stopped that from happening.* We tell ourselves that next time we're not going to be caught unarmed or off-guard. We're going to make sure we're ready at all times. We constantly fortify our protective walls. Think of the saying, *This weighs heavy on my heart*, or even, *I just have to get this off my chest*. These phrases relate to Stage Two in Alchemy.

Building Up the Fortresses

As life progresses, we may have quite a number of these fortresses built up on our chest—all of these ways we habitually watch and protect. But what are the consequences of constantly trying to prevent bad things from happening and to keep everything at a distance so we are not hurt emotionally or physically? The cost is that the armor, the fortresses, and the protection prevent us from being able to truly open our hearts and live full and happy lives. We end up missing out on the beauty and wonder of life, love, and happiness.

Living in a fortress is cold, dark, and gloomy. Unfortunately many people suffer from this kind of unhappiness everyday. It can be the way they live without even being fully aware of it. They are certainly not free like children frolicking in fields of flowers on a warm summer day! They are not "dancing like no one is watching." They are not daring to fall in love with anything or anyone. They are living in fear with the curtains drawn and peeking through peep holes drilled into the thick walls of the fortress. Maybe they can look out and see those beautiful flowers, but there's no chance of being able to actually touch them, smell them, or pick them. This is what we refer to as *living a fear-based reality*.

Stage Two is about a simple yet seemingly impossible new way of living life with a mind free of the fears, trauma, and past events that caused pain. We can sum it up with one sentence. *The best protection is no protection.*

What? No protection? Best protection? How would that work? You mean live life completely vulnerable and open? What? How could that even be possible? We always recognize when we say this statement that it might take a while for people to understand it. How is no protection any kind of protection?

And Taking Them Down

Well, here's how we think it works. We like to use several examples: a Tai Chi Master, like our favorite, Sun Lutang, who created Sun-style Tai Chi; Yoda from the Star Wars movie series, or Neo from the movie *The Matrix*—pretty cool right? So, Sun Lutang, Yoda, and Neo walk into a bar and get into a fight... wait, that's another story! We're joking of course, but imagine if someone throws a physical punch at Sun Lutang, the Master simply moves just out of the line of attack, and the attacker loses balance and falls to the ground. It's easy and effortless for the Master. As a Master of the internal arts, Sun Lutang always had such confidence and was deeply centered. Sometimes when you see Tai Chi Masters give public exhibitions against opponents, they are laughing while they fight. They're having nothing but fun, while the opponents fall and flounder around. Now, think about the Jedi Master Yoda—tiny and wizened and frail-looking. He may appear to be quite vulnerable and weak. He practically hobbles along with his cane, but make no mistake, he could absolutely kick your butt if you tried to attack him. He knows no equal in combat, because he's energetically in command.

> Master Yoda believes everyone and everything in the universe is the same and connected energetically, through the Force.

No one could ever truly hurt him. For him, every battle is the battle of the mind over matter. He effortlessly lifts Luke's giant ship out of the swamp with his tiny hand. Physical size does not matter. His world is ruled by the energy, by the mind.

Another example of *the best protection is no protection* that we like is from the sci-fi movie *The Matrix*. In the scene where Neo is being showered with a million bullets flying at him, the bad guy is absolutely blasting him. But Neo simply moves and bends out of the way, and he's never hit by a single bullet. He energetically bends time and space to move out of the way, no problem. He doesn't try to stop the bullets. He simply shifts his place in reality itself, and then there is no target for the bullets to hit.

Okay, so maybe you're thinking, "I'm not Neo from the Matrix movie and my multi-dimensional bending skills are still pretty dormant." But why not embrace this new concept in your life? The only way something can *hit* you is if you present yourself as a target. Your armor is heavy and actually makes you more visible, and since you think it will protect you, you don't move out of the line of fire. In fact, you hold your armor up to the attack and you let yourself be pummeled. You think this behavior keeps you safe. In fact it's the exact opposite of what you want! Then you wonder why you keep getting hit over and over, and why it hurts so much. And if something does manage to break through your armor, then it *really* hurts, and you're angry at yourself for having weak armor. The cycle just continues.

Living in this kind of reality, the problem is: there's always something out there stronger than whatever fortress you've built. Always.

But let's say instead of focusing on blocking the attack with your armor, you begin to think of yourself as open space or full of big holes. We are all actually just a bunch of molecules and atoms with an awful lot of space around them. If you're not trying to protect yourself and youyour're mostly open spaces, then an unwanted attack, like those Neo bullets, will just pass right through you. In other words, if there's no protection, then there's nothing to hit or break or hurt.

Let's take it to the non-physical level, since maybe that's a bit easier to understand. Someone can only hurt your feelings if you let them hurt your feelings. If you're actively trying to stop someone from hurting you, your protection is actually creating more pain than if you just didn't take anything personally. It's also painful to never let anyone actually get close to you, because you're afraid of getting hurt. Barbs being thrown at you only hit their mark because you have given them a place to land by trying to protect against them. Otherwise, they could just fly right by you, as if you're the Tai Chi Master, Master Yoda, or Neo. The only reason we think we need protection is that we don't want to be hurt. But ironically the only thing that can hurt us is our own protection being hit, pierced, or destroyed.

So what does it take to live with *no protection*?

Here is our big thought:

Being present and in the moment with the strength of your own vulnerability.

We also recommend watching Brené Brown's first TED Talk, *The Power of Vulnerability*, which is one of the most watched TED talks of all time. Brené believes that vulnerability is the key to having a happier life and that hiding behind protection leads to feelings of disconnect and unhappiness. We just love how unprotected she was when she presented this talk! She definitely showed her own vulnerability. She made a very good case for how exhausting and tedious it is to constantly need to put up a protective front. Living a care-free life is so much more fun! This one TED talk changed the lives of millions of people and shifted their perspectives on how they could live more joyfully.

The goal or purpose of Stage Two is to release the baggage of this lifetime. This means releasing the chest protections you've built up over the years—the armory that is protecting your heart. The way to do this is to begin addressing the heart pains you may have stored there. Many of these pains are actually caused by disliking yourself. The hurt you feel is because at some point in your development, you started to believe the negative things people said to you or about you. You began to believe the story that all the bad things that happened to you were your fault.

You lost your ability to believe in and embrace your own goodness. This stage is about learning to love yourself *despite* what anyone else may think of you.

If you learn to love yourself *unconditionally, then you will not need to* *protect yourself from others.*

The Elemental Theme for Stage Two—Fire

The overall theme of Stage Two is all about loving yourself, and therefore it embodies the number one lesson of the Fire Element, which is to actually love yourself and experience total self-acceptance. It's one thing to love others, and Fires do that easily. To accept and love yourself is the ultimate love in the universe. Feeling that you need to protect yourself ultimately comes from a lack of self-acceptance and the desire to hide your flaws from the world. This level of vulnerability can feel very risky for many people. In fact feeling vulnerable is likely to be the most challenging part of any Fire person's life. The theories and themes in this stage require that the Fire Element energy inside you stops protecting you, no matter whether it's first or last in your energetic stack-up. You can do this because your self-love becomes undeniable and true.

Stage Two has a two distinct steps:

1. **Building Your Cauldron**—creating a safe space to do deep work

2. **Releasing Protection**—removing the armor that protects you

Step One: Building Your Cauldron

The first step in Stage Two is learning how to build a safe container for your Alchemical transformation. Feeling safe is a prerequisite to self-love. Remember we mentioned the challenges of vulnerability? Alchemy, especially Stage Two, requires your willingness to undertake a deep and profoundly honest self-inquiry. How easy or challenging this turns out to be is a reflection of your relationship with yourself. It is paramount that you are completely willing to suspend all self-judgment as you search inside, which requires a certain awareness of your comfort levels with yourself. So the first question to ask yourself is: *Does it feel safe to look inside yourself?*

Before we describe more about Stage Two, it's important to note here that if you're feeling suicidal or even depressed, you *should not* begin working with this stage just yet. You must first do some preparation work that will help you to find islands of safety within yourself. At the end of this book, we discuss a treatment called The Thirteen Ghost Points, that addresses trauma, and having this treatment may be necessary and helpful at this phase. At a minimum, seeking therapy or some sort of somatic work on your emotional state is often called for here.

If your answer to our above question was a "yes" and you are ready for Stage Two, then the first step is to consciously build a safe container for your self-inquiry. In ancient times when Alchemists were creating their own Stone Medicine elixirs to drink, they first had to create their Alchemical cauldrons. These were very specifically designed and built. They had to be made out of the right materials that could hold the intense heat that was required to make the elixirs. They also had to be able to withstand radical temperature changes, since some of the elixirs required a cold stage as well. For this type of Alchemy, think of yourself as the cauldron.

Your first step is to set up this cauldron inside to contain your own internal Alchemy process. Can you create a safe space inside yourself where you can put aside all self-judgment and look at your life with an open heart? You may not like what you see, but are you willing to engage with it? In some cases, it may feel like you're about to open your proverbial Pandora's box of memories and negative thoughts that you closed—and indeed nailed shut and hid in the back of the closet—a long, long time ago. If this is the case, what is your level of willingness to open this now? If you feel apprehensive, then embrace that as *the truth* and respect it. One way to proceed from here is to ask yourself what you would have to do within yourself to feel a wholehearted desire to engage with your past.

And here we arrive at the actual goal of this step, which isn't so much to create the cauldron itself, but to ask yourself if you're truly ready to engage. If you've gotten this far, life is already quite a bit easier than when you began. There is really no rush to proceed. Building the cauldron could take years for someone who has had a lot of trauma. Take your time. Examine with all honesty whether you can feel safe with yourself. Are you going to beat yourself up or be accusatory to yourself with every memory that comes up? If so, then it's not yet time for this work. The Alchemists definitely took their time building their cauldrons. There could be no cracks that would have allowed the elixir to drain away. You, too, must make sure that your internal vessel is fully prepared and intact.

The Building Your Cauldron Meditation

Sit quietly in a chair or cross-legged on the floor with your journal. You may want to begin with a short relaxation meditation in order to make memories of the past more accessible to you.

When you are ready, start by focusing on your chest and your heart within your chest. Without a need to achieve or accomplish anything, allow your presence to settle in this area. Simply be present with yourself. Take five to ten minutes to rest in this heart space.

When you are done, write about how you felt while being present with yourself. Did you feel safe and relaxed? Or did you feel anxious, scared, or unsettled?

If the latter is true, continue to do this meditation daily, each time allowing yourself to feel more settled and safe in this space. This meditation is a way to ease into the kind of presence and intimacy with yourself that allows you to feel safe inside. For some people, it may be quite emotional at first, but as long as you are progressively feeling more at ease and safer, continue to explore your safe space inside.

What is this "safe space"? One of the Thirteen Ghost Points that we use for trauma represents this safe room that we all have inside us. It's the ante-chamber of the heart, where you are completely free to be yourself. No one is going to poison your food or stab you in the back. This is the room of intimacy. And right now, the only person that you need to feel safe with in that room is you.

If you don't seem to be making progress, consider taking a break from Stage Two and working on past traumas that might have made your trauma response too strong to proceed. Greater healing of past traumas might be needed before you can build your cauldron and will certainly benefit you in many other ways.

Step Two: Releasing Protection

This step is a two-part process. As you work through this process, you're going to allow whatever arises to arise. Remember, you don't need to go digging around in your past to find all that baggage, root it out, and toss it. Alchemy is an organic journey, not a forced one. We simply facilitate opportunities for you to move in the direction of the Alchemical roadmap. Do you recall those signposts the Alchemists left us? They're simply saying "T*his way please. Move along when you're ready.*"

This step requires a deep examination of your lifetime and your memories. This is a similar process to the one we did in the Letting Go meditation where you're remembering your day and letting it go. Only this time, you're going to be remembering the whole trajectory of your life.

You're going to want to proceed slowly through this step. You can only take on a little bit at a time. You might start with your earliest memories, remembering the times that "caught your breath." Perhaps you were scolded and shamed. Or perhaps you remember the perfect nostalgic day when you felt elated and overjoyed. Any event with significant emotion attached can be released. We always say that the memories don't go away entirely, but they no longer have a hold on you.

The Life-Review Journaling Meditation

Sit quietly in a chair or cross-legged on the floor with your journal. You are going to be using the journal in the meditation. You may want to begin with a short relaxation meditation in order to make memories of the past more accessible to you.

When you are ready, start by taking a gentle journey through your life, in the same way that you reviewed your day in the Letting Go meditation.

Make this a gentle review. Don't try to force any particular kind of memory. Just allow yourself to let memories come up however they may. Trust that the order might not be chronological, which is just fine. Practice trusting that what needs to come up will come up at the right time.

As memories begin to surface, ask yourself whether the event was one that you felt you wanted to prevent from happening again. If it was an event you decided to avoid repeating, bring to mind the little fortress on your chest that you created to have protection from future similar events. Remember that we are becoming aware of these fortresses so that we can learn how to dismantle them and still feel safe. As you discover these painful events, make a list in your journal of some of your fortresses and protections. What are the things you *never, ever* want to have happen again?

Take your time. You may repeat this exercise over several days or weeks. It may take some time to review your life, especially the longer you've lived or if you had a lot of trauma early on in life. Also be gentle with yourself if you've had a lot of trauma. You may not be ready to allow these memories to resurface. Remember that you are building trust with your body's responses. This is a good place to practice your belief in that possibility.

After working on your Life-Review Journaling meditation, the next step is to do the Best Protection is No Protection meditation. The goal of this meditation is to release the protection you're wearing—to step out of the heavy armor and put it aside.

The Best Protection is No Protection Meditation

The goal of this meditation is to open your heart and release the old heart pains you may have stored there so that your heart can be repaired, rejuvenated, and reborn. Then you can begin to love yourself again, or maybe you can start to love yourself for the very first time. If you can love yourself, you do not need protection.

The Heart Pains result from the difficulties you encounter in the fulfillment of your Nine Palaces. These heart pains clog up your beautiful spirit home. We like to have people visualize heart pains as if they were dusty and bulky old furniture that crowds their home and really needs to be moved out. They're limiting your spirit's freedom to move. No fresh air or Qi can flow if bulky, old, outdated furniture has filled up the space. Some redecorating is in order!

If this is your first time doing this meditation and if you have had many serious and traumatic events in your list, you may want to focus this meditation on a memory that is not too upsetting. Small steps are best here. As you continue using this meditation, you will be strengthening your ability to allow any memory to arise and be released.

Begin with the Relax Your Body, Clear Your Mind, Open Your Doors meditation on page 79. When you are ready, start this meditation.

Bring your attention to your heart, specifically the center of your heart—the hollow space where the blood flows through. We call this the Void of the Heart. In Chinese Medicine, this hollow space is called Spirit Hall, the home of your spirit, which is your higher being. This is the place where all magical healing takes place.

> The Void of the Heart is also the space where you may have stored your past hurts and heart pains.

Breathe deeply into your Void of the Heart. Keep focusing on this space inside your heart. Allow thoughts to simply arise inside you. If any uncomfortable or disturbing memories surface, see if there's one in particular that your mind wants to focus on. If a very upsetting memory comes up first, just gently put it aside and wait until a memory surfaces that's not too upsetting. This can be the focus of your meditation for today.

If you wish to continue, breathe in again, and return your focus to the Void of your Heart. Relax and begin to open your heart enough to allow the feeling of protectiveness that is trying to stop this bad memory from ever happening again to arise. Ask yourself why you don't want a similar event to happen in the future, and how you've been keeping yourself on guard to avoid similar circumstances from happening. The memory will likely make you feel tightness and stress in your chest. Breathe in deeply, and on the exhale, consciously relax that tension in your chest.

If you have difficulty relaxing and opening, this is perfectly natural. You've been guarding your heart against future pains for a long time now. If you decide that you want to stop here this time, which, of course, is always perfectly fine, wait until the tension in your chest has lessened before you end the meditation.

If you have decided to continue, imagine a similar event in your future threatening to unfold again. But this time you know that you have changed. You are older, more mature, and wiser now. You are much more like the Tai Chi Master. You can easily sidestep this future danger without even trying. You are smiling. You now have a whole new set of choices.

In your mind's eye, allow your imagination to envision a different, positive outcome to this similar future event that you just imagined. You are so much wiser now. You know yourself and love yourself more than you did back when this event first happened. The circumstances are completely different now. Can you change your reaction this time and not even let it affect you? Just because you had pain then, doesn't mean you'll ever have to repeat that pain again. Like magic, you can now redirect the unfolding of that negative event. Feel the relief of never having to protect yourself against this happening again.

Now focus on opening your heart. Can you be fully open again? Can you let yourself be true and authentic?

Take five to ten minutes, and just breathe fully while relaxing. Imagine letting go of the old pains and hurts that have weighed you down for many years until you start to feel a great sense of freedom. See what's possible now. Feel how much lighter and freer you can be now.

If this part of the meditation has been difficult, just be present with the difficulty. Be kind to yourself. You may have very strong barriers around your heart. You may have wrapped it in cellophane to keep everyone and everything at a distance. It's fine if you feel like it's just not safe to open your heart yet. You may need more time. Today just sit and see what's possible. Can you release some of the protection? Can the barriers around your heart begin to melt away? Can you lessen the tentacles just a little bit?

Next, focus on your energy. Allow the energy to flow through you and fill your body with light and love. Repeat these affirmations in your mind:

I am worthy of love.
I deserve love.
I am lovable.
I love myself.

How do you feel? If you want to smile, then smile. If you want to laugh, then laugh. If you feel tears coming, let them flow. It's all good. Breathe! When you are finished, open your eyes and write about what you experienced. Remember, Stage Two takes time, so *take your time. You can't release the baggage of a lifetime in one day.*

For some people, this stage takes months or even years to complete! You may even need many days, months, or years to release just one specific incident. Nevertheless, what you're looking for is a real change in your attitude and perception toward anything that reminds you of old events. If you can release your fear and the need to self-protect, then you can begin to feel much more confident in your walk through life. Once this happens, you've completed Stage Two.

Ultimately, in this Stage you fall in love with yourself and become complete in yourself. There are so many people who are always looking for a perfect partner to "complete" them. That's never really going to work because the partner could always go away and leave them incomplete again. You have to be the completion for yourself.

Being complete in yourself means being 100% confident in who you are. This is the essence of Stage Two. Then if someone comes along and throws you a hurtful comment, you can smile and not even feel the pain of the words. Why? Because you're loving you. You don't *need* them, or anyone, to love you anymore in order to be fulfilled and happy. This powerful self-love allows you to waylay your fears and to truly accept yourself just the way you are—which is perfect.

Kim's New-Found Self-Love

If you'd asked Kim whether she loved herself, she would have said "Yes, of course!" However, Kim didn't *behave* as if she loved herself. Kim had an incessant need to please everyone all the time, and to be liked 100% of the time. She gauged how good she was by what others thought of her. She may have thought she loved herself during times when no one was really upset with her. But it was clear that when she fell out of favor with her co-workers, friends, or family, she would feel devastated, and true self-hatred would ensue. In fact, a recent family disagreement that broke down lines of communication with her siblings left her utterly bereft. Kim was so distraught she could barely function.

When Kim started Alchemy, she sailed through Stage One, finding it relatively easy to work through the various steps. She did her homework, started self-cultivating more, and started to feel more in control of her life. At the beginning of Stage Two, Kim started reviewing her life. She had many, many heart pains in her past, some of which were quite traumatic. Every mean thing that anyone had ever said to her, she remembered in great detail. She had not forgotten any of the mean barbs, fights, or betrayals. They were all right there under her armor and fortresses. A lot of them stemmed from her childhood where her father's alcoholism led to many scary and mean behaviors that as a child she wasn't able to comprehend. Even though he didn't harm her intentionally, the original pain still created a lifetime of mistrust and fear. She went through her life making extra sure that nothing like that would ever happen again. She found that by being the nicest, sweetest person ever—no matter what—she could feel somewhat safe in her relationships. However, this often meant that she got lost in her own shuffle. Being so nice to everyone all the time, no matter what, left her feeling empty, lonely, and confused. She had no real life for herself. Where was there time for Kim in that scenario?

After her initial struggles with Stage Two, we decided to do another Alchemical treatment called The Healing Heart Pain treatment.

After this Alchemical treatment, she felt greatly changed, but it was difficult for her to articulate how. She had a profound transformation that day, and she *felt* completely different inside. However, it wasn't until after three months had passed that she began to understand what had actually changed in her life. She said it was as if she'd been hiding from all emotions and feelings her entire life, and now she felt a deep sense of calm and security in herself that she'd never felt before. As a result, she could let her light shine out. She was no longer afraid to show anyone her true self.

It took more time for the deep shift we had made in the treatment to filter up to her consciousness, but once it did, she never went back. She said, "I was really surprised when you initially asked me if I loved myself. I couldn't imagine that I didn't. But now, looking back, I can see that I didn't at all. Now it feels totally different, and I truly love me!"

Many people think they love themselves, but upon some self-examination, they realize they don't even like themselves, and that they even have ways that they can be mean and actively destructive to themselves. This is usually learned behavior leftover from earlier life traumas. Alchemical treatments, like the Healing Heart Pains, can sometimes help facilitate new thoughts and a new perception of loving yourself.

The Healing Heart Pain Treatment

For some people, the possibility that you could fall in love with yourself seems very remote. Self-hatred can be a very real thing, especially for those who have had parents, lovers, or other people who've abused them and told them how horrible they are. And they then internalized those beliefs about themselves.

If you have some aspect of this kind of self-conflict, there is more work to do for Stage Two. Another more powerful technique for healing your self-hatred may be required. We think of the Healing Heart Pain treatment as a way to connect your spiritual umbilical cord to what we like to call Source Energy. Some might choose to call that Divine energy or God. For each person, the name may be different.

Before you were born, when you were in your mother's womb, every single thing you wanted or needed, including all your nourishment, was instantly given to you, through your umbilical cord. You were connected to your mother and to Source Energy through this cord. You had complete, unbroken access to love and light.

Self-hatred, on the other hand, is disconnectedness. You feel as if you're all alone, like that little tiny boat on the big, tumultuous sea. You feel you're not like anyone else, and that you don't truly fit into life's bigger picture. This is the essence of self-loathing and self-hatred.

What you don't see from this narrowed perspective is that you and even your boat are just tiny molecules that are part of the whole sea of existence! You *are the sea*. You *are* connected to everything, and you couldn't be separate even if you tried. When you connect your spiritual umbilical cord back up to the Whole, or to God, the Divine, or to Source, or to the Mother—whatever term you want to use—this is like finding yourself sitting in the lap of Oneness, where all is profoundly well. You experience complete and heartfelt connectedness. *You are home: safe, sound, loved, accepted, and held.* For many people, this is a concept and feeling they have rarely experienced.

So what is the journey to connectedness? It's a journey of the heart. There are two aspects of the heart. The first is the Heart Protector, which is the aspect of the heart that interfaces with people, and gets heart-broken over and over again.

The second aspect, which is the Inner Heart, on the other hand, has nothing to do with the events of this life. The Inner Heart rules your incarnation in this lifetime and your relationship with the Divine. This is that place we call *the home of your spirit.* Your spirit is your own piece of the Divine that lives inside of you for this lifetime.

Imagine there are two paths. One is the path leading from the wholeness of your mother's womb—where you were so warm and cared for and connected—to separateness, which is where you find yourself now—on your own and perhaps feeling disconnected from everyone and everything. However, ideally this path is leading you toward greater self-realization and individuation *without* feeling alone.

The second path winds backwards in the opposite direction. It starts from separateness–from where you stand now with all your heart pains and loneliness–and travels back to the experience of wholeness, where your heart can be healed.

In Alchemical Healing, we do the Heart Pains treatment with a series of acu-points that delineate these two paths, and there always an accompanying soundtrack of random music. In ancient times several hours of nonstop music was improvised by a group of musicians in the same room, and what they chose to play helped shape the course of the treatment. These days we use the whole Alchemy Healing Center's music library on shuffle, and then let "the cosmic DJ" pick out the songs, which always informs the whole trajectory of the treatment in a magical way. During the treatment, the two paths metaphorically cross each other, to bring that separateness back into the wholeness and the wholeness back out to the separateness. At the end, the individual finds they can feel themselves reconnected to the Whole, or to Source itself. There, in the lap of God, self-love can return.

The Healing Heart Pain Meditation

This is a meditation for healing your heart pain. As usual you can begin with the Relax Your Body, Clear Your Mind, Open Your Doors meditation. Refer to page 79 of this book for instructions, or you can find a recording of the guided meditation at the Alchemy Learning Center Website: AlchemyLearningCenter.com.

When you are ready, start this meditation.

Now imagine two pathways in your body. One starts in your armpits at a point called Utmost Source, which is another word for Divine or God energy, and moves down to your pinkie fingers, to the point that represents the little boat all alone on the big sea. The second path starts from a point on your middle finger that symbolizes the most heart pain—there's a reason we give people the middle finger when they hurt us—and it moves up to a point on the breast, which is the source of mother's milk, symbolizing pure love and total connectedness.

Now imagine all the heart pains that have caused you to have self-hatred and pain. Starting at your middle finger, think of all the difficult choices you've had to make that resulted in the loss of things you really, really wanted or loved. Bring to mind any horrible statements from friends or family that you may have somehow internalized about yourself. Slowly, one-by-one, take each pain home to your breast, and allow the nurturing and loving energy of mother's milk to heal them.

You can also imagine yourself in your mother's arms being nursed. Or if your mother is the cause of some pain and suffering, imagine a kind, loving person who loves you unconditionally as a substitute. Take your time. You are waiting for a feeling of immense lifting relief. It could feel like a wave of emotions. When you feel yourself coming home to that feeling of nurturing, you are receiving love and coming back to wholeness.

Next, imagine the Utmost Source spot under your armpits, and feel energy flowing down from there to your pinkies. Source energy floods down to that little boat lost on the sea and envelops you, in a feeling of belonging. Feel what it would be like to release separateness, and simply be part of the whole. The vastness of life IS you. You are not separate from it in any way. You are sitting in the safe and wonderful lap of God, or the great Spirit, or whatever image you'd like to use that feels safe. Stay still there and soak in the feeling of being the one within the all.

This meditation can be practiced over a very long period of time—weeks, months, or even years. You can do it as long as necessary, until you truly feel yourself connected up to all that is. Sometimes it can happen in an instant, and it sticks. Once it does connect or reconnect, you won't ever go back to the loneliness, because your spiritual umbilical cord is once again connected.

Stage Two Homework: Affirming Your Life

The homework for Stage Two supports the development of self-love and helps you let go of the influence of the significant baggage and major traumas in your life.

To most efficiently work on releasing the baggage of this lifetime, your daily meditations should now focus on reviewing your lifetime in chronological or sequential order, as if you're reading a mental journal from beginning to end. See the Life-Review Journaling meditation above.

In addition to all this letting go, Stage Two is also a prime time to work on affirming your life. Affirmations are not prayers or wish-lists. Affirmations are positive statements that acknowledge all the good that's happening, or that you want to happen, in your life. Affirmations can be used repetitively, as mantras, to create more positivity in your mind. For example if you regularly have anxiety about your safety, you can repeat the mantra I *am safe* over and over in your mind many times a day, especially when you may be doing something that makes you nervous or frightened. We have both used this mantra extensively over the years with amazing results! Using this mantra every day for a long period of time, can really eliminate generalized anxiety. Once it does, you can begin to make friends with fear, which actually serves to keep you safe when real danger is near.

You can also use affirmations to manifest an outcome you would like to have happen. Instead of praying for that outcome, which is acknowledging the lack of the thing you want and praying for that lack to change, affirmations help you focus on knowing that the thing you want has already manifested. You imagine and feel the outcome you're wishing for, as if it already exists. It's important to practice feeling the positive emotions you would feel as if it all came true, while you imagine your desired outcome.

For example, if you want a new job, imagine you just got the job, and now you're planning to go out to celebrate with your friends. How much detail can you envision? Maybe you're jumping up and down, calling your parents, and picking out your favorite outfit to wear. Maybe you're laughing and telling your sweetheart all about the new job! What does it feel like? What helps you to *really* feel the joy and excitement of your dream arriving? This is a powerful way to affirm your success and happiness.

If you realize that all things change, there is nothing you will try to hold on to.

If you are not afraid of dying, there is nothing you cannot achieve.

– Lao Tzu

Stage Three: Divine Influence

Now that you've learned to release the baggage of each day, and you've let go of the baggage of *this* lifetime, it's time to move on to releasing the baggage from previous lifetimes. One of the signs that you're ready to move forward is that you might find yourself thinking about issues or challenges that seem to have always been with you from birth.

Everyone is different, and there are countless examples. "I've always been afraid of snakes, even though I've never really encountered one in real life." Or "I've always struggled with people telling me what to do, since my very first memory." Or "I'm terrified to drive across bridges, and I don't know why."

These issues have nothing to do with the kind of baggage we addressed in Stage Two. These are more the things you carried with you from your last lifetime, or your ancestors' experiences, going back as far as five generations. These are burdens you inherited at birth. In other words, this is all the unwanted stuff you brought into this physical incarnation with you, and Stage Three is when you begin to unload it all!

When you were born into this lifetime, you came into your physical body inside your mother's womb. It would have been nice for us to all to come in with a completely clean slate, right? But no, that would just be way too easy!

Almost everyone brings some baggage along the way that has nothing to do with them per se, and seems to pre-date even this lifetime. We often explain these as past-life influences, or as the impact of your ancestors on your current experience in this lifetime. If you think about it, these things really don't belong to you. That irrational fear of flying or that food allergy could simply have been inherited from your grandmother. Yet somehow they need to be released in order for you to truly live this lifetime in freedom and joy. Essentially, you can think about Stage Three as forgiving yourself for who you are, including all the mistakes you think you've made in the past, and including the burdens you may have carried in from before your incarnation into this body. It's about setting yourself really free.

Stage Three opens up with three steps that are called called the Three Elixir Fields:

The chest (Man),

The lower abdomen (Earth), and

The Head (Heaven).

Once we open them, we will begin to circulate the energy through all three in Stage Four so you can see the world differently and react to the world differently. You are going to be given a clean slate so to speak.

- The first step, Man, refers to your relationship with yourself.

- The second step, Earth, is your relationship with nature and the earth plane of existence.

- The third step, Heaven, is your relationship with Spirit.

The challenges of Stage Three occur because this stage addresses the kind of deep darkness within us that has its roots buried beyond our known reality of this lifetime, and so it may also be completely unconscious.

> *With some work and a vigilant mind, from the darkness rises a new sense of hope and a new state of love.*

The good news is, that you will finish Stage Three feeling more loving and more hopeful, ready to live in a child-like state of innocence in Stage Four.

The Elemental Theme for Stage Three— Earth

The overall theme of Stage Three is learning to give to yourself, so that your inner strength can fuel your transformation. This is a transitional stage—and the Earth Element is all about transitions. Transformationally speaking, this is also where the rubber meets the road. All the changes you've made so far have been amazing, and here's the great thing about that—you are bringing all the new strengths and tools with you from Stages One and Two that arose out of all the challenges you've successfully embraced. Hang onto your hats though: this next phase of your transformation is going to be *miraculous*. And this is going to require a bit of work. You must first build your inner strength in order to be able to do this part. You need the Alchemical Fire in the cauldron to be so strong that a huge catalytic shift can occur within you.

If you're like most of us, you've been giving and giving, to everyone and everything else in your life. Now it's time to give to yourself. To do this, you really have to embrace the Earth Element within you. Earth must receive in order to give.

> *This is a really good time in your life to put aside the needs of others and receive all the abundance that the universe is offering you.*

As you move through this stage, your strength will grow, and you will accumulate power in your lower abdomen, where your cauldron is located. In Stage Two, you created and completed the cauldron. In Stage Three, you allow your Earth energy to begin to stoke the cauldron.

Here are the names of those three distinct steps of Stage Three again so you can see how you are going to accomplish this:

1. **Man**—releasing whatever came with you into this lifetime that has an influence over you

2. **Earth**—building your qi in your lower abdomen

3. **Heaven**—moving the qi up to your head to begin the process of birthing yourself

Step One: Man

This step releases any ties you have to the time before your birth that are holding you back from being completely authentic. In this step, you release your Akashic records, which are believed to hold all of your experiences from every single lifetime. Akasha is a Sanskrit word that means aether, sky, atmosphere. In Chinese Medicine, it's believed that when you die, a part of your spirit stores the memories of this life, and adds them into a vault of all of your many lifetimes' memories. The Akashic records, are the inscribed content of those memories, the "atmosphere" that you brought with you at birth.

Even though we don't necessarily remember our past -life experiences, they are kept for us so that we can keep track of the continuity of our development from lifetime to lifetime. Our Akashic records transcend time and space.

There are many different ways to access your Akashic records. One way is to participate in a past-life regression hypnosis session, which can take you back into your past lives. This might allow you to see recurring themes showing up that are strongly affecting your current lifetime.

Past-life regression is an extremely powerful technique, and you may want to explore it if you sense that a major issue from a past life is currently holding you back on your current journey. However, Stage Three isn't really about understanding or knowing how your past-lives influence you in this lifetime. What we're really aiming to do in this stage is to completely free ourselves from the influence of the Akashic records over our current lifetimes. The past lives will still exist, but the experiences from those lives will no longer have power over us.

As you work through Stage Three, you'll find that thoughts or experiences that might have often upset you or challenged you in the past, now seem less important or relevant. You'll find more freedom in your relationships and interactions with the people around you, especially family members.

Releasing Your Akashic Records Exercise

The link to your Akashic records is on your chest. You can begin the process of releasing your Akashic records by working with this area.

You can gently press your finger on the point just an inch above the nipple and an inch to the outside (lateral) to the nipple. This acu-point is called Pericardium 1.

To locate an acu-point on the body, it helps to lightly slide your finger over the area and feel for a slight depression or a feeling of qi that to some feels like a pulse or a buzzy feeling. You can also try pressing more deeply to find the spot that is most tender. However, it can sometimes be difficult for some to locate the point under dense breast tissue. And in the case of this point, the entire area is tender for most people. If this is the case, you can use an alternative point. You can press your fingers into your ribs, directly under each breast, just lateral, which means toward the outside, from directly under your nipple. There is a tender place that is just where the bottom of a bra would likely fall, if you wear one. It's an acu-point called Liver 14.

When you hold these points, you gently vibrate them with your fingers to help release those ties to the past. If you're doing this for yourself, we recommend holding these points while meditating in the morning. Do so daily, over an extended period of time. We recommend no less than 30 days.

While doing this morning exercise over time, pay attention to your day-to-day activities. See if any of your behaviors, or your responses to events and people, begin to change. We suggest you write in your journal every day, paying special attention to any changes you notice. You may perceive that you're starting to feel less rigid about your life. Maybe you're less reactive around your parents or your siblings. Maybe you're less sensitive to perceived slights in the world around you. Perhaps your irrational fears or phobias, like a fear of heights, start to ease up. Maybe you have no distasteful reaction to Brussels sprouts anymore. These are all events you can observe and write down.

Step Two: Earth

This step helps you to build the Qi or energy in your belly. You must have strong belly Qi to move onto Stage Four, because this phase requires a lot of energy to rise from your belly and lower abdomen all the way up to your head. This is where we talk again about *proper firing time*, which refers to the care the Alchemists took to get their cauldrons hot enough to create their special alchemical potions. One of the famous elixirs contained mercury, which of course is extremely poisonous. However, according to legend, if you got your cauldron to just the right temperature, and all the steps were correctly and meticulously followed, mercury could be transformed into the elixir of immortality–a secret potion that the Alchemists claimed made them able to live forever. As a metaphor, Stage Three heats up your belly so that you can have the proper temperature to move onto Stage Four. In essence, you're working on skills to contain or consolidate Qi in your cauldron, or lower Dan Tian area, which is located in your lower abdomen.

During this Earth step in Stage Three, we often do a lot of moxibustion in sessions, which is a technique that heats up acu-points around the belly button by burning little bits of the herb mugwort, also known as *artemisia vulgaris*.

NOTE: Moxibustion is best done by a Chinese Medicine practitioner due to possible contraindications. Many of our clients do their own moxibustion during this stage, but only after consulting with us for specific instructions and safety protocols.

Another approach to building your Qi in this stage is to use stone medicine, which is the practice of using healing stones to support and treat your body. We use it differently than the ancient Alchemists did, however. There are many stones that could be useful at this juncture of your journey. For example, Stibnite, which is also called Antimony, is a stone that helps us build energy. You can place it just below your belly button or about three inches to either side of it, to strengthen the Qi or fire in your lower abdomen. Here we are not talking about internal use, but please note that these stones can be toxic if ingested, so please talk to a Stone Medicine practitioner prior to using this technique or any Stone Medicine treatment.

A third approach is through Dao Yin exercises, also known as Daoist Qi Gong, which is the practice of moving your Qi to achieve healing results or to do Alchemical transformation. One way we build the Qi in the abdomen is through Tai Chi Dao Yin, a form of Qi Gong. In one exercise, you hold your hands just below the navel area, about six inches away, and simply concentrate on building the Qi there. There are many Tai Chi Dao Yin exercises that would be useful in Stage Three and for overall general health as well. They are quite gentle and easy to learn. If you're looking for a good starting place, we have created an instructional video on our Alchemy Learning Center website, which shows how to do some Dao Yin exercises that can help you move Qi and build and strengthen the Alchemical cauldron.

A great way to work on your belly Qi is to focus on your digestion. If your digestion is strong, that is a good sign that you might work through this stage rather easily. If your digestion is weak, you will need to look at how to improve it before you proceed. How can you do that?

First, it helps to assess your diet. Are you eating well in general? From a Chinese Medicine point of view, we want to make sure our diet is *balanced*. We use tongue diagnosis to help identify strengths and weaknesses in the diet, the organs, and the body as a whole. For example, if your tongue is thickly coated in white, has a crack down the middle, or is extremely wet looking, that indicates that your digestive "fire" is weak. In this case, you may want to consult a Chinese Medicine practitioner about ways to increase your digestive strength in this stage.

Stage Three heals your gut by addressing the emotional baggage you've stored in your body. The Sitting on Eggs meditation is a powerful tool you can use every day for releasing the "old stuff" you have stored in your lower abdomen. We like using this "stuff" metaphor, because many people "stuff" their emotions down around the belt area of the body. We attempt to store the toxic things that were too physically or emotionally overwhelming. Since there was no available way to purge or manage this toxic emotional material, the body must find a place to put it away in deep storage.

The area where you store this stuff is what in Chinese Medicine is called the Belt Channel or the *Dai Mai* channel, which wraps right around your waist. It can contain whatever emotional baggage you have so far accumulated in your lifetime; you may even have ancestral or past-life material hidden there as well. Much of the emotional content stored in the Dai Mai is repressed and so you may not be consciously aware of it. Stage Three releases this unconscious accumulation of stuff. People with acute or chronic digestive issues often discover that working with Stage Three clears up these problems.

One thing to remember is that there is *no hurry*. If your digestion has been very weak, it might take you months or even years to improve and strengthen your digestion enough to proceed further with this stage. Remember that Alchemy is never something you tackle and "accomplish" within a set time period. You must always allow the body time to adjust and heal itself.

Life is a journey, not a destination.

–Ralph Waldo Emerson

Alchemy could take many lifetimes beyond this one to complete. In fact, you may have been introduced to this book because you've already been working on an Alchemical path in previous lifetimes, and now you're returning to the practice. At Stage Three it's more important than ever for you to take all the time you need.

Emotionally, Stage Three begins to signal its completion when you feel a lightness, like some weight has lifted off of you. Old, deeply rooted pain that you once felt about your family members dissipates, or sometimes even family curses seem to disappear. Typical emotional or psychological triggers suddenly lose their charge. You just aren't as reactive to the world around you, and you may feel that there is some kind of light emanating from you. People may start wanting to spend more time around you. You may start enjoying family events with others that would have disturbed or triggered you in the past. If these things are happening, you are getting ready for Stage Four.

The Sitting on Eggs Meditation

Begin with the Relax Your Body, Clear Your Mind, Open Your Doors meditation as described on page 79. When you are ready, start this meditation.

Begin by imagining you're a hen sitting very lightly on her eggs. A hen can't sit too hard on those eggs or she will squash them. She has to lift up a little bit even as she's sitting down on them.

Imagine pulling up inside from your groin area, specifically your perineum, through your belly area, which may feel a little more taut than usual, and coming up all the way to your heart. Many of our meditations focus on grounding and moving energy downward. This meditation has very different energetics. When lifting upward, you may feel some lightness, and some hope coming up. Sit on your eggs with an awareness of that feeling for a few minutes.

Now you're going to add another energetic dynamic. While continuing to lift up, imagine a bright light shining down and out from the bottom of your body, specifically your perineum. You can also imagine warmth emanating out from that same area, downward and outward to warm and incubate your eggs. It's a nice, warm, lovely feeling of healing and nurturing energy.

So now you have the energy lifting up and the energy of light and warmth emanating downward. Your waist is the halfway place where these energies are pulling up from and moving down out of.

NOTE: Don't think too much about the actual eggs. You don't need to take care of them. You won't break or squash them. The analogy of sitting like a chicken doesn't come with any parental responsibilities toward the eggs or to ensure their safety. They are perfectly safe! They are all good eggs. You don't need to worry if they hatch, and you don't have to take them all the way through to chicken high school! Yes, we have heard all of these thoughts from our students. After all, this is an Earth Element Stage and Earths pride themselves on being very good parents. You're simply developing the ability to lift up while sitting lightly the way a hen would, and at the same time emanating the kind of light and warmth that could incubate eggs. It's a great meditation practice to build body muscles for good meditation posture too.

Now that you have the energetic dynamics set up, and the eggs are indeed safe, we can begin the meditation. Begin by once again allowing all thoughts that arise to pass through your mind. This time, however, as a thought arises, ask yourself, "Is this thought a relatively unimportant one?" An example of this would be, "What's for lunch?" If so, recheck your alignment inside to make sure you're not squashing your eggs. Lift up and shine the light and warmth down. Then un-focus your mind again.

When a thought emerges that is about something that feels particularly important—especially something from the past that was a big deal, perhaps even something you haven't thought about in ages—just pause and examine that thought for a moment. Sometimes you need to allow it to fully surface, especially if it's an old memory. Once you realize what it is, it's time to clear it. To do this, you push it downward into your incubator light. The light evaporates the thought, and it simply and easily disappears. Often you can't even remember what it was. You just stop thinking about it. You can either continue and allow another thought to arise, or finish and write about that experience in your journal. For the next session, simply set yourself up as you did before, and when new, significant memories or feelings come up, give them to the light again. Repeat and relax.

We suggest you practice this meditation for a minimum of 100 days. This is a great but challenging 100-day goal. Are you ready for it? We think you are!

Step Three: Heaven

The last step in Stage Three is the step of Heaven. During this stage, we return once again to our memories, especially those times of our life when we felt blocked or disappointed. Heaven is represented by your head, and this stage initiates the movement of Qi or energy from your lower abdomen up to your brain, so that you can move into Stage Four.

When the brain opens, you can experience a sense of rebirth. The ancient Alchemists felt that this was the process of giving birth to your own spiritual life.

> When you were born into this body, you had to come down to this earth, through your mother's birthing canal. But to birth your spiritual being, you move upward through the top of your head toward heaven.

Because this stage is about moving the Qi upward, some physical responses are not uncommon. For instance, this opening of the brain often helps to ease or even relieve depression. You also may feel shaky or a little disoriented at first when you move through this step. But it's imperative that you open up the brain, in order to move on to Stage Four.

Case Study: Andrea Takes Her Own Path

Andrea came to Alchemy after her mother died from a long and debilitating disease. Andrea was in her thirties and the death hit her hard. She had a good relationship with her mother but they were not "super close," since they'd had a somewhat up-and-down lifetime journey together. Andrea was quite afraid that she would someday become depressed like her mother had been, or that she would even eventually die of the same disease, because of their genetic connection. Something was haunting her but it wasn't necessarily her own stuff—it was more a fear that forces from her ancestral lineage would take her over somehow and ruin her life.

Andrea did a number of Alchemical treatments initially, including a Grieving treatment to help her release her stuck sorrow and the Thirteen Ghost Points treatment to release the trauma of the death. She immediately had a huge shift and started to feel more like she had felt before her mother's death had so affected her. However, some of her fears about her mother's legacy still hung around, and continued to somehow haunt her.

When Andrea was ready to begin the actual Stages of Alchemy, she sailed through the first two stages over a period of several months. Easy peasy! But once we started Stage Three, it was immediately apparent that she would need to slow down and do a lot of work in this phase. In fact, her Alchemical work came to a screeching halt, which is a very common occurrence—many people, practitioners and healers find Stage Three very challenging. A huge amount of blame and anger towards her father surfaced, and she suddenly realized that she'd been blaming him for her mother's death. She was also angry at her longtime boyfriend, who in some ways reminded her of her father.

The anger was visceral, and made her whole body shake during her sessions. It took over a year for her to work on these challenges, sometimes even needing to avoid contact with her father, who she genuinely loved and wanted to have a relationship with. She finally ended the relationship with her boyfriend. Even though it was a difficult stage for her to go through, she reported that she actually liked the process, and in line with that, she was one of our clients who did in fact feel a sense of rebirth during it.

After that year of intensively working to untie the knots that had been holding her to her old beliefs, she reported going home to see her father and feeling completely free and unaffected around him. Her release of these struggles and traumas let us know that she had made it through Stage Three.

Let's look at some of the ways Andrea undid those knots. During this year, we worked on building her weak stomach energy with moxibustion and acupressure points. She had been plagued with lifelong digestive issues that often crippled her and kept her from working. Perhaps her mother's depression had led to some deep soul malnourishment in childhood? Or maybe the thread of what caused her mother to suffer was woven genetically through Andrea as well, until she was able to free herself from that influence. We will never know the exact story but it was clear she needed to rebuild, strengthen, and restore her Alchemical cauldron.

After another full year of sessions and personal work, her stomach was much more normal and her emotions were much more positive as we worked with Step Three (Heaven). She was a totally new person, free and clear from her mother's influence from the past. For the first time in her life, she could own it and live it as truly hers and she was ready to move on to whatever the world would bring her, including Stage Four. She was a little nervous but mostly excited to see what would come her way.

Advanced Forgiveness: Ho'oponopono Homework

For homework in this stage, you're going to move from affirming your life, the process of Stage Two, to working out your deep traumas using the power of forgiveness. It's not just forgiving the people who did you harm, but also forgiving yourself for whatever poor judgment, lack of self-worth, or lack of self-love constituted your own part in it. We all make mistakes, but what really hurts us is when we burden ourselves with our mistakes, and never set ourselves free. Stage Three helps us change all that. It allows us to release the rigidity so that we can transform the guilt and blame that resides inside us.

Part of being free is not just forgiving our perpetrators and ourselves, but also forgiving the Divine, the all-powerful governing force of the universe—by whatever name you may call it—that we believe puts us in those bad situations to begin with. This is an especially important step if harm was done to you as a child.

The most powerful exercise we like to suggest for this stage comes from a Hawaiian Shamanic tradition called Ho'oponopono. In this wonderful tradition, the underlying belief is that we create our realities. In this empowering model, anything negative that has occurred or is occurring in our lives is completely our own responsibility. In other words, if we are having trouble releasing a deep, old trauma and its effect on us, then we have to claim responsibility for it.

This philosophy is closely aligned with the Daoist Alchemy idea that everything we see in the world is an illusion, and when you *wake up from that*, you become disillusioned. Suddenly you can see the truth about this non-reality that we all agree to believe is so real. Because the Daoists believe we come into this life to have experiences that we will learn and grow from, it stands to reason that we picked these experiences before birth. We chose that unloving parent. Or we decided on that horrible car accident because we stood to learn something very important from it. Following the Daoist understanding, we also, in our current physical reality, are empowered to heal whatever it is in us that required traumatic experiences to teach us lessons in the first place.

For many of our clients who have traumatic stories from their pasts, this can be a hard pill to swallow. How could this trauma be the fault of the victim? We agree, it's counter-intuitive and doesn't seem rational. And it's not that we are saying it's the *fault* of the victim in a traditional sense, at all. Instead, the Hawaiian "Advanced Forgiveness" practice of Ho'oponopono is simply about acknowledging your part in the creation of your own reality. Both the good and the bad things that appear in your life are ultimately your own lessons, that were laid out to engender great learning and growth during this lifetime. Many, many people find relief in aligning with this form of healing, and it's a very gentle approach.

Advanced Forgiveness is not about forgiving the perpetrator of your trauma, but instead forgiving yourself for creating that traumatic experience. A basic tenet of Advanced Forgiveness is that we create all experiences for the fulfillment of our own purposes. Everything that exists in reality is said to serve us in some way or another.

Advanced Forgiveness Exercise

This exercise is one of the most powerful exercises you can do to release yourself from the guilt and blame of past traumas. It works best if you do it in conjunction with Stage Three, which energetically requires you to release things from a cellular level, not just intellectually.

Take some time to do this exercise, perhaps a half hour or more. Find a quiet place to sit or lie down. There are three parts to it.

First, begin by reviewing your life from the start. Go as far back as you can remember, and then try to go back even further. This usually takes some time and practice. Go through each year of your life, and when you find a moment that was particularly painful for you, spend some time there. This might be quite painful, but try to look at all the people who had a role in that event. Do you hold any grudges against any of them? In other words, who are the people you are still mad at? If you're not sure, could you make this statement?

"If only _____ hadn't done _____, everything would have been so much better."

If you find you can fill in those blanks with a particular person from your memory, then you need to practice Advanced Forgiveness with that person.

NOTE: You can also try filling the blank in with your own name. And when you've done that, also try filling in the blank with the Divine. It is extremely powerful to do the Advanced Forgiveness exercise for yourself, and for whatever your conception of the Divine may be.

Now think about the person you need to forgive. Imagine them standing right in front of you. You can often feel the emotions of anger, resentment, and blame. You see that person only from your vantage point, from the lens of what they did to you. You cannot see them as a whole person.

Repeat the following phrases slowly:
I'm sorry.
Please forgive me.
Thank you.
I love you.

It might be difficult to say these words at first, to a person who caused you pain and trauma. It can almost seem ridiculous. What you are saying is, *"I'm sorry I created you to be* such an awful, mean, horrible, person in my life." And "*Please forgive me* for creating you this way." And "*Thank you* for healing me through your existence in my life, because as I begin to forgive, I heal, and your actions have helped me see that I created this." And then finally, I *love you* really means, "I can transcend this illusion and love the pure spirit of who you are, which sets me free."

Continue to repeat the words "I'm sorry, please forgive me, thank you, I love you" as part of your meditation over and over, for five minutes or more. At first it may feel like nothing is happening. After awhile though, you should begin to feel something shifting, as if some lightness or softening is slowly coming in. They say that it's as if something comes down from heaven, and is delivered to your mind, and you begin to shift. I find that that the rigid identity I had subscribed to that person ("bad," "mean," "messed up," or whatever) begins to soften. There is an opening that will allow you to see the divinity, the true spirit, and the inherent goodness of that person. It's as if you can see that person as their own loving mother and father would see them, acknowledging their foibles and negative attributes, but still finding love and appreciation for their human spirit and for all the good parts of them.

Essentially, what you're doing here is reclaiming your innocence. You aren't seeing all the complications of the "evil" that you remember. You're seeing the goodness. You return to seeing things the way a child who has never been hurt, sees things. It's a return to innocence and, in a sense, a recalling of all that was lost, or stolen. Again, this may take time, especially if the grievance you are holding is deep and longstanding.

Once you feel a big shift and a sense of love for this person, you may notice that you feel more empowered within your own life. Keep repeating the exercise and continue scanning your lifetime. When you come to the next painful moment in your life, repeat the steps above, even if it involves some or all of the same people.

Homework 2: Mabu - Horse Stance Training

In addition to your forgiveness homework, we often suggest *Mabu* (horse) stance training, which helps you to become more grounded and connected to the earth. You will need to be strong for the next Stage of Alchemy. To find your Mabu stance, you stand with your knees slightly bent, and your tongue on the roof of your mouth, while focusing on feeling rooted into the ground. If someone came up and pushed you while you were standing this way, you wouldn't budge. You are grounded, and your feet are completely rooted to the earth. You are connected to the power of the earth's energy. Studying and practicing more Dao Yin or Qi Gong stances will definitely help you to build this rooted feeling in your life.

It's the art of not consciously moving.

–Master Jeffrey Yuen

Please go to our Alchemy Learning Center Website for more information and videos about Dao Yin and Qi Gong practices you can do on your own: AlchemyLearningCenter.com.

He who is in harmony with the Tao
is like a newborn child.

—Lao Tzu

Stage Four: Circulation

The first three stages of Alchemy are a trinity of releasing and letting go. In Stage One, you released the day-to-day memories you used to cling to your own identity. In Stage Two, you let go of the protections and armor that were weighing you down. In Stage Three, you purified the guilt and blame held deeply inside you. Having worked through those three stages, you are now ready for the next trinity of stages. Stages Four, Five, and Six show you how to expand your mind so that you can change your perception of the world, and therefore, change your reality by learning how to circulate your Qi in a different way. So why change your reality? Well, maybe the first question to consider is:

"How real is reality?"

Is our perception of the world really the true reality? Or is life really an illusion of our own making. Ponder this for a moment: scientists have found that people with multiple personalities can have one disease within one of their personalities, and not have it in another. They can actually have a blood test, such as for diabetes, and one personality somehow comes back positive, and the other negative. Same blood, different personality. Perhaps a better question to be asking is:

"Do we create our own reality?"

If you are unwell and you are able to change your mind and your perception of reality, do you have the powerful potential to recover from any illness?

Stage Four, the first of this next group of stages, is one of our favorite stages. Having released your guilt and blame, you will begin to sense of new-found freedom in your life. It will lead you to experiences that are fresh and unique, like those of a child. Think about how children interact with the world for the first time as they explore and discover things. Can you remember what it's like to experience something for the first time without any preconceived notions, without any judgments, or biases? What would it feel like, right now, to return to that innocence? Now that you've released all the old pains, you can reclaim that sense of wonder.

Stepping into the world of Stage Four is a huge shift in consciousness from the previous three. This is why it's important not to rush into it. Before you engage with the power of Stage Four, you must first ensure that your lower abdomen Qi is strong, which is indicated by good digestion and a feeling of having lots of energy. In Stage Three, you build your energy, especially your digestive energy or *digestive fire*, as we call it in Chinese Medicine. That belly cauldron we've been talking about is fully stoked and the proper firing time has been reached. This ensures that when you get to Stage Four, you have the energy to shift your consciousness.

This next stage can feel like you're taking off a pair of blinders that you've been wearing your whole life. Your habitual way of seeing the world is stripped away. Those blinders had been making it impossible to see what is actually there. Without them, you begin to see that all your life experiences and all the things your parents and teachers told you were the true reality, aren't necessarily real. With your eyes now wide open, you can suddenly see the gloriousness of what is really all around you. You see the world as a small child would—a big place full of magical things. It's your wonderful spatial and cosmic awakening.

The Elemental Theme for Stage Four—Metal

The overall theme of Stage Four is to feel safe enough in life to be free and easy like a child. It's not difficult to become over-attached to our parents or caretakers because it seems scary to explore the world on our own. The Metal Element in particular is acutely aware of themes of attachment and freedom. They want to fly through life on a magic carpet ride, but they also want to feel deep connections with others. This stage requires that you resolve the the Metal Element issues inside you and learn how to connect deeply within yourself—like a child with its parent—so that you can feel free to explore the world like a young one who has internalized that parental love and protection and knows that it is always with you inside. Attachment and detachment are the lessons we learn from the Metal Element.

Stage Four has a five distinct steps:

1. Innocent Child

2. Wind Screen

3. The Microcosmic Orbit

4. Exchanging Desires for Wisdom

5. Rejuvenation

Step One: Innocent Child

Step One of Stage Four in Alchemy opens your eyes and creates renewal; it's a rebirth, returning you to the state of an innocent child. A return to innocence means that you've not yet been contaminated by negative experiences. You don't even have an idea of negativity. You are clean and clear. All is good in the world.

The child-like mind represents our ability to be immortal. We pass our genes onto the next generation and continue to live through them. It's our eternal legacy. The next generation always comes up with new and better ideas, new ways of experiencing life that are even better than before. The child is our hope for the future. New generations give us new ways of living life, new ways of healing the old illnesses that were passed on in our genes. But what if we could become our own hope for the future? In our own personal rebirth, can we become like a magical, innocent child again? Can we transform *ourselves* and take on the role we usually give to the next generation? Can we come up with radical new ways of living without having to die? If so, then our children don't have to carry our torch or our burdens because we have let go of these in this life.

Becoming the Innocent Child is also a way of releasing your immense potential. Children still have all possibilities at their disposal! They don't see limitations or obstacles. They *know* deep in their bones that they might become the greatest singer, athlete, or politician that ever lived.

Anything and everything is possible to them. They don't know that they can't grow up to win The Voice or to be the prime minister of their country. They don't know what they *can't* do. They only imagine what they *can* do. For an innocent child, limitlessness is a reality.

In the limitless mind that is awakened in Stage Four, you approach everything with curiosity, with no memory of it ever happening before. You experience all the beauty and wonder of the world, as if it's an utterly magical place!

This is such a different way of thinking and being. Here's an example of how we have experienced the world up until now. When you're about to eat a blueberry as an adult, you have a memory and a thought process about what a blueberry is and what it tastes like before you even put it in your mouth. You can't help but apply that memory to the experience of tasting the blueberry. You don't have the child's complete unknowing of what's about to happen to your mouth and senses. You know pretty much what your mouth is in for. You expect and anticipate that flavor that you've come to know. You may even compare the flavor you taste to past blueberries you've had. You definitely don't taste it like it's something new. The old filters of your past experiences interfere with your actual present experience. You are subconsciously pre-judging that little blueberry before it lands on your tongue.

Innocent children have nothing to compare their experiences to. For them, that first blueberry is a completely new experience. Children approach things with complete openness and awe—like tasting this brand new little round fruit. They might roll it in their palms and examine it and marvel about its beautiful dusty blue color, having never eaten something blue, squishy, and round before. What an amazing world to have created this thing called a blueberry!

Children aren't jaded yet. They don't have any agendas. As they get older they may tend to get emotionally entangled with parents and authority figures, but very young children are more clear and clean, and have no guilt. Guilt is an emotion that can besiege your life and take away your freedom. The first step of Stage Four is to return yourself to that level of innocence, where you are pure and free, uncontaminated by past experiences and habits of thinking, free of guilt.

When you achieve the ability to truly practice innocence in your life, the colors around you might start to appear brighter, more vivid, even psychedelic. The sounds are more prominent and sharp, less faded into the background. Your taste buds are attuned to every nuance of flavor in the food. Your fingers become more sensitive to all the different textures you touch. This all sounds quite experiential and pleasurable, but be forewarned!

> *If you truly opened all your senses this much all at once, you would be completely overwhelmed!*

This is why it's so important that you are completely ready before you begin this stage, so you can handle the experience. Water Element people tend to have a bit of an advantage in this stage if they are living authentically in their Element. Water lives in a state of limitless potential all the time. That's why it's somewhat advantageous to be a Water person while doing Alchemy, especially Stage Four. However we don't all have to be Water people to be prepared and ready for anything!

In this step, you can give yourself permission to truly savor all the nuances of the experiences we take for granted every day in our lives, but without becoming overwhelmed.

Homework: Be the Child—No Preconceived Judgments

Set aside some time every day to practice being the innocent child. Let yourself be innocent and naive without premeditated thoughts adulterating what you're doing or diluting your experience. Let yourself have a reaction in every cell of your body to something new. Before you do something, clear yourself of all expectations about what you're about to experience.

You can try doing this in several ways.

1. You can embark on doing something you've never done before. You may wish to try something thrilling or exciting, or simply something new or out of your ordinary routine. Don't prepare mentally by setting expectations of how this new experience might feel. Get into the open mindset of a child as much as you can. What would it be like to experience something brand new?

2. You can also attempt to do something you've done many times before as if you've never done it before. You can practice this daily. Try it with driving the car. Can you see the blurred landscape going by as

if it's the first time? Can you feel the force of gravity pulling as you round the curve? You can even simply go outside, like a child, just to play out in nature. Resist the adult desire to squash your sense of play and instead turn every trip outdoors into a fitness mission. Learn to play and explore again.

3. Try choosing to have a sensory experience as if it's the first time. Pay fresh and intense attention to every texture, sight, and sound. When you eat your dinner, are you just trying to satisfy your hunger? Are you even present while you're chewing and swallowing? Try really concentrating on the tastes and textures of the food in your mouth. If you're with friends, try to focus on experiencing the food with all your senses, as much as you're focused on whatever people are saying at the table. The food can have as much meaning as the conversation.

Case Study: Playing with Newness

Lindsay really got excited about the "Being the Child" homework. When she was little, she was never really allowed to play freely or behave like a child. She was constantly told to be quiet and act like a little lady. She remembers going into the kitchen where the family cook would sometimes let her eat candy and sweets. She felt the most like a child there, out from under her mother's stern gaze.

When she started Stage Four, she learned to embrace the concept of the Innocent Child and the exploration of her senses with enthusiasm and gusto. She not only tried eating a blueberry as if she'd never tasted one before, she went even further and packed herself whole picnics full of yummy treats! "Raspberries," she exclaimed, "are simply amazing!" She walked through nearby hills and trails, found lovely overlooks, and ate her delicious picnics all summer long. She was essentially discovering how to play, and she was seeing through a child's eyes for the very first time. It was a delightful and glorious summer of adventure.

Step Two: Wind Screen

Step Two of Stage Four offers ways to address any overwhelm that may arise from this stage in Alchemy. There are various reasons why you might experience this.

Over the course of your lifetime, you've developed filters that are beneficial for you. You've chosen, for example, not to hear the sound of the refrigerator running in your kitchen or the occasional sirens, trains, car alarms, or lawnmowers droning on your street all day long. If you suddenly removed all those filters from your senses at once, it could easily overload your circuits.

If you've been confined to a very narrow way of experiencing life until now, this much change may even be frightening. You need to have a way to mitigate these changes. Change in Chinese Medicine is likened to the Wind. The Wind brings changes, and sometimes these aren't welcome. Imagine driving fast down the road in a car without a windshield. Sometimes we need some protection from too much change. We need a shield, so to speak, to help buffer the incoming stimulus from the chaotic, busy world.

We often resist all kinds of changes by bracing ourselves and tightening our muscles, usually in our shoulders and necks. Fear causes that resistance. If we feel fear when we're practicing being the child again, we need to put up a *wind screen*. We need a break from all this change. We don't have to be the innocent child all the time, all at once. We can pull the covers over our heads and block out all the input to our senses, so that we have a little time to adjust. This step is only here to use in case the fears come up or our senses feel too overwhelmed.

Removing the Blinders

The Innocent Child step may also release latent things you've stored deep in your bones. Perhaps there are things from your childhood that you blocked out because you didn't want to see them. You created those blinders in the first place so that you wouldn't have to see certain things. Removing the blinders and becoming the innocent child again requires great bravery for some people. Letting go of the expectations that the old, bad things might happen again, and daring to be wide-eyed and embrace whatever will come without knowing what it is, or without even trying to know—that takes a profound level of courage. It might take more courage than you feel you have. That's alright. If these feelings begin to surface, just return to Stage Three. There is more healing to be done. You don't even have to proceed to Stage Four. You can spend your lifetime healing in Stage Three. That might be all you are destined to do. Sometimes the injury or pain was too great to return all the way back to the innocent child. Be kind to yourself. Be true.

Standing in Limitless Potential

Opening up your immense potential in Step One of Stage Four can feel freeing and invigorating on the one hand, and at the same time it may also feel overwhelming. You might not be able to accept this feeling of unlimited potential in yourself, after a lifetime of trying to subdue it and hold it down. You've been told that you can't feel, say, or do what you want, and you've really taken that on and believed it.

Feeling a sudden, big surge of your own potential rising up can be disorienting or regretful for some, or it might be a wonderful uplifting feeling that is familiar, but you haven't had it in a long time. Again, be kind to yourself. Give yourself time.

The Wind Screen step of Stage Four is here to say that you might need time to block out all these Winds of Change. Some of us go too fast. If we open our eyes too wide, all at once, then suddenly, unexpectedly, we may feel completely unsafe. This step is saying, please take your time with this. It's a big consciousness shift to return to the Innocent Child after living a life of self-protection and insecurity.

Letting Go of Distracting Thoughts

As we cultivate the child-like mind, our thoughts may tend to feel a little more erratic. We can sometimes feel distracted by our own thoughts if the Winds of Change are blowing too much. The idea of giving yourself a wind screen is to release these distracting thoughts that we keep hearing inside our heads. It's key to practice quieting the mind, to help us let go of any over-stimulation from opening our portals and letting our brains take in so much visual information.

Homework 1: Adult Time vs. Play Time

As much quick progress as you may make in Stage Four, you also need to allow yourself plenty of time to transition. Moving too quickly in this Stage is not necessarily a good idea. While it can be a lot of fun to return to a child-like state of innocence and openness, you will of course need to return to your adult self frequently, to attend to your everyday life.

This homework is about that part of the transition—returning to your adult self and handling your life as an adult. While you do so, try to keep in mind the feelings from your *Be the Child* homework. You don't need to let go of everything at once and be reborn into someone new. You can fall back and rest in the comfort of who you've been. As you do so, keep in mind how it felt to be a child and how you may have enjoyed life differently in that mode of being. Maintain that link to your child self, while activating your adult identity. Watch for the differences between how you behave and feel as the innocent child versus how you feel living in your adult identity. What is the difference? Keep a daily journal about the contrast between the two states, and how it feels to be in each.

Homework 2: Practice the Relax Your Mind Meditation Again

If you are finding it challenging to open up your life to living life as a child in this Step, return to the more adult nature of meditation in your daily practice. Practice our Relax Your Body, Clear Your Mind, Open Your Doors meditation from page 79 of this book, several times a day to release the distracting thoughts from your mind. Life as a child may feel exhilarating, but too much exhilaration isn't always helpful here. Use this meditation to help calm your mind and stay grounded. It can be a good idea to continue alternating between being the child and the adult until being the child feels easy and fun but not overwhelming to your mind.

Step Three: The Microcosmic Orbit

As you move through Stage Four, there is an even greater transformation that's occurring—think of it as something brewing under the surface. The experience of this stage is not only about becoming an innocent child, but it's also about becoming someone you have not been before. You are leaving behind your old, adult-only identity, —and your cherished old ideas of yourself. If you're going to be the child, you have to give up the adult you spent many years developing. Whether these constructs you've carefully built about yourself were good or bad, they made up your ego identity. You held them tightly because everyone needs an identity in order to move through the world. You needed to be able to say to everyone around you, *this is me*. You've carefully constructed and protected these adult ideas of yourself. And now, in this phase of Stage Four, you have to let all that go. A child's identity is not constructed, it simply is. The child presents a raw and unfiltered "me" to the world.

If you are to be able to return to the innocent child self, you will see that you really do have to let go of many of your old ideas about who you are—even your old preferences. For example, if you like blueberries in a pie, but not raw blueberries, you have to let that go and taste the blueberry innocently, as a child would. You release preconceived notions of what you do or don't like. And in fact, you may find that you now love raw blueberries picked right off the tree—sweet and sour alike. That's the new potential of everything in the world that arrives in this stage. You now have the potential to transform. You can *do* things differently, and you can *be* someone completely new. Once you've embraced yourself as a child with unlimited possibilities, you begin to move the Qi and circulate it through your body in new ways.

As you begin to experience this new circulation, practicing The *Microcosmic Orbit Visualization* every day is very helpful. This process serves to move things up and out of you as you release that old identity, and all those specific parts of your personal story that you grasped and held onto so strongly. In order to do this, you have to begin to take all that Qi you have stored in your lower abdomen and move it upward to your head so it can be used there. It's time to put the fire you created in your belly in Stage Three to work.

How does a child come into existence? In procreation, the sexual fluids mix together, to create something from two things, the parents, that becomes one thing, the baby.

The number two is the number of Yin and Yang, which then merge to create the number one.

Seeing this through the lens of this Stage of Alchemy, it's as if you're having a child, but you're also actually the child itself. You're birthing and rebirthing yourself. Children carry on our legacy after our deaths. Only this time, in a sense, you're living out your own legacy, by becoming your own child. You're recycling yourself, your essences, which is how you get younger, not older using Alchemy–like the character in the Benjamin Button movie. You circulate your own essences to feed and enrich your brain and your organs so you can rejuvenate yourself.

We've talked quite a bit about the fact that to become an innocent child, you must release your "accrued" identity. You also have to release any intense desires or lust. Lust is not something an innocent child even contemplates. Children's desires are fleeting, and they are easily distracted from them. Adult lust is something that can withstand all distractions and be quite overpowering. It's not just sexual lust that we are talking about here. We can also lust after all sorts of material things. These deep desires need to come up and out, so that they can be released.

This is a different kind of letting go than we did in Stage Two. This isn't just the old stuff we're protecting ourselves from and the armory we carry. Now we have to let go of the stuff we want and are really chasing after–the things we're lusting after. They also form our identity. The phrase "I've always wanted _____," also helps to form our identity. To keep that desire is to be who you've always been. To let go of that desire is to change.

In Chinese Medicine, Wind is change. But desire and lust can also be conceived of as Wind. Letting desires and lust affect our bodies can deplete us, which leads us sooner to death. For example, you may have devoted all your essences to a relationship that was ultimately draining. Maybe you feel like you wasted those ten years, and in the end you broke up anyway. What happens to those essences you invested in that relationship? Like investing in the stock market just before it suddenly drops, you can lose all you've invested. It's one thing to take a risk and spend ten years devoted to building a relationship. But what if you actually knew the relationship was bad for you from the very beginning? Why did you invest yourself emotionally and physically in the first place if you knew deep down inside that it wasn't healthy? Maybe you just wanted so badly to have a relationship, you lusted for it, and you overlooked the signs that it wasn't right. Maybe desires overrode your common sense so much that you decided to do it anyway. A child entering that relationship wouldn't have needed to force it to work, because those fresh eyes would have been sensitive to the negative signs from the start and most likely would have turned in another direction, one that was naturally satisfying and pleasing.

Maybe you're chasing after another promotion in your career, or the idea of some lover you haven't met yet, or you are craving the peace and quiet that you so wish for in your life. Or you may even be chasing after this theory of Alchemy itself. No matter what they may be, you have to try and let these desires go, as much as you would your pains and grievances. You can't experience Alchemical transformation from a place of desperately needing to change. Alchemy must be approached from a place of lightness and freedom. This stage is where we let go of the lusting and I *have to have it* feelings. The Microcosmic Orbit movement can help free us from these feelings and move us into the natural, organic peace and ease of the childlike mind.

Microcosmic Orbit Visualization Exercise

One of the most important components of Stage Four is the practice of the Microcosmic Orbit. This is an exercise that moves the Qi through your body in a specific, circuitous pattern, by using visualization and a kinesthetic body awareness. You imagine the Qi moving, and you attune your senses to what's happening in your body in that area. As you focus on it, and then sense it, soon you can feel it moving and circulating.

This is an extremely powerful meditative exercise that you shouldn't do until you're ready, that is until you have done all the prep work from the previous stages and you feel ready deep inside yourself. Even if you are reading this book for the first time and have not yet begun to work on the first three stages but find yourself "lusting" to do this stage right now, definitely do the work of the first three stages first, before embarking on this part of your journey. We cannot stress this enough. Every Stage of Alchemy builds on the one before it. You are practicing self-cultivation, and gardeners know that the plants will be healthy and lush only if the soil has been properly prepared. From an Alchemical perspective, you can't easily release what's in your abdomen in Stage Three until you've first released the protections in your chest in Stage Two. In all of these advanced stages, proceeding too quickly can cause a lot of mental stress and anguish. Be honest with yourself. Or even better, work with a skilled guide or practitioner. Find someone who can be impartial and assess your progress without pushing you to move forward too quickly.

In traditional practices the Microcosmic Orbit is different for men and women based on the Chinese Medicine understanding of how Yin and Yang relates to gender. We describe the traditional practices followed by a discussion of how to approach these practices for non-binary and transgender individuals. The idea here is that you move Qi from your strength and use it to feed your weakness. In Chinese Medicine, it is believed that masculine energy is more Yang, which we will call Yang Dominant, and feminine energy is more Yin, which we will call Yin Dominant.

The Yang Dominant Approach

Start the Microcosmic Orbit Visualization Exercise by touching the tip of your tongue to the roof of your mouth. Now focus on the perineum, the spot between your genitals and your anus. You can imagine there is a ball of energy sitting there, and you begin to move that energy up your back, up through your tailbone and sacrum and into your spine in your lower back. Go slowly. If the ball of energy is having difficulty moving slowly up and through an area, it may mean that area is blocked. Slow down even more there and allow the energy to find its way through the blockage. In other words, you don't want to just quickly move the energy up your back without any awareness of what's happening along the way. Allow the sticking points some time to unstick. Let the energy knots release and relax.

Continue to move the Qi energy up your spine to your mid-back, then your upper back, and finally let it flow up to your neck. Again, you focus on the movement of the Qi, and slow down for any stuck areas to let them unstick. Allow the Qi to move up the center of the back of your head, and up and over the crown of your head. It will then tip downwards onto your forehead, down between your eyes, and along your nose to a point directly on the center of your philtrum, the groove between the base of the nose and the border of the upper lip. You can even hold that point to familiarize yourself with the sensation there. This point is called Du 26, or GV 26, also known as The Middle of Man.

Now continue the Qi or energy ball moving downward, to the center of your upper lip and then on to the center of your chin. You can touch this very important point as well, which is found on the center of the chin crease, to familiarize yourself with the sensations there. This point is Ren 24, or CV 24, which is also called Receiving Fluid. Continue moving the Qi down your throat and then into your chest. Let it flow down the center of your chest and into your belly to your belly button, and from there down through your lower abdomen, until it reaches the starting point, the perineum. That is one complete cycle of the Microcosmic Orbit Visualization Exercise. Continue to cycle this energy up the back and down the front. You can start doing this visualization for five to ten minutes at first, extending it up to twenty minutes over time.

The Yin Dominant Approach

Start the *Microcosmic Orbit Visualization Exercise* by touching the tip of your tongue to the roof of your mouth. Now focus on the perineum, the spot between your genitals and your anus. Imagine there is a ball of energy there that you begin to move up the front of your body to your pubic bone and into the area in front of the uterus. As you do this, you really want to take your time. If the ball of energy or Qi is having difficulty moving slowly through an area, that may mean the area is blocked. You want to slow down even more and allow that energy to find its way through the blockage. In other words, you don't want to just quickly move the energy up the front of you without any awareness of what's happening along the way. Allow the sticking points time to unstick.

Continue to move the Qi up your belly to your belly button, then your chest, and finally into your throat. Again, pay attention and slow down in stuck areas, allowing extra time for the energy to loosen the blockage and flow through there. As the energy moves into your head, begin by moving it up to the center of your chin. You can even hold that point on the center of the chin crease to familiarize yourself with the point's sensation. This point is Ren 24, or CV 24, which is also called Receiving Fluid.

At this point, re-check to make sure your tongue is touching the roof of your mouth. Now continue upward, to a point directly on the center of your philtrum, the groove between the base of the nose and the border of the upper lip. You can touch this very important point as well to familiarize yourself with the sensations. This point is called Du 26, or GV 26, also known as The Middle of Man.

Continue up the center of your face between your eyes, then up your forehead and over the top or crown of your head. Now continue down the center of the back of your head and bring the energy into your neck along your spine. Allow the energy to follow your spine downward through your back, slowly, into your tailbone and finally back down to the starting point, the perineum. That is one cycle. Continue to cycle this energy up the front of your body and down the back. You can start doing this visualization for five to ten minutes at first, and extend if up to twenty minutes over time.

Energy Reversal

After doing this meditation for a fairly long period of time, you may find that at some point the energy naturally wants to reverse itself. If this happens, and you are certain you are not forcing it in any way, you can allow the energy to reverse directions. In advanced Alchemy, this is a sign that your body has begun reversing the cycle of aging. With the Yin Dominant Approach, the Yin usually feeds the Yang. With the Yang Dominant Approach, the Yang usually feeds the Yin. When that pattern reverses, your energy is rejuvenated. Remember that this takes time and extensive practice. Don't rush it or push yourself ahead. Always seek a practitioner who understands and can guide you in these more advanced meditation practices.

Gender and the Microcosmic Orbit

For individuals who are in the process or have transitioned their gender, we've given a lot of thought about how to apply the very binary approach that Chinese Medicine takes to healing according to gender. We have yet to encounter anything in the classics that indicates the best approach to take. But here is the common sense wisdom we've gained from working with many transgender and non-binary individuals.

The idea behind the classical Microcosmic Orbit is that women have more Yin energy and men have more Yang energy. Women have more Yin because they have a womb on the front side, and in Chinese Medicine the front is the Yin side. Yin is a consolidating energy, a cocooning, gestating, creation energy easily symbolized by the womb. Men have more Yang energy, which is upward and outward surging energy. The penis and the erection is representative of this kind of energy.

There are a number of ways to approach this as a non-binary or transgender person. Some people take the stance that the physical Yin or Yang predominance that you were born with never changes, even with gender transition, so they practice the Microcosmic Orbit in the direction of their original gender assignment. Others feel that their Yin or Yang orientation changes along with their gender during a transition, or according to which gender feels most dominant to them at any given point in time.

If you believe your energetic nature doesn't match your gender assignment at birth, due to hormone enhancement, or your own body/mind/spirit shifts, or simply by nature, then you can do the Microcosmic Orbit according to your new Yin or Yang orientation. This could correlate with your declarative gender, but could also correlate with your own assessment of Yin and Yang in your body, if those are different from each other. In other words, you can choose the direction of your Microcosmic Orbit based on your current gender, or you can base it on your own assessment of whether you are currently embodying more Yin or more Yang.

Step Four: Exchanging Desires for Wisdom

Now that you've established the movement of Qi in your body, you might discover that there are substantial areas that are holding back a lot of deep desires, areas that in Chinese Medicine are described as places where dampness accumulates as excess fluid and fatty tissues, which serves to hold down those desires. Dampness is something we create when we have a great desire *that we don't actually believe we can fulfill*. We don't want to be disappointed, so we may eat sugary, heavy, and glutenous foods or create some other kind of addiction to help us neutralize or cover up and subdue our intense and uncomfortable feelings. Want that lover you can never have? Eating muffins, cakes, and bread will soothe your emotions for the moment. The desire isn't gone though. It's now just buried deep within your fatty tissues. For many people this can be an endless cycle—until they find a way to exit the dampness.

Step Four is one of those ways. You can move out that dampness that's helping you hold onto those deep unmet desires by burying them inside deep inner spaces. The most important thing to remember is that these desires distract you from what's really important—YOU. They cause you to focus outward, hoping to find solace there, instead of looking inward and tending to your own spiritual evolution. Buried desires take you on detours along your destiny's road. They waste the precious time you have on this planet to evolve, and to even become immortal. *I wasted three years in that lousy relationship.* They lead you to addictive, distractive behaviors that rob your time and energy. *I wasted a whole weekend trying to win at the casino.* To let these deeply buried desires go is to embrace real change. To keep them and repeat them over and over is to stop evolving.

Taking on Step Four is like going to the market and exchanging the dampness and unfulfilled desires for something better. You can trade the dampness for wisdom and positive change. In Alchemy treatments, we use fire, in the form of moxibustion, to dry up that dampness. There is also a Chinese Medicine treatment that is very helpful in this phase, especially if you have a lot of fatty tissue holding onto your unfulfilled desires around your waist, at the Belt Channel.

We mentioned this *Dai Mai* or Belt Channel treatment earlier, and it can be quite powerful and successful in allowing you to "comfortably tighten your belt" once you have dried up the dampness and let the desires go. Once you are at that point, it's suddenly easier to let go of many things. And how do you know what to let go of? Two important questions to ask yourself are:

"What is there to want in this world anyway?"

and,

"Once I have it, will it really make me happy?"

You realize that true happiness is something that comes from inside not outside of you. Chasing external happiness can leave you with many restless, unfulfilled desires. Finding and securing internal happiness offers peace, spiritual bliss, and simplicity.

Homework: Drying Up the Dampness and Letting Go of Desires

While doing your *Be the Child homework*, you will be practicing seeing the world as a child does. After a while, one of the feelings you get from doing this work is a sense of lightness and freedom. If you feel like you have an excess of outward desires that are weighing you down, then you can practice meditations to help you let them go. Begin with the Relax Your Body, Clear Your Mind, Open Your Doors meditation on page 79 if you haven't practiced it for awhile, or you can find the recorded guided meditations at the Alchemy Learning Center Website: AlchemyLearningCenter.com.

When you are ready, begin this meditation.

Start by slowly making a review of where you stand in your life. Make a mental list of the greatest desires you have in your current situation. Maybe you want more money, for example, or you've always wanted to put on a backpack and travel around the globe. Whatever these desires are, make a mental list of them. Now notice which is the biggest desire. This is the thing you believe will bring the most happiness in life, and the lack of it seems to bring you the greatest pain.

Imagine yourself letting go of this desire. If you no longer wanted that money, could you simply be happy with what you have now? If you no longer wanted to travel, what fun things could you be doing with all your time at home? This exercise can bring about a sense of relief, and ultimately happiness. You will no longer feel driven to make big external changes, and you won't be left with a sense of resignation from "giving something up." You make a choice. You choose to let go of the desire, so there's no feeling of losing, or giving it up because you can't achieve it.

We recommend doing one desire per meditation session. You do not have to "remember" the mental list that you came up with in the previous meditation. One helpful guideline for this meditation is to use the Nine Palaces as a starting point. Go through the list of the Nine Palaces to review and release what you still desire for each one.

Step Five: Rejuvenation

Once you are free from these desires, you can begin to utilize your physical essences to increase your longevity, to aim for becoming physically immortal. The Alchemists didn't just want to find spiritual immortality, they wanted physical immortality. To accomplish this, your body or container of your spirit—with all its physical essences—needs to reverse the process of aging and begin rejuvenating itself.

As we talked about above, Step Four shows you how to clear away all of those unrequited desires. Now you can begin to learn how to rejuvenate yourself. Every cell in your body already has the capability for renewal and rejuvenation—if they didn't, we wouldn't last very long. However, over time, as we age, we accumulate so much physical, emotional, and spiritual "gunk" in all kinds of places in our body and mind that hamper the ability of our cells to renew themselves, and the rejuvenation process begins to break down. The Alchemists believed that with the right attention to our physical essences, we can maintain the rejuvenation process and stop the process of aging altogether.

In Step Four of the fourth stage of Alchemy you begin to consolidate your essences. You begin to be the person you've always wanted to be and do the things that matter most to you. You start spending less time wasting your precious essences, which means you're not focused on needless desires and distractions. It's important to do the Microcosmic Orbit before beginning this stage because that helps to jumpstart the rejuvenation process and to have it continue throughout the step to support your efforts here.

One of the areas where the Alchemists believed that we waste our essences is in sexual activity. Remember that metaphorically here, you're creating your own baby, which is your true self. In males, the physical essences are contained in the semen, so the Alchemists learned to hold back orgasm and recycle those fluids back into the body to prevent wasting precious essences. This is called injaculation by some.

Step Five, the last step in this Stage, is about learning to recycle your essential essences so you can conserve and consolidate them and therefore increase longevity. This is the secret to becoming younger.

While it's true that your lifespan is getting longer because you're not distracted by your desires, abstinence can be problematic because it's a denial, not necessarily a release, of your desires. You have to bury that desire deep down in order to avoid feeling it.

For example, if you decide the best way to let go of your desires is through denial, you might become celibate and deny your body's craving for sex if it feels like it's addictive for you. But your body may not ultimately cooperate. You may still have sexual dreams at night—and still lose essences in the form of sexual fluids, through nocturnal emissions, and other symptoms may arise too.

In other words, your body may still be losing essences if you simply deny those desires. The desire still exists although you've tried to bury it. The Wind will come, and you'll feel the lust for sex again. Abstinence can be good to help you stop wasting your essences on activities you don't want to be doing, but it's tricky if you bury the desire deep down. Your body will have issues as a result.

The Daoists would ask this question:

Why are you denying yourself something
that you really want?

Can you resolve this desire and let it go? Or is it truly your heart's desire and you're just denying it? To really let go of your desires is totally different from simply abstaining from them. This step helps you release those desires in a healthy way and thereby keep your essences.

Is Sexual Activity a Deposit or Withdrawal?

As a side note, there are many famous Daoists who believed that sexual activity was key to personal development. In fact, one of the most famous Alchemists, Sun SiMiao, was an advocate of what's called Daoist Sexology. On one of Leta's trips to China, her group visited his home, which is now a museum. There they saw many small statues of the various sexual positions he advocated plus a huge statue of a man with a ten-foot long erection!

He and many others believed that, if practiced correctly, sexual activity could replenish your bank account instead of draining your essences.

Homework: Consolidating Your Essences

Essences are your building blocks. They are the physical matter of you, plus all your essential Qi. They are your most precious gift in life—the body that was given to you at birth. You need to care for your essences, just the way a gardener tends to their garden.

If you begin to develop a relationship with your essences as if they're valuable resources that are in limited supply, like iron or oil or coal, you may start to go about living your life a little differently.

In this stage, as part of your work to consolidate your essences and rejuvenate yourself, you need to start tracking how exactly you spend your essences on a daily basis. If we told you that you were given a deposit of essences at the beginning of life, and you've been making deposits and withdrawals on that bank account your whole life, but that the balance has been steadily decreasing, would you still keep spending in the same way? Would you stop and assess your spending habits and be more careful?

This is not as simple as it sounds because you are probably assuming that the answer would be yes (and you would be right) and that the outcome would be further abstinence so that mostly you would be making deposits. And that's not necessarily the case. Let's say you really want to travel to Bali. That's a financial expenditure, but it might be worth it to you. It's on your bucket list! Another person might think it sounds fun, without really feeling a deep need to do it. They'd rather do something else with their resources. But you can't imagine anything else you'd rather do. For you in particular, the expenditure could be beneficial.

Knowing that we all are going to be making withdrawals from our essence account, let's take a look at what you're doing with your body day-to-day that ensures as many adequate deposits as possible. First, getting enough sleep, eating healthy food, and maybe having relaxing baths or massages are all great choices. Every time you sleep deeply, you're saving up energy and depositing it into your personal essence account. Second: Are you doing more than you need to do all the time? Are you running around doing things for everyone else and nothing for yourself? Maybe you're all wrapped up in things you think you have to do and ignoring the things you really want to be doing. If so, there might come a day when you're finally ready to do the "important" things and find that your resources are depleted or even worse, that your essence account is empty.

Do an evaluation of how you nourish yourself and also how you spend your resources. What more could you do to nourish and replenish? Make a list of things you'd like to do and how you can make the appropriate changes to allow these into your day-to-day life. In your journal, create an accounting ledger that has a deposits column and a withdrawals column. At the end of the day, enter your life-affirming activities into the deposit column and your energy-wasting activities into the withdrawal column. Try to do this without any judgment. Don't punish yourself for making what appear to be bad choices (remember that upon greater reflection tomorrow or the day after or farther along, they might not turn out to be bad at all.) This exercise is simply about watching your activities and then making the conscious choice to add more life-affirming activities into your daily life, while cutting out some of what may be wasting your energy. Keep this in mind; spending energy is *good* when it's in alignment with your values and mission for this lifetime. We came here to live out our curriculum and applying our energy towards that aim is life-affirming.

Case Study: Jade's Blocks Get Unblocked

Stage Four took a long time for Jade, who we mentioned at the beginning of this book. She had had a very difficult childhood. She was given up for adoption at birth and wasn't adopted for several months. The family she was given to really didn't match her energetics in any way, so she never felt at home. Jade was not looking forward to the Stage called, "Innocent Child." Anything about her childhood could make her feel uncomfortable and scared.

Interestingly, when we started working on this stage and she tried to do the Microcosmic Orbit, she felt like she couldn't even get her energy to go one circuit around. She was so blocked in so many areas that her energy kept stalling, and she was very frustrated.

The first few times we did the Stage Four treatment, for about a day after, she would feel really great. She really felt childlike and innocent—better than she'd ever felt before. But it would vanish after about 24 hours, and she'd go back to being uncomfortable again. Strange things happened. She spontaneously started smoking again, for no apparent reason. She started seeing her old lover again, even though they had no intention of getting back together and it was uncomfortable and emotionally draining.

Jade was a musician who hadn't been playing much for years before she first started treatment. She'd been extremely sick for about four years, so much so that she barely got out of bed. We had done a lot of work over the timespan of a couple of years to get her well enough for her to begin to step back into her life before we even started the Nine Stages of Alchemy. During that time, she started playing guitar again, even taking lessons on a weekly basis.

One day, right after a Stage Four treatment, she came back in for a follow-up visit very excited. She wanted to play me a song that she had written and then recorded on her phone. The song was stunningly beautiful. But for her, the sound of the song itself wasn't the amazing thing, as beautiful as it was (she is an incredible musician). What was truly astonishing to her was that she had written it at all, after not having written a new song in many, many years. She realized that she had always been trying to "make" a song, as if her intellectual mind was doing it, and then she'd talk herself out of it due to her low self-esteem. "Who am I to make a great song?" she'd think. But this time, she realized that she had simply allowed the song to happen. She didn't push it. She just let it flow through her. "I waited and listened for the song," she said. She was so excited too because she knew now she could write other songs in the same way. It took the pressure off her. She was listening for the song, and channeling it from some higher place far beyond herself. Jade had not only mastered Stage Four, she'd moved on to Stage Five, which is all about listening and channeling what flows through you from the Divine.

Moving onto Stage Five

As with all the stages, you definitely don't want to move on to Stage Five before Stage Four is fully completed. Here are some indications to help you know when you are ready to proceed.

At the beginning of Stage Four, you may experience a lot of physical irritation. You may even have red eyes and a dry mouth for awhile. This is because there may be a lot of heat coming out of your body as you let go of your desires. There is a point, directly in line with the center of the pupil of the eye and lying above it, just inside the hairline, that mitigates these symptoms. It's called Head Above Tears, or Gall Bladder 15. Releasing this point lets some of the heat move out.

Eventually you will begin to feel lighter, and you'll notice that people may start commenting on how great you look. You may also begin to notice that more and more people want to be around you. The new sense of lightness you have feels easy and uncomplicated to other people, and they want to hang around you.

In general, you may also find that your mouth has more saliva. This stage is very moistening, which is different than dampness; in Chinese Medicine we say your body emits a golden fluid. The fluid causes an aromatic, pleasant floral scent. As your essences are circulating more and more, your body is renewing itself. You begin to sometimes even smell like a newborn baby.

When you talk, you are only repeating what you already know. But if you listen, you may learn something new.

–His Holiness the Dalai Lama

Those who know don't talk. Those who talk don't know.

–Lao Tzu

Stage Five: Ear

Whereas in Stage Four you become the Innocent Child, we think of Stage Five as the place where you become the Elder, the Wise Person. You gain so much knowledge throughout your life, both helpful and perhaps not so helpful, and then in old age you let it go and return to your childlike self. The whole point of each of our lifetimes is to fill up with wisdom and then let it go. When you have lived so long that you no longer care so deeply about the outer world or want to be so involved in it, then there is also an innocence about you.

In Stage Four, you learned to be a child again, one who could simply play and have fun. In Stage Five you have to let go of all that. You can't just hang onto trying to do only the things that give you pleasure. To be fully yourself, you need to be willing to experience something totally new every moment.

Society generally wants you to sacrifice your individual self to serve the communal good or greater humanity as a whole. But instead of making sacrifices for society, like going to law school so you can be a public defender, this stage is about sacrificing yourself for the Divine, through things like daily meditation practice, sacred movement, and self-cultivation. It's a celebration of the Divine that results in joyfully surrendering. It's a full reunion with the Divine.

The previous stages have served to purify you so that you are able to come to this moment. This is a big transition. You're on the way to a new vision of yourself, a new you. But this new you is not static. It's the authentic you, but it will always continue to change. You may even contradict yourself in the future. In fact, you're completely unlearning all you've learned. One of the most important things you can do as a wise person is contradict yourself and be comfortable with that.

Enlightenment is never a static state. After Buddha became enlightened, he taught others what he had discovered. These teachings continued to grow and change daily as he walked the earth. You have to be comfortable doing the same–making the effort to come to major conclusions and really believing in them, and then changing those beliefs, again and again. In this stage you learn that you can be true to what you believe and at the same time know with wise certainty that your belief will eventually change. Today I'm sure that something is true, and tomorrow I'm not so sure. Welcome to the absolute certainty that there are no absolutes in Alchemy.

Alchemy is not moral or immoral. It's amoral, which means that it's utterly unconcerned with the rightness or wrongness of things. Another way to say this is that Alchemists aren't invested in the dualistic system that traditional morals represent. Therefore, Stage Five teaches you how to acknowledge the truth that there is no good or bad. Everything in the universe is either all good, or neither good nor bad.

Does this sound challenging? In fact it is a concept that can be extremely hard to embrace for most humans. However doing so is worth every bit of effort.

How can things like cheating, stealing, murder, and rape be anything but bad? Think of someone you would call good, for example, Mother Teresa. She is Saint Teresa according to the Catholic religion and in the minds of millions of people–but if you suddenly found out that she murdered someone, would she suddenly be bad? How does reality, or your perception of it, change based on the story? If you could travel back in time and have a chance to kill Hitler before millions were murdered in the Holocaust, would that be a good thing, because the result would save millions of lives? Or is that a bad thing, because you killed another human being? Can a bad action turn out to be good? Can a good action turn out to be bad? What if you were a healer, and someone like Hitler really needed your help? Would you help him if you knew what he was going to do in the future?

This stage teaches us how we can sidestep our constant habit of making judgments. It's about humbly taking yourself out of that equation. Who are you to judge what the world should be like?

> *If you remove yourself from judgment, you free yourself from the shackles of judgmental behavior.*

The Elemental Theme for Stage Five—Water

The overall theme of Stage Five is to come into the possession of true wisdom. In the Nine Palaces, the Palace of Wisdom is ruled by the Water Element, which is all about the power of timing and fluidity. In order to gain wisdom, we must first let go of our rigid attachment to knowledge or what we believe to be knowledge. By recognizing that facts are not the truth, we realize we actually know nothing. However, we can touch into the deeper plane of wisdom. Water Element people hold this deeper wisdom inside their bodies. They don't always feel the need to articulate it, and words are often inadequate to express it anyway. However, they will offer this wisdom when they are inspired to do so. This stage requires that you embrace the power of the Water Element inside you and allow yourself to detach from right and wrong. Instead you'll learn to simply go with the flow.

No Good, No Bad

The leader of the Eight Immortals, Zhongli Quan, was the teacher of Lu Dongbin, the great Chinese poet and scholar. Zhongli Quan wanted to test Lu Dongbin's ability to achieve this state of no good, no bad. He devised for him what came to be called the Ten Trials, during which Lu Dongbin was tested with many difficult, painful, and challenging situations to see if he could maintain a state of peace without judgment. He had to undergo the death of close loved ones and endure the loss of all his money and everything he owned. He was verbally accosted by strangers daily. These are just some of the difficult trials he had to face. In all of these examples, Lu Dongbin was an extraordinary student, as he remained emotionally unflappable, refusing to construe any circumstance as either good or bad. He simply let life flow, and he carried on seeing everything as good.

There is a goodness that has no enemies.

–Anonymous

Another example we like to share is the story of the Taoist farmer whose only horse runs away from the farm. All of his neighbors gather to tell the farmer how unfortunate he is to lose his only horse. But the farmer does not concur. He simply answers, "Well, maybe." Then his one horse comes back to the farm with a pack of many other wild horses in tow, and the neighbors then come by to celebrate and tell the farmer how fortunate he is to have all these new horses. But the farmer simply replies, "Well, maybe." Then his only son gets on the back of one of the wild horses to ride it, and he falls off and breaks his leg. The neighbors are once again dismayed and pronounce that it's such bad luck to have your only son injured, but the farmer just says, "Well, maybe." When the army comes into their town and conscripts all the young men to fight, except the farmer's son because his leg is broken, the neighbors exclaim that the farmer has such good luck. But still the farmer replies, "Well, maybe," because he knows that life is cyclical. It's about the balance of all things in the world. Yin and Yang energies are always exchanging. What may appear to our eyes as being something good follows what we deem to be bad and vice versa. The farmer doesn't know the future. He only knows that in the moment, everything is simply as it is. The only way to escape the cycle of "good and bad" is to step beyond Yin and Yang into a state of oneness where all duality is transcended.

> *From there you can see that all is good in*
> *the present moment.*

As you enter Stage Five, you will likely still see the flow of the universe through the eyes of dualism—Yin and Yang, good and bad, life and death, dark and light. In this stage, you learn to simply embrace the rightness of all of that: of all that is. This can be very difficult to understand and even if you do, it can still feel scary to embrace. If this is the case for you, you can return to Stage Three and practice the Ho'oponopono Advanced Forgiveness exercise, and work on releasing any strong judgments you're carrying.

Stage Five is also the time to begin to develop rituals that remind you of and enhance your new devotion to living the Truth of the Divine: that everything in the universe is either all good, or neither good nor bad. Rituals give us sense of consistency, yet at the same time, the lessons of Stage Five teach us that we must be flexible in our willingness to acknowledge when it is time to change them. Nothing is ever absolute. In Stage Five, rituals are done without judgment or rigidity; instead, we carry them out with flexibility and fluidity and that requires a wide open mind.

> To have an open mind, you must first open
> your ears and listen to the environment
> around you.

When you were born, the first thing you experienced was the sound of your own first breath entering your lungs and then the sound of your first cry. Now that you have learned to become the innocent child again, it is time to open your ears so that you can hear truth as you did when you were still a baby. Stage Five opens the ears in a way that you can do this.

Stage Four is a very active, outwardly focused stage, with emphasis on the eyes and seeing and experiencing the world differently. Stage Five also focuses on seeing, but not on seeing out into the world around us. We will share

partner besides financial or material things. He had light and love emanating from him.

He and the woman had a great time together. She was the first woman he'd felt passionate about in decades. They had a wonderful summer fling. The relationship didn't last past the end of that season, but he was in such a good place with himself that when it ended, he was totally okay with it, and so was she. He was surprised at how okay he was, in fact, since that wasn't his usual pattern with breakups. He said that in the past, he would have been very upset and probably would have fallen into a bout of melancholia or even depression. This time, he knew she wasn't the right long-term person, so he immediately got back to dating and looking for the one who would be. He barely skipped a beat. Soon afterwards, he started Stage Six, found his life partner, and they're now very happy in their new life together.

The Steps of Stage Five

Stage Five has a two distinct steps:

1. **Opening the Ears**–learning to listen

2. **Opening the Third Eye**–for illumination

Step One: Opening the Ears

The first step of this stage is to open up the ears. There are many acu-points on the head all around the outside of the ears. The idea is to use them to open the ears. They can also help with some of the symptoms that may have developed from Stage Four, some of which we already mentioned, such as red eyes and dry mouth. However, there can also be sleep issues, toothaches, jaw pain, tinnitus, headaches, and difficulty hearing during Stage Four. These are sometimes referred to as the Fire Toxins, and they are the poisons that your body couldn't get rid of because they were put away so deeply in a kind of protective storage. When these begin to release they can cause some uncomfortable symptoms as they rise to the surface. Stage Five can alleviate much of this because it continues to clear things that are being released from deep down in the body. Various acu-points on your head will help your body expunge whatever still needs to be removed, and we recommend you work with a Chinese Medicine practitioner if you feel this is the case for you.

When you open the ears, sounds begin to change, similarly to how visual perceptions shifted in Stage Four. You may hear music, for example, in a totally new way. You may hear overlays and harmonies, and experience music as more profound, like a direct communication from the Divine. You're able to listen now at a completely different level than you did before you worked through the first Four Stages. Musicians may sometimes already have this ability to some extent, but they will also experience an enhancement to their listening in this stage.

Case Study: Katherine's Refusal to Take Sides

Katherine was a dedicated activist, invested in multiple causes, who spent years of her career and volunteer life working to help those in need. When she first began Stage Four, she had a lot of fun with it. She loved the feeling of being the Innocent Child, and many aspects of her life felt new and exciting as she explored this new way of being in the world.

Then all of a sudden, all hell broke loose in her life. Her brother, whom she was very close with, became quite ill and passed away. She was extremely sad about his passing, and on top of that, it took an entire year to facilitate and administrate his estate.

Then, in the middle of that emotional turmoil and grief, Katherine's spouse was injured and couldn't work for almost a year. Katherine had to increase her workload and take on fully supporting the family on a single income. We didn't see her in the clinic for sessions very often during this tumultuous two-year period of her life, but Katherine was still working away on her Stage Four homework.

Eventually things smoothed out. One day, when Katherine came in for a session, she recounted a story that she thought was interesting. She began talking about a friend who was angry with her because she wouldn't take a strong stance during an important political election. Katherine said, "I just don't feel like I can be the one making change on the front lines anymore. I have fought those big battles in the past. I understand the viewpoints on both sides. I think I'll do my work behind the scenes and just listen to both sides. I can make the most change by listening and finding opportunities to say the right thing at the right time." Her angry friend couldn't understand what Katherine was talking about, but it was clear to Katherine and to us. Katherine was ready to begin her Stage Five work.

Homework: Just Listen

The first step of listening is closing your mouth. The second step is opening your ears.

Some of us have an incessant need to talk. Try spending some time everyday curbing that impulse, and focusing only on listening to those around you. Ask some questions, and then try to actually listen to the answers. Make a point of not offering any opinions. Don't come up with advice, solutions, or fixes for whatever challenges someone is facing. Just try to deeply listen and understand another person's experience.

After you practice this for awhile, what do you notice in yourself? How does it feel not weighing in with your own opinion all the time? It can be a challenging shift for many people, who truly think that their logic will help someone figure things out. Can you start letting that impulse go now and listen instead for the Divine voice inside you? See if you can *know* what to say from a place that is not your logical, practical mind. Keep listening until you're sure you can hear something that is not necessarily *your opinion,* but something you're *receiving in the moment.* Imagine you have *an antenna that receives just what is required in perfect timing.* It will simply come to you. When a thought like this arises in your mind—one that feels inspired rather than fabricated by your logical reasoning—then slowly speak the words to the person you're talking with. Then stop and start listening again. Don't get overcome by the need to make your point.

After allowing yourself to have a few conversations this way, evaluate how it works. Compare it to how you would have normally contributed to the conversation. Is this new way different? Evaluate the reactions you're getting. Are your words more effective than they used to be? This homework can take a bit of practice and may need to be done for a while before you really start to perceive any changes.

Step Two: Opening the Third Eye

Now you are ready to move your work from your inner hearing of Truth to your inner seeing of Truth. In this step, you open the first of three levels of the third eye. This first step represents illumination and begins to prepare you for Stage Six, where we open the second level of the third eye. This first step illuminates your eyes. It begins to feel as if your spirit is shining out from them.

As you do this step, your body will experience new sensations as the brain continues to open up to you. Each day may feel different than the last because it will not necessarily resemble the routine experience you've been used to. You're deconstructing and unlearning all that you've learned, which is what the wise person has to do. You're not making any judgements about what to keep and what to let go. You are letting go of all of it—all of your memories—not just the traumas, but the wonderful remembrances too. This frees you to live fully and do that kind of living completely in the present moment. Just because you had fun doing something yesterday doesn't mean that it will be fun today. And it doesn't have to because something new will arise that will be just as much fun—maybe even more fun!

> You let go of trying to achieve pleasure by repeating the same old things that gave you pleasure in the past. You enter into the ritual of being yourself. Each time you experience something completely new, you are celebrating The Divine.

Homework: Third Eye Meditation

The Third Eye meditation focuses on bringing light into the third eye. This advanced Alchemical meditation requires significant preparation and is best done with some guidance. If you do the Third Eye meditation without proper guidance, you risk developing some unusual symptoms, such as premature graying of the hair, or a feeling of deep, pervasive anxiety. Go easy and go slow! Make sure you're truly ready. With this stage, we actually recommend that you check in with a practitioner before you start. One of our favorite meditations to revisit for this stage is the Sitting on the Eggs meditation that we described in an earlier chapter. This practice helps you begin to work with light and prepares you for higher level meditations that bring light into the third eye. Revisiting the Sitting on the Eggs meditation at this point can help you build your strength and your ability to manage the light skillfully. We really mean it when we say that this stage requires a definite level of preparation.

There are many versions of meditations to use at this phase of your development. Some Daoist practices work with different colors of light or geometric shapes. We like to encourage simply focusing on white light without any thoughts, actions, or reactions. Just pure focus and pure light. This advanced meditation process is described in the book: *The Secret of the Golden Flower: A Chinese Book of Life* translated by Richard Wilhelm.

Repeating Stages 1-4: Back to the Future

At this point in your Alchemical journey, if any symptoms are presenting themselves to you, assess them, remind yourself about which stage addresses those issues, and return there so that you can practice doing those meditations again until symptoms clear. This is one of the many gifts of the Nine Stages of Alchemy. Each stage is always available to revisit to help you undo or release any new issues that arise along the way. So please remember, no judgment! Celebrate the concept that you are working on your Alchemy and your life!

> *Alchemy isn't a once-and-done kind of practice. It's a circular or spiral process that winds and unwinds throughout one's entire life.*

Here are some examples of how to know if it would be helpful or even necessary for your Alchemical journey to incorporate some of the practices from past stages. Stage Five requires you to let go of all the events of your day on a daily basis, so you don't carry them into the next day. If you find you're perseverating or even dreaming at night about something that happened during the day, you need to return to Stage One and do the Letting Go meditations. This just means old habits could be insinuating themselves back into your life.

If old traumas and emotional pains start to make you feel defensive, or you find you can't affirm your life in the present moment, revisit some of the Stage Two practices. Try working on "The best protection is no protection." What inside of you is feeling inferior so that you feel the need to protect it? Remember to do your affirmations. Spend some days or months affirming your life, until your core feels stronger again. Take as much time as you need. There is never any hurry or rush.

Sometimes old traumas can surface and haunt us again, and challenge our sense of groundedness. This is addressed in Stage Three. Get yourself rooted in your three Dan Tians—your lower abdomen, chest, and head—by working with the stance training you did in Stage Three. You may need to build up more cauldron strength. If there are old resentments and anger coming up, return to the Ho'oponopono Advanced Forgiveness work.

Are you circulating your energy and are your portals open? If not, it's important to engage again in Stage Four practices and work on the Microcosmic Orbit. Stage Five is above all about detoxifying the contaminants that are polluting your mind. When you open the portals, these toxins are going to be released. Returning to the practices from earlier stages will help you clear away any obstructions that are showing up right now.

Along with the above suggestions, if you feel overly challenged and you're struggling to move through Stage Five, we recommend the *Thirteen Ghost Points* treatment to help you purify and release any persistent factors obstructing your path forward.

Stage Five Homework: Neither Good Nor Bad

Stage Five is about learning to see everything in the world and in your life as good or *neither good nor bad.* This is downright challenging for many of us. Our minds are trained to be so quick to judge, process, and label everything as either good or bad. How do we see news headlines and not think good or bad? We are constantly bombarded with other people's judgments and thoughts in the media and from within our own circle of family and friends. Modern life can feel like an emotional rollercoaster, and the challenge is to be able to find peace and quiet within your own mind.

We live in a world of Yin versus Yang. We learn to see everything in comparison or opposition to something else. Stage Five may be the first time you step away from the division of the number two and into Oneness or Wholeness of the number one. This is how you become a messenger of Divine inspiration. You can't receive inspired messages if you are rigidly holding judgments about the people you're talking to or even about the information you're imparting. You have to stay out of the equation, in neutrality. You can do this by learning to experience the world as *all good.*

Start by practicing seeing things this way for an hour or two a day. Maybe try it while watching a movie, or during a meeting at work where you don't have to be too involved. Simply observe the world and pay attention to how you feel about it. Try to notice the thoughts you're having and the judgments that so easily surface about everything you experience. What if you could just let them all melt away? How would it feel to free your own mind from the constant barrage of judgments?

Begin to practice listening to your own language when you're speaking to yourself and to others. How often do your phrases reflect dividing things into categories of good and bad? It's a strong habit in our culture to use these terms in almost every sentence.

Now, that's not to say you have to give up having preferences. But just because you prefer tomatoes and have an aversion to peppers doesn't make tomatoes good and peppers bad. They are equivalently good in the big picture. You just know that you have a preference. You may have a preference for love and peace, and a distaste for hatred and war in the world. But in Stage Five you transcend seeing them as *good or bad*. Of course you might prefer to see one rather than the other, but they both simply exist. Conceptually, this idea is challenging for many people, but once you embark on Stage Five, the understanding happens with ease. The homework becomes easier and easier as you work through this stage. You definitely can't move onto Stage Six until you're able to truly see the world as *neither good nor bad*, or *all good*.

Moving onto Stage Six

How do you know you're ready to move on to Stage Six? You're cultivating the *all is good* belief in your life. You have appreciation and gratitude for exactly the way things are. Divine Grace is ever present, and you find it everywhere you look. Your every perception is evidence of the Divine presence, and you bow to the perfection you see. Immortality is your present state, not a future state. You celebrate the innate and precious goodness of everyone you meet, and your life becomes an unfolding prayer of gratitude. Everything is as it should be. From this vantage point, there is no wishing that life could be better, because that would take away from the perfection of all that is.

You were born
with wings,
why prefer to
crawl through life?

-Rumi

Stage Six: Flying in Your Life

Stage Six is the point where you have achieved immortality because you truly believe in it and can experience the feeling of it in present time. Now it's time to practice it, train it, and emanate it. You are getting younger and younger as time goes on. You see everything fresh and new each day. You are so pure and clear that the Divine simply comes through you and emanates out of you.

Stage One was about discovering the entryway to the Divine Mystery at the Mystery Gate. Now you've discovered that you, yourself, are Divine. In Stage Five, you became a messenger for the Divine. In Stage Six you're moving that Divinity into the very presence of your being.

Now there is no longer any separation between you as an individual and the Divine Whole. The Divine is inside you. You have the seed of immortality within you. We *can* be immortal. How? By embodying Divinity itself.

At this stage of Alchemy you are already experiencing heaven on earth. You're aligning yourself to the reality of heaven on earth. You know the ways of heaven without leaving your house or even opening the windows. We are all connected to Source, and when we're truly aligned with it, everything comes from the One. You can predict the future because when you're in Oneness, all time and all of eternity exists in each moment.

Microcosmic Orbit Reversal

At this point in your Alchemical Journey the Microcosmic Orbit visualization will often naturally reverse its direction, as discussed in Stage Four. You'll find yourself getting younger and younger over time as you practice seeing everything fresh and new each day.

When the Microcosmic Orbit cycles backwards, it moves down and away from the brain, which means that the brain will no longer be "contaminated" by life's daily experiences. Every day of your life, your brain experiences a buildup of many concepts, ideas, and beliefs about the nature of reality. Sometimes they don't "consciously" stick. But if you see something or someone tells you something with a strong charge that hooks your brain and infects it, you can become obsessed with it. When the Microcosmic Orbit reverses, you are releasing these obsessive thoughts.

Flying

In ancient times, it was believed that the Immortals could fly. As late as the 1950s, a Japanese man in China documented seeing one of the Immortals flying through the mountains. As we said much earlier in the book, we haven't seen anyone practicing Alchemy actually fly through the sky yet, but as a metaphor for flying in your life, we've seen many of our clients really take off in their lives.

It's always an amazing thing to watch one of our clients move into Stage Six. Everything in their lives falls into place and the runway is cleared for take-off. Whatever they have wanted to do, they simply do it with ease and grace. They do it happily, without complaints. Their relationships run smoothly. The difficult ones often simply fall away.

What's your full potential? How do you move into it and then live it? It definitely takes a little practice to fly. You don't just suddenly jump off the roof while flapping your arms. The true name of this stage is understood as practice. Practice makes perfect! As we worked with more and more clients over the years, we began to see that it would be helpful to offer other ways to support our clients in their practice besides the ways that we can help them on the treatment table.

What is Alchemical Life Strategy Coaching?

We have referred to Alchemical coaching before. Here is the point where it can really help, so let's look at what the Alchemical Life Strategy Coaching we offer at the clinic is, why you might need it, and what it can do.

People often need some practical guidance and life advice to direct the big energy of potentiality as it's emerging during the stages of Alchemy. Clients may find themselves taxiing on the runway and feeling like they can't quite get enough momentum going—likely because of practical obstacles still standing in the way here and there. You need to know how to clear the runway so that you can finally achieve liftoff.

You've seen those airport marshallers who wear the yellow vests and help guide the pilot as they back the plane out of its berth. They are there to alert the pilot to any obstacles that they would otherwise bump into. And the dispatchers in the tower are there to make sure that the pilot knows when to cross lanes and when to wait. This team of workers is crucial for a successful lift-off. We feel the same kind of advance team is important to have in place for our clients in general and especially as they approach this stage of Alchemy.

Alchemical Life Strategy Coaching is an approach that helps you identify your authentic energy temperament, by figuring out your own personal energetic stack-up of the Five Elements. We focus especially on the client's signature three elements, which always determine how an individual can best and most authentically move through the world and function effectively.

With this understanding of your signature elemental nature as a base, we can begin to address any major life issues you're facing through the lens of the Nine Palaces. The system of the Nine Palaces makes it easy to see where any trouble spots and challenges are. Sessions can be ongoing, but they truly work best after you've cleared away your baggage in Stage Two and worked through any past-life issues in Stage Three. This is true because even if you can see strategically that you need to make major life changes, you're often unable to actually achieve them until you've done the letting go work in Stages Two and Three.

Alchemy Life Strategy work provides crucial guidance and well-timed insights to keep you connected and moving down the runway in your life. Alchemy-specific coaching is invaluable to help you harness and direct your transformational energy, and to truly take flight when you're ready.

Case Study: Always Waiting for Bad Luck Turns to Good Luck

Dennis came to us many years ago with a pain in his arm. It was in his elbow to be exact. Leta worked on the physical pain for many months with no results. Every time he came in, he claimed there was no emotional reason why he had the pain. He insisted it was from playing golf which he did every week with his friends. So every session, Leta worked on the physical pain, but she couldn't help wondering if there was something else brewing, on an emotional level, deep inside him.

Finally one day he came in and told Leta a story. His employee of fifteen years and a close friend of the family had stolen a very large sum of money from his company. Not only did she steal the money, but she proceeded to gamble it all away in a short period of time. Dennis was devastated by the whole situation and was currently attending her court case. She was likely to serve jail time for her crime.

Leta suggested an Alchemy treatment, and they started that very day. Leta began by doing some of the ghost points, which started to relieve some of his emotional pain. When she got to the ghost point that is located on the elbow, which is called Ghost Official, and is known as the point for addressing legal problems, his elbow pain vanished immediately! He became a somewhat reluctant believer and decided he wanted to continue this work. Some ten years later, the pain hasn't ever returned, even though he still plays golf.

Leta worked through the Stages of Alchemy with him over a number of years. When he got to Stage Six, some radical events happened in his life. He had suffered a lot of financial woes after the money was stolen from his company. Suddenly, literally the day after he started the Flying Stage, Stage Six, he got a million dollar contract for his company, and also sold his house for a large gain.

He was giddy the next time he came in to see Leta. He thought his bad luck had turned to good, but really *he had changed his own fate.* If he had never started Alchemy, thoughts about the betrayal and the loss of his money could have crippled his financial stability and plagued his happiness for the rest of his life. That was the story he'd been telling himself and everyone around him, for years! Now, he had the chance to embrace prosperity again and to feel himself flying into a new phase of life. His business has been successful ever since—even during some hard economic times—and he lives with his wife in a lovely new home. They travel together and live a very happy and contented life. He is no longer waiting in fear for betrayal and misery to find him in life. He's flying free!

Becoming Limitless

This Stage teaches you how to bust up all the limitations and obstacles you believe you have. What's one of the biggest limitations every person on this planet is bound by every day? Gravity! So the concept of flying is the perfect limitation buster. In Stage Six you can defy gravity in your life. The ability to release limitations that used to seem undeniable is the metaphoric secret to Stage Six. There are no obstacles anymore.

Remember, there's a lot that has to happen before you get here. There can be years of work leading up to this time in your life. One of the most important concepts to master and embody comes during Stage Five, when we learn to let go of the duality belief of good and bad. From the earlier perspective of Stage One or any of the earlier stages, you could easily think: flying is a good thing! *Well, maybe.* You learned in Stage Five that it's neither good nor bad. *Well, maybe.*

Now in Stage Six, there is a level of ease and a true belief that *it's all good.* So now you believe that you can fly. You can't come from the place of the duality of good and bad in order to overcome your obstacles. When you believe obstacles are bad, you will only bang your head against them over and over again. They become the bedrock of the all the stories you tell yourself. *They exist, therefore they limit you.* Gravity exists, therefore I can't fly.

If you remove the obstacles in your day-to-day life in Stage One, release the baggage of this lifetime in Stage Two, eliminate the influence of past lives or your ancestry over your life in Stage Three, remove the blinders blocking your sight in Stage Four, and embrace the *all is good* mentality in Stage Five, then nothing can hold you back!

> *Spontaneity is about living in the present moment, all the time.*

When you get to Stage Six, life is all about being spontaneous. You've let go of your desires. You've opened up all your sensory organs. As a result you can now come into a state of complete freedom and spontaneity in your life.

This is the key to Stage Six—to be living with freedom in the present moment. If you have a dentist appointment at 10:00 a.m., at 9:00 a.m., you remember you have to get in the car at just the right time to go to your appointment. You don't need an appointment book or a to-do list because you trust that in every moment you're led to do the next thing. This is a Water Element quality. You're completely guided by Spirit in each moment. You've become a realized human being—a *Zhen Ren*—a wizard in your own life.

If your mind is no longer making to-do lists and carefully checking things off, then you have completely surrendered to The Divine flow. In Stage Six, you simply *feel* at any given moment what the next right thing to do is, and you're completely guided in each moment. This is the *Xuan Ji* or Mystery Power of a realized human being. If you follow the *Xuan Ji* in an undistracted and untainted way, it will take you on the perfect journey of its own spontaneity.

You will notice you are no longer at all concerned with the past. You give up every *ago*. Five minutes *ago* I was thinking about this, or ten years *ago* I did that. You no longer need to reference the past.

It takes time and training to learn to fly—and then practice, and practice, and practice. You have to get used to this new orientation.

The points of the Stage Six treatment represent the shape of the Big Dipper, mapped onto the body. In Chinese culture, you obtain wholeness by being in alignment or synchronicity with the Big Dipper. In acupuncture, practitioners typically use gold needles to needle the Stage Six points. These points activate all the stars of the constellation, which are like chakras or energetic centers. It's believed that a Divine Presence lives in each of the points, of which there are ten. They are represented by seven points on the front and three on the back. Once the points are activated, they begin to spin, creating symmetry in the body.

Ten is the number of perfection, which is the Five Elements multiplied by two. The Five Elements represent life, which is always moving forward toward death. Immortality is achieved when the Five Elements begin to reverse and move backwards toward immortal life. The Microcosmic Orbit connects the circuitry that governs your aging and its reversal. Each orbit connects with each point representing one of the Big Dipper stars, touching each one with awareness and energy. Each point is the abode of a Divine presence, an awakening presence. So energy is circulating up and down with the Microcosmic Orbit— lifting up to heaven and dissipating back to earth—and in this circular motion, a tornado begins to spiral.

Two Parts: Preparing to Jump and Jumping

There are two parts to Stage Six. Before you can fly, you need to prepare to jump. Whenever you jump, you first bend your knees to get the power to jump up. In fact, you'll find you can't jump at all if you don't go into a semi-crouch position first. We once heard a story of an old Tai Chi Master who would allow a small bird to land on the palm of his hand. Every time the bird tried to squat down to prepare to fly, he would relax the palm of his hand downward. The downward motion of his palm did not allow the bird the push-off energy it needed to jump into flight. The bird stayed in the palm of the Master's hand until he let it fly. In other words, like the bird who couldn't squat to push off the Master's hand, we can't fly unless we bend our knees so that we can push off the ground.

Therefore we start Stage Six by focusing on Alchemical Life Strategy work. This is the preparation time—the taxiing on the runway before takeoff phase. We focus on training ourselves and practicing how to be someone who can fly in their life.

Once we are prepared and ready, we will move the energy upward to fly in the shape of the spinning Big Dipper. This looks like something you have probably seen in a number of Kung Fu action movies—there is a tornado-like movement in the air. Often the martial artist winds down like a screw turning in one direction and then bursts up into the air, whirling in the opposite direction. If you slowed this movement down, the motion would look like it was happening in two separate parts. Part One is a *downward* squatting and coiling movement in preparation for the jump. Part Two moves *upward*, uncoiling and jumping towards heaven to fly, in the same way water moves to heaven by evaporating, which creates clouds.

Moving Beyond the Five Elements and the Nine Palaces—Connecting Your Circle

In Stage Six, you've mastered all of the Five Elements within you. We call this, "connecting your circle."

NOTE: If you're interested in learning more about the process of developing each of the Five Elements within, you can read more about that in our book *Connecting Your Circle*. It's listed in the Our Reading List section at the end of this book.

By allowing yourself to equally embody the qualities of all Five Elements at any time, you free yourself from your own default behaviors. You're no longer confined to living only from your own particular innate nature. First you affirm who you truly are, and then you detach from it. Now you can fly free in the world. Your Nine Palaces are in balance, and you've arrived at the final *Home Palace* at the center of The Magic Square. *You've come home to the Divine.* You no longer need anyone or anything to take care of you and keep you safe.

> *Now you are sitting in the lap of God in every moment of your life. Stages Six through Nine are not associated with any particular Elements. Rather, they are ruled by the magic that transcends our DNA and essential nature.*

Stage Six has a five distinct steps:

1. **Opening the Third Eye**–detachment from the need to know

2. **Spirit Burial Ground**–letting go of desires and connecting with the Divine

3. **Groundedness**–anchoring your energy and finding ground to push off of

4. **Liftoff**–taking flight effortlessly

5. **The Gate to Flying**–transforming yourself into a

bird

6. **The Source**–connecting with Source energy

7. **Accessing Heaven through Flight**–crouching before you jump

Step One: Opening the Third Eye

You begin Stage Six by continuing the opening process of your third eye, located between your eyebrows and behind your forehead. There are three levels of activation of the third eye. The first level is the most shallow level, just under the skin. It is activated at the end of Stage Five. It is the step of illumination. The second level, which we open at this stage, is located about two inches further inside the head, and is activated by the Purple Palace point on the chest. It represents detachment. The color purple is the color of the crown chakra, the highest chakra. Purple is a combination of red, which is the color of the Spirit, and blue, which is the color of the Mystery with a capital M. The third level, located even deeper, about three inches inside the brain, is an entranceway to the Dao. When you activate it in Stage Seven, you have access to all information, which at this level of reality, beyond duality, is the same as no information.

> To know is not to know.
> To not know, is to know.

What does it mean when we say that we become detached when we open the second level of the third eye?

Attachments are the things that you cling to because you have a desire to remember them, and the presence of that kind of desire creates a hitch or blockage in your system that can stop your Qi from circulating. Opening this deeper level of the third eye allows you to detach from the memories that create the blockages. In this part of Stage Six, you're no longer relying on memory to power (or disempower) you. You are living in the present, acquiring experiences without having to store them consciously as a memory. As a result, nothing stops the power of your Qi as it moves throughout your body.

> *You become completely spontaneous. This is not forgetting like dementia would be. This is choosing not to hang onto memories through your advanced cultivation.*

Serving the Spirit

Our life-force energy and the essences of our physical body are here with the sole purpose of serving our Spirit. Our spirit believes it is limitless. But our physical body does indeed have limitations. Our spirit then has to be in balance with our physical essences. That way our desires are tempered and don't kill us. This "limitless Spirit," that we call our Big Shen, lives in our head, or the Upper Dan Tian. It's associated with the Fire Element. Our body's physical essences that are given to us by our parents at birth, are stored in our kidney area, or what we call the Lower Dan Tian. The kidneys are associated with the Water Element. No matter what Elemental temperament you are, your Water element tempers or slows down your Fire element desires. This function of the Water Element balances our spirit with our physical elements.

The space that lies between the Upper and Lower Dan Tians is called the Middle Dan Tian and is located in the chest. We must open the chest where the Heart lives as well as the throat, which is the bridge between the Upper and Middle Dan Tians, to release all of our fears, whether they are of success or failure, love or solitude, inclusion or exclusion. Opening the chest, or the Middle Dan Tian, allows better communication between the body and the spirit through the magic of the heart.

Your spirit comes to a physical life with a curriculum, and your body and its energies are here to serve that higher purpose. However, when the events of the years and days before this day, also known as your memories, are clogging up your Qi circulation, it becomes difficult and sometimes impossible to follow your pre-conceived curriculum. This is where the opening the third eye becomes so very important. At that second depth level, it helps us to "see" what is distracting us so that we can obliterate those blockages.

How does the body actually do this? Well, the body feeds energy to the organs that are associated with your Elemental makeup. So if you're a Wood Element person, your energy is distributed more to the organs associated with the Wood Element than to the other organs. As a Wood person, your energy will be delivered to the Wood organs, the liver and gallbladder. As a result, you'll experience the need to have goals and fulfill them, and you will be filled with what we like to call assertiveness, but many might translate as anger. Pursuing goals is a strong driving force of humanity. But our need to fulfill our goals, which is a Wood virtue, must be tempered.

Wood needs to fulfill its goals, but fulfilling goals is a desire. We receive our desires from heaven. Our Big Shen Spirit is associated with the Divine presence within us. It sets the path of our destiny and our curriculum for this lifetime. But then we have to make choices about how we're going to fulfill that destiny. And we can also get distracted by our Little Shen spirit's goals. Our indiscretions and squandered energies are our own choices too. And so when the Wood person's need to fulfill goals becomes more of an obsession than a tempered balance between the physical body's needs and the Spirit's purpose, the heart can mediate.

First, you learn to come into alignment with your spirit, and then second, you learn how to make choices that help you follow your true path in this life, your Big Shen Spirit, instead of being sidetracked by your own distractions and indiscretions.

By opening up the chest, we are actually opening our heart to learn to listen to our own spirit's guidance. We are coming into a deeper level of communion with our higher self. Our ability to live in complete spontaneity comes because we trust that our higher self is guiding each step on our path. We no longer have to do all the planning ahead and strategizing that we thought we had to before we began our Alchemical journey. Actually trusting that we will take the next right step in every moment is one of the highest levels of cultivation a person can attain. It requires our mastery of each stage of Alchemy, and here in Stage Six, the balanced partnership of an open third eye and a completely open heart.

Step Two: Spirit Burial Ground

> *The secret of life is to "die before you die"–*
> *and find that there is no death.*
>
> **– Eckhart Tolle**

The next step is what we call the "die before you die" step. In Alchemy, you have to bury the person you used to be along with all the remnants of your past lives. You're essentially burying your past-life karma. When you do, you're setting free your essences and spirit so that they can move freely in a balanced relationship. This freedom is built upon all the hard work you did in Stages Two and Three, which released you from the baggage from this lifetime and from past lives.

This step also unbinds and opens your chest even more, to increase your level of communication with your higher self and the Divine. We might say your heart and kidneys have to have good communication, because the heart represents your little *Shen*/spirit, or the spirit of your incarnation, and the kidneys represent your Will. This means the Will to live, and the Will to do what you need to do in life. Before Alchemy your little *Shen*/spirit might enlist your Will to do the things that you desire, but that might not be in alignment with your higher self or *Big Shen/Spirit*. You might have addictions that you can't kick, or become otherwise distracted away from your true path.

By surrendering yourself to the Divine in Stage Six, you come face-to-face with Divine Love in the present moment. In order to connect with Divine Love, you must overcome any fears of inadequacy or failure. This means you no longer experience the "sins" of desire itemized by many religions, such as pride, gluttony, or sloth. It's not that you stop having desires. Desires actually cause the movement of life. We need desires. When we desire something, we move toward it. That is our Will moving us to do what our heart desires. Without desire, there would be no movement.

But in Stage Six, you no longer let these desires control you. For example, if you're Wood and enjoy being successful, how do you keep your ambition in check so that you don't begin manipulating the people around you? Or if you're Fire, how do you enjoy the pleasures of life like food, partying, and sex without them getting out of control so that you become overweight or self-absorbed, forgetting your compassion for others? If you're Earth, how do you help and give to others without becoming empty or needy?

You let go of the weight of previous lifetimes in Stage Three. In Stage Five you accepted who you are. Life became your celebration. Now in Stage Six, when you no longer let desires control you, you can experience *direct contact* with the Divine. This may happen during a fleeting moment in meditation. You start to take flight! You're like a bird catching air as it's learning to fly. You feel lightweight, as if you could just lift off! Actually, as a side note, it has been said that The Immortals ate very little, especially no cereals or grains, the heavier harvest of the Earth. No wonder they could fly! Yet, as wonderful as these moments of pre-flight are, the connection often disappears as quickly as it appears. It's impossible to hang onto it, though you may instinctively want to try. You want to take flight and soar through the air with your wings spread. It feels exhilarating! But the truth is, you're more like a baby bird, who is a little wobbly, and inexperienced. The bird may just keep trying until it succeeds. That is *its* curriculum. However, until we are very clear about our curriculum, very sure about our direct contact with the Divine, we discover in Stage Six that it is critically important not to let any of our desires control us.

Step Three: Groundedness

Perhaps more than any other stage so far, Stage Six exemplifies the ongoing practice of Alchemy, which is always about letting it all go. As the famous writer Jack Kornfield describes in the title of his book *After the Ecstasy, the Laundry*, there will be many amazing moments of ecstasy that feel like flying and being completely connected with the Divine. But there's no hanging onto those moments—in fact trying to hang on to them will surely cause them to disappear from your grasp. After the ecstatic moments, the sense of connection ends and you drop back into regular life, and into the mundane daily tasks you have to accomplish. It's easy to fall out of the present moment and even feel unsteady or judgmental when this happens. This takes you out of alignment.

In order to keep moving, you must continue to "rectify" your Qi, which is about transforming and correcting any wrong motives, choices, or attitudes you notice in yourself. This ability to accept and forgive yourself gives you that feeling of being weightless and ready to fly.

In this third step, you continue to open your heart so that you increase your ability to be at peace with any disappointment that you're not very adept at flying and staying aloft yet. With an open chest, you realize that it's okay when you fall out of alignment. With the heart-mind, you can clearly see each of your choices and understand that you did the best you could, even when you made choices that were out of alignment. You see yourself with kindness, as if you're watching a baby bird learning to fly. You see how unsteady you've been in your learning process, not really knowing how, but still trying to fly. You see and fully understand how life events influenced you and shaped your path, and now you can accept with equanimity any and all of the choices you made in the past.

In the first and second steps, we spoke about the importance of balance. With all this upward expectation, it makes sense to also learn how to anchor your energy downward to become steady. An experienced bird is not unsteady on its feet. It firmly plants itself on a branch or on the ground, and it knows exactly how to use that solidity underneath its feet to support its takeoff.

This phase finds you grounding inside yourself, in the safety of the rectified you. This version of you can now see that even the mistakes you made were good or neither good nor bad because they brought you safely here to your present moment in time. You understand that grounding is the downward movement that must come before every move toward heaven.

Why did you make the choices you made? Often they were based on the desires of other people around you. These were either people you loved and cared about or people who threatened you in some way. Many Alchemists of antiquity recognized that living among other people could easily take them out of alignment. It's tempting for all of us to say, "I'd be enlightened if it wasn't for my crazy boss/spouse/children!" Some Alchemists ran off and lived hidden away in caves to seek solitude in order to stay in alignment. But they began to realize that the truly *enlightened being* could walk among humans and still stay in alignment. This is a much bigger feat than maintaining alignment in solitude.

Step Four: Liftoff

Many people ask us what we mean when we say someone is *flying in their life*. What we mean is that when a person is working through Stage Six and their life seems to become effortless. There is no sense of *gravity* weighing them down. They are living their potential fully and with joy. Their path is wide open before them. They are soaring.

In order to fly, we must have wings and a tail. This step represents the development of our flying apparatus. We are humans, and as such we are not born to physically fly. But we have ribs that are the human equivalent of wings. And we have a little piece of cartilage, called the xiphoid process, extending down from our sternum, which is our human equivalent of a tail. In a sense, our *Middle Dan Tian*, which is the chest area and abdomen, is the area that we can *fly* from. It's the residence of our spirit, inside our heart.

When we open our chest and allow our metaphorical wings to elongate outward, we become free to take to the clouds. Each rib is like a feather of a bird and the xiphoid process is our little tail that helps us to steady out any wobble in our flight. It's like a rudder on that little boat on the sea that we talked about. It means that we can not only fly, but we can fly in a particular direction!

In the beginning, we may feel emotionally unsure about the freedom of flying in our lives or living our full potential. We may not be able to believe that it's real or possible at first. Emotions may come up that cause us to falter and fall down. Remember, flying takes practice! Before we get used to it, we may have more than a few false starts. What beliefs about the nature of gravity and the universe are weighing us down? The area around the xiphoid process is associated with what Chinese Medicine refers to as our *heart protector.* Its job is to protect us from Heart Pains, and fear of failure is one of the most common heart pains to have. We must release these fears, and the negative beliefs and judgments we hold about ourselves and others as we attempt to fly.

The work of this step is to transform any heaviness, dampness, or phlegm left in your body after Step Four from the habit of being judgmental. Whatever may have come before no longer has to weigh you down. You are resolving your judgments. Being in judgment keeps us from being in the present moment.

This lightness of being is still just a start. We can't get carried away yet. We don't want to feel so light that we feel ungrounded. Remember, we're just launching into flight for the first time, not yet soaring. We have to continue to harmonize our Earth Element so we can feel like our feet are still standing on the earth–this is groundedness.

You also want to make sure you have the energy to fly. Some people have had their energy heavily taxed. Taxation can come from many things such as a poor diet, excessive sitting or lying down, excessive staring at screens, excessive sexual activity, excessive work, or excessive exercise. *Everything in moderation* is definitely the key to not becoming taxed physically or energetically. In order to fly, you must first go through Stages One through Five, which hopefully will have addressed any heavy taxations and brought balance to the energetic body. If not, you must do some additional work in those stages, especially Stage Three, which really works on building up your energy.

Step Five: The Gate to Flying

As you know from your reading so far, each stage serves as a transition, a gateway, to the one that follows it. In Stage Six, you are undergoing the transition to Stage Seven, which is about becoming softer and more changeable. In Stage Seven you will be working on developing the ability to morph and change the shape of your body. In essence this allows you to sculpt the form you want to take. In the big picture you are in a sense morphing into a bird, as you transform yourself into a being that can metaphorically fly. So for just a moment, let's step over the gate and learn a little bit more about Stage Seven's morphing so we can see how what we do near the end of Stage Six enhances our next steps.

How does morphing work? Try first thinking of stone. It's clearly something you cannot change. Or can you? Stone does get broken down by the weather and by water. It gets chiseled away.

Can you pass through a barrier of stone? Stone is a symbol of the rigidity and weight that has defined the limitations of your life. We believe that stone is subject to the laws of gravity. But in reality, gravity is not an absolute. For example, the process of osmosis defies gravity, when water travels upward from the ground and into a plant. If we can see the existence of exceptions to the rules of physics and physical laws, we can acknowledge that there is a possibility of flight, even for a human.

There is an old story of Pan Gu, who was a giant born in pre-creation times, whose huge body morphs and becomes the planet Earth as he dies. As the legend goes, his bones become the mountains, his sweat becomes the rivers, his body hair becomes the forests, his eyes become the sun and moon, and the maggots on his body become the humans who inhabit the Earth. Pan Gu's transformation in this creation myth symbolizes our ability as humans to transform and change. Like the earth being chiseled everyday by the elements such as wind and rain, we also can become chiseled and changed, and re-create ourselves.

Remember that Alchemically, you are creating your own immortal fetus. In this case, of course we're not talking about trying to create an external baby. You're simply re-creating yourself within yourself. This is the immortal you emerging, a brand new baby you.

To do this, you must take your essential energy and move your essences. What are you devoting your time to? This is a foundational question to ask during this phase, because this stage requires all your time. You must devote your will and your essences, or all of your mind and your body, to this transformation.

Your will functions in present time. It directs your essential energy to go where you want it to go in an instant. The act of flight is all encompassing and unified. You can't have a split mind, or split energy, and be able to stay in the air. It requires one hundred percent focus. If you still have strong desires, such as sexual ones, this step helps you break through those desires so that they do not split your energy.

Essential Qi

In Chinese Medicine, your real fears of inadequacy or failure are said to stem from the underlying fear of letting the "true you" get out of control. Let's take a minute to review what you have already read about the Five Element theory. Your Elemental constitution is based largely on one of the Five Elements: Wood, Fire, Earth, Metal, or Water, although all of the Elements are present in your being. The first Element in your Elemental stack-up is the most prominent in your constitution, followed in order by the second and third, and so on. Each Element has a strength that can be your greatest gift—or your worst nightmare. Inside, you fear that if you let the quality that is your greatest strength get out of control, it will cause you to fail. So taken all together, you're terrified of what would happen if you let yourself be truly, deeply, authentically you!

Each Element has its own fear of failure or of being out of control. These are fears of deficiency or excess from too much desire, similar to the idea of the seven deadly sins, where hunger could become gluttony, and the need for rest could turn into sloth.

Here is where the work of Stage Six complements your quest to calm this fear. In this stage, you want your essential Qi to flow freely to your Element so that you can feel comfortable being your authentic self and overcome your fear of failure. You want to feel comfortable allowing yourself to be completely yourself, so that you can connect with Divine Love.

Below is a list of all the places and situations that cause fear and blockages in each of the Five Elements. You might want to bookmark this list as a great reference—its application is valuable for any part of your life as well as your specific Alchemical journey. One more note: At this point in the book, you might wonder why we almost always start with the Wood Element in our discussions of the Elements. Wood symbolizes the season of Spring, which to the Chinese Medicine Ancients was the beginning of the life cycle.

- **If you're a Wood Element person**, then your biggest fear is of being too big and successful in the world. For you, losing control would mean becoming controlled by your own desire for success, and turning into someone who manipulates others. This would mean losing your Benevolence, which is the great virtue of the Wood Element. In this way, the fear of failure leads you to always try to control your desire to win at all costs. Often Wood people can feel out of control in the arena of achievement and success. Because Metal controls Wood in the cycle of the elements, Woods may choose to surround themselves with Metal Element people who can control them, so that they can't be too assertive in the world. For a Wood person in Stage Six, the kidneys need to deliver essential Qi to the liver to keep a Wood person from being afraid, or what the Chinese call being *timid*, so that they can in fact be big and successful in the world. In order to really connect with Divine Love, you have to allow yourself your full expression without being afraid you'll hurt other people.

- **If you're a Fire Element person**, you are afraid that you won't be able to stop if you allow yourself to experience the full amount of joy and pleasure you want to experience in the world. Unbridled eating will hurt your health. Too much partying and sex leads to a focus on pleasure, which could make you lose sight of Compassion for others—the great Virtue of Fire. Because Water controls Fire, some Fires may surround themselves with Water to temper their desires and thus remember their Compassion for others. In Stage Six for the Fire person, the kidneys need to deliver essential Qi to the heart to help a Fire person overcome their fear of too much joy and pleasure.

- **If you're an Earth Element person**, your biggest fear is that if you keep giving and giving, according to your natural way in the world, then eventually you'll give everything away and not have anything for yourself. You're afraid you'll be left feeling too needy or greedy. The fear is that if you allow yourself full self-expression, you'll be the one left with nothing. Because Wood controls Earth, many Earths surround themselves with Wood to temper their giving and learn to be a little less selfless. Wood knows you have to receive nutrients from others to grow and thrive. In Stage Six for an Earth person to connect with Divine Love, the kidneys must deliver essential Qi to the spleen so that they feel that they have a constant stream of goodness to give away, without ever becoming empty.

- **If you're a Metal Element person**, your biggest fear is that if you are true to your authentic nature you'll just blow around in the wind and let life lead you from place to place, doing whatever you want to do in the moment, and society will ultimately reject you. You might even become a wanderer or a hermit without any focus or guidance or family. Because Fire controls Metal, many Metals surround themselves with Fire to temper their non-attachment and develop connections to life, so they can partake in society. In Stage Six for the Metal person, the kidneys need to deliver essential Qi to the lungs to help them become comfortable with their true self, which may not fit into the society around them.

- **If you're a Water Element person**, then you have an innate power that if left unchecked could hurt those around you. It could be your physical power that could hurt someone—you have the kind of might that lets you lift a car off of someone in an emergency—it's the tidal wave state of Water. Your intense energy might be overpowering to those around you. You may feel like you're constantly holding yourself back. What if you let yourself just be that intense? Because Earth controls Water, many Waters surround themselves with Earth to "bank the waters"—contain that intense energy in a safe channel—the banks of the river. For Water people in Stage Six, the essential Qi needs to be delivered to the kidneys in order to release the constant need to hold back, so that they can feel free to be their true intense self.

Case Study: Freedom Flier

Many of our clients who have reached Stage Six have truly miraculous, successful lives. But sometimes their successes aren't what society would necessarily recognize as such. One woman got to Stage Six and simply walked out of a thirty-year-long marriage that wasn't working for her. She then proceeded to leave a job she'd had for over twenty years and disliked and resented. She became what she always had wanted to be—an artist, a writer, and a creator. She dared to become someone who let go of monetary concerns and began to contribute in what she saw as a more meaningful way in the world. She wanted to guide others to the understanding that there is more to life than being defined by materialistic goals and desires. She wanted to give hope to others that life does not have to be a struggle all the time. Living free and authentically in the present moment was her life goal. Sometimes leaving everything in your old life behind is how you learn to start flying in your new life. It can be scary, but if you make the motion, bend those knees, take a deep breath and leap, you can truly take off and fly!

Step Six: The Source

Before Creation, there has always existed something mysterious and impossible to understand—something we could call the One, or the Dao. Out of that one-ness, two things emerged: something ascended and created heaven, and something descended and was formed into the earth. Out of the dichotomy of heaven and earth emerged the dynamics we associate with humanity, which is movement, or Qi.

In the beginning of our Alchemy experience we entered the Mystery. But that was just the beginning of a journey to the deeper mystery, which is sometimes called *the emptiness* or *the ultimate one*. It represents the beginning of everything that is.

At this point, in Stage Six, you're connecting for the first time with this Ultimate Source where something becomes nothing. This comes from your center—your belly, your cauldron. The very real transformational process inside you is digestion, which comes from the strength of your Earth Element. Think of the miracle of digestion. Something identifiable goes into your mouth, let's say an apple. And by a mysterious process it gets completely transformed into essences and energy that become YOU! This is the gift and miracle of the Earth Element and the digestive power of the spleen and stomach organs.

Being in harmony with the Earth Element allows you to slow down and do things at the right pace. Digestion involves the breakdown of the food, which takes time. It's important to keep in mind that you can't rush through digestion—it just takes as long as it takes.

Human beings love to take short cuts. We always want to rush and hurry things along. Now you've had a taste of what it's like to fly! And the over-excitement and exhilaration of the flying experience may have overcome you. This step is about calming your heart down so that you don't rush. By calming the heart, your anxiety disappears. There's no more asking, *what's next...what's next?* Ultimately this step allows us the time to slow down and let things proceed at their own pace. Your transformation deserves the gift of time.

Step Seven: Accessing Heaven Through Flight

As we mentioned before, in order to ascend toward heaven, you must first go down. You have to crouch down before you can jump up. You must bend at the knees and the waist to squat in order to prepare for the leap heavenward.

So far in the process you've detached yourself from the past and from long-term memories, from both this life and your past lives. Your soul is cleared and you are living in this present moment in time. You're no longer influenced by past or future expectations. You got rid of all the *agos*, such as ten or twenty minutes or ten days or years ago. You're just no longer concerned with the past. You don't take on strong opinions or choose sides, which would require holding on, memory, and judgment. You have become effortless. Stage Six requires no effort.

In navigational terms, when you're in alignment with the North Star of the Big Dipper, you know how to *course the wind*. You look for the North Star to guide you home. You return to that state of Oneness with heaven. You are now pointing yourself to heaven like a rocket ready to launch, because you no longer need to be confined by the limitations of earth. There are no obstacles, and you can easily find whatever passages and gates you need. In fact, you can *make* passages wherever you need them. You can metaphorically drill a hole or mine a tunnel without collapsing the earth. You can even work with your own essences and dig a tunnel or passage through *yourself* that then allows you to take flight and ascend to heaven. You've completed your Nine Palaces, which are the nine curricula of life. The last curriculum is called *Home*. We must find our way back home, like a homing pigeon.

> *The famous Alchemist Ge Hong said, "You have to abandon the Nine Palaces to travel the Alchemical path."*

From here it's time to purify your Essences and Spirit. In Stage Seven, you will go into solitude so that you can truly and completely forget the past. This is called *sitting in oblivion* and *forgetting*. In Stage Six, you release yourself from the Nine Palaces, and in Stage Seven you retreat from the world, and go into the cave to be purified.

NOTE: Stage Six can comprise an excellent treatment for post-traumatic stress disorders (PTSD). It frees the client from having to relive the past again and again. A person can release a traumatic memory and stop carrying it with them all the time. We have seen much success over the years in efforts to treat PTSD, once a client has gotten to Stage Six.

Homework: Wu Wei is the Way

In Stage Six you come into alignment with the North Dipper, which means that in any given moment, you will be guided to walk the next perfect footstep on your path. If you are totally in the present moment, and you are receiving instructions for each next step directly from the Divine, then you are truly being guided. It looks like you're being spontaneous, but you're actually practicing Wu Wei. As we previously pointed out, Wu Wei has been traditionally translated as non-action or non-doing. But this sounds like you're doing nothing at all. We prefer to translate it as inspired action. We even used Inspired Action for the name of our podcast, to highlight this foundational concept. Living from the place of Inspired Action or Wu Wei means that you are only doing what you're inspired or guided to do. Living in the Wu Wei is effortless and full of Grace.

We've said it over and over: This stage requires "practice" because the focus is on practicing being fully present. It's being in the Power of Now, as Eckhart Tolle talks about in his famous book of the same name. Being present in the moment requires no effort. It asks only that you pay attention with simple awareness. If you're not fully in Stage Six, this can be very difficult to achieve, and it's even more challenging to maintain. Once you attain Stage Six, it gets easier and easier and eventually requires no effort at all.

When you're fully in this Stage, you don't concern yourself with whatever emerges in your mind, from the past, present, or future. These are just distractions. *Oh no I forgot to do that* or, *tomorrow I have to get on a plane!* These thoughts pull you out of the moment. You simply let go of time, in order to be fully present.

For homework, start by trying to spend an hour a day being totally spontaneous. This is a meditation of sorts. Just do whatever occurs to you in the moment. Once you get more familiar with this mode of being, you'll begin to learn to trust that the Divine is guiding you to do whatever you need to do in any given moment. As we mentioned before, you don't have to set a timer to remind you of your dentist appointment. You can trust that you'll be reminded to move in that direction at the exact right moment.

Work up to spending an entire day not pre-planning anything—tap into the Metal Element, happily going wherever the wind takes you. Can you spend a whole day living that way, with no plan and no agenda? You can't say, *Oh I can't just let myself wander about* or *I have work to do* or *I need to do this thing for my mother.* You fall out of the present moment just thinking about it. Don't let yourself labor or make an effort to get through the day.

See if you can spend a whole day being totally spontaneous.

If you find that you want the day to quickly end, you're not in Stage Six yet. We can't rush through creation. Stage Six completely changes our relationship to time.

Here is our suggestion. Start with an hour of total spontaneity each day. If you can't do an hour, start smaller. Then as you're able, work up to two hours, four hours, eight hours, and beyond—until you no longer want to rush through the day.

Gradual change – free and unfettered body.

Be detached–free and unrestrained body.

—Lu Dong Bin

Stage Seven: Softening

Stage Seven is about leaving society, going into the cave, and living like a hermit on the top of a mountain —alone. Despite whatever the stereotype might be, the hermit is not indifferent to life. Things can affect the hermit, but the hermit doesn't become attached. When you spend months in a cave all by yourself with no interactions, you must develop a deep connection with yourself and a presence with all that is. This can certainly also be done without entering a physical cave.

Many of the ancient Alchemists actually did go to the cave though. On Mount Hua Shan where many Alchemists practiced, there are caves tucked away in the mountain where, to this day, Alchemists still retreat for long periods of time. Other practicing Alchemists bring them food and water that they slide through a small hole. But other than the food exchange, there is no interaction with the outside world. It's just you, and the darkness of the cave, and the air you breathe.

One of the legends of The Immortals is a story of a middle aged man who was out walking in the woods one day when he met an Immortal who had suddenly appeared out of nowhere. The Immortal saw the quality of sincerity in the man's face, and decided to tell him the secret to immortality. Upon learning this, the man rushed home and went to bed, pretending to be sick so that he could be left alone to ponder what the Immortal had taught him. He vowed not leave his bedroom until he could literally walk through the walls to get out. He stayed in that bed for ten years, with his wife and family members taking care of his every need. They thought he was deathly ill and that he wasn't able to get up. But in fact, he was simply lying silently in his thoughts day after day, never saying a word to anyone. Then one day, he stood up and literally walked through the wall to leave the room. He figured out how to change his molecular structure so that he could morph into another shape to achieve that unbelievable feat! We know this sounds crazy, but this is the kind of crazy that Stage Seven is all about.

> *The art or way of softness is about softening the body, becoming malleable, and morphing. The body can take any shape it wants to. This stage is also about softening the mind, so it becomes less stuck in permanency and the ego.*

When we say *less stuck in the ego*, we're not talking about losing the qualities that make you your *Self*. The process is really about finding *wholeness* instead of *individual-ness*. It's like dying. When you're buried in the ground, your body begins to decay and become less permanent. It's a softening of the body, mind, and ego. In another spiritual sense you are becoming *more* present. And then, even presence is impermanent.

In 2015, Jaye and Leta travelled to China with Master Yuen, and visited *Luofu Shan*, which was the mountain home of the famous Alchemists Ge Hong and his wife Bao Gu. We climbed and walked all around the mountain. We visited many temples and shrines there. We sat in front of one of the Alchemist's caves where Immortals are said to have transcended to immortality. It was a beautiful and peaceful space. The only entrance to Ge Hong's cave was a very small opening, much smaller than any human could fit through. Inside the cave they found a large cauldron that was much bigger than the tiny entrance to the cave. How was he able to get himself and his cauldron through an opening that size? He did it through malleability, or the ability to morph his body into something as small as a mouse, which has no collar bones, and can change its shape to get through even the tiniest hole.

Water overcomes hardness and permanence. It makes things soft. It can break things down. It can even make stone soften. In the body, the kidneys are responsible for softening things, because they control the water in your body.

Your essences signify your permanence and the physicality of the world. Your essences are your physical body, or what we call *Jing* in Chinese Medicine. The water in your body, on the other hand, is the impermanence factor. The kidneys are responsible for your essences—your *Jing*—and the water in your body. They are holding both the permanence and impermanence of you.

Stage Seven has two distinct steps:

1. **See-Saw**–becoming less permanent

2. **Returning Home to Die Before You Die**–completing your curriculum

Step One: See-Saw

Step One helps you ease into the changes that are about to take place. So initially, we are not trying to become less permanent. Instead we start out like water lapping the shores. The shoreline definitely and solidly exists. It has some permanence. But then a wave comes, and just for a moment the shoreline is impermanent. It shifts just the tiniest bit.

Step One of Stage Seven is a juxtaposition of these two factors: permanence and impermanence. Qi creates manifestation by giving it energy. But manifestation also creates Qi by giving it the physical essences that can carry out or express the *movement* that Qi fundamentally is. So it's the classic chicken and the egg scenario. Which came first? Qi or Essences? Energy or the body?

This step makes the body lighter and softer, alternating back and forth between the solidity of the body and the softening of the body, like a see-saw. By doing this, you're generating warmth in the lower abdomen that stimulates and arouses the kidney's essential Qi. As that happens, the kidneys begin to soften things. It's the juxtaposition of what is most magical about the kidneys— they are the organ that has both Yin and Yang Qi. The Yin is the solidity of the essences, and the Yang is the movement of the Qi, which is ultimately the cause of change in the world. Practicing this alternation back and forth between Yin and Yang in the lower abdomen promotes longevity, which is one of the reasons that Alchemists can reverse the aging process. This is how you begin to create that immortal fetus within yourself. It also changes your ideas about manifestation. You realize that you *are* what you think and feel.

Sometimes while you're practicing this, you can lose your connection to your own Divinity and start to feel judgmental again. If you're feeling sad, you're creating or attracting sadness. You will resonate with sadness in the world. This may mean you need to return to Stage Five— there is no good or bad.

Homework: Breath of Fire

There are breathing meditation practices in almost all spiritual traditions. With the simple focus on the breath, much can change throughout the body and mind, in ways that sometimes happen subtly and sometimes more dramatically. A good one to start practicing is called *The Breath of Fire*, which comes from one of the oldest yoga traditions, Kundalini Yoga. This exercise can be practiced slowly over time and with the guidance of a practitioner who is familiar with this breathing technique. Sit cross-legged or stand. Breathe in and out quickly through your nose while pumping your navel area and lower abdomen in and out. The goal is to breathe rapidly in and out while lifting and pumping your belly. If you have difficulty doing this through your nose at first, you can begin by breathing through your mouth. Open your mouth wide and stick your tongue out, like a dog panting on a hot day, and breathe quickly while pumping your belly.

As you pull back and pump your navel area, think about the solidity of your body alternating with the immaterial nature of the spirit. Breathe in the spirit and expand beyond the boundaries of your body, then breathe out and feel the solidity of the body again. Alternate feeling the impermanence and the permanence. The goal is to continue until you generate warmth in your abdomen, in the Lower Dan Tian.

Step Two: Returning Home to Die Before You Die

In this stage, you are returning to Home, the final curriculum of the Nine Palaces. You return to your own inner sanctuary, allowing yourself to metaphorically die so that you can be reborn. This is where you *die before you die*, so that you can live forever.

> The secret of life is to "die before you die" —
> and find that there is no death.
>
> **– Eckhart Tolle**

Wholeness transcends time and space. In Chinese numerology, we say the One gives birth to the Two, which are Yin and Yang. Therefore, we live in the duality of Yin and Yang—simply to be born. At the time of our birth we actually leave wholeness (the number one), to become a separate individual (the number two, separate from the wholeness).

In Stage Seven, we return to the wholeness and embrace the broken parts of us. You see yourself as deeply loved and then let the loved part hold the part that isn't loved. The love in you heals the unloved part of you. And this healing can only happen in a safe place—that's the sanctuary, your retreat, your Alchemical cave.

It's through safety, acceptance of who you are, and self-love that you heal. You have to provide your own safety and love. All you need is yourself in a safe place in order to heal yourself.

Acceptance means self-acceptance. Both positive and negative thinking come from inside you. The Divine is all-accepting and all-healing. In your Inner chamber, you can be in contact with the Divine. When you accept yourself, you're holding onto your integrity and what you believe about yourself, regardless of anything anyone else might tell you. If someone says you're ill, and you feel good, you have to hold onto your integrity, your acceptance of yourself as you know yourself to be, and continue to feel good, without letting that other person's opinion negatively sway you.

We explained that Step One of Stage Seven generates a lot of new energy in the front of your abdomen. In Step Two, you play dead, which is metaphorically the ultimate return journey to Home. You lie like a corpse, face down. You take all that Qi in the abdomen and circulate that energy to each of the Five Elements within you. Working from the bottom to the top, you bring your Qi from your lower back to the residences of each of the Five Elements, to each of the organs associated with a particular Element, as the energy moves up your back. You are allowing this newly built Qi and vitality to embrace and nourish all the organs.

This nourishment helps you to overcome the fears that are associated with each individual Element. These are the remnants of fears from this life or previous incarnations that you haven't yet cleared out.

Start with the kidneys, the Water Element. The kidneys are associated with your Will, also called the *Zhi*, which is the aspect of your spirit that gives you the *will to live*. It's your fight for life! It's the aspect of you that holds the hand of the of the part of you that is afraid.

Next you move to your spleen, the Earth Element. This is associated with your Mind, also called the *Yi*, which is the aspect of your spirit that gives you the ability to think, analyze, examine, and philosophize. This is where you listen to the part of you that feels ignored.

Then you move onto your liver, the Wood Element. This is associated with your Spiritual Soul, also called the *Hun*, which is the aspect of your spirit that gives you the ability to plan for the future and even predict what will happen. Now you give the part of you that's been angry a big selfie hug.

Next, you deliver your essential Qi to your heart, the Fire Element. This is associated with your spirit, also called the *Shen*, or the aspect of your spirit that is your unique individual piece of the Divine. Here you love the part of you that's felt unloved.

Lastly, you deliver your essential Qi to your lungs, the Metal Element. This is associated with your Corporeal Soul, also called the *Po*, which is the aspect of your spirit that gives you your animal instinct. This is when you embrace the part of you that's been sad.

As you embrace these parts of yourself, you are returning home to your sanctuary. The opening to this sanctuary is accessed through the back of your head, in the cerebellum area, connecting to the hypothalamus and the midbrain, which controls hunger and many other functions like temperature control. In this stage, as you connect with your cerebellum and hypothalamus, you begin to be able to control your body temperature and to withstand very cold or hot temperatures. You overcome survival issues. In the Tibetan mountains, monks would practice something called *Tung-mo*, which is the ability to warm the body through meditation. Herbert Benson of Harvard studied this amazing practice. To read more about Benson's study, see the book *Healing Anxiety* by Dr. Mary Ryan-Friedman, page 87.

Depression, lack of hunger or anorexia, and lethargy are all symptoms that you can't maintain balance in your life, which points to issues with the brain. The cerebellum is the part of your brain that maintains posture and balance. If you fall down, it's because you have no sense of your gait, or how each step needs to be so that you can maintain your uprightness. You have to adjust every step when walking to balance your gait.

The skill of balance is extremely important in flight. It's imperative that you are not off balance when you're flying! If you find yourself off balance during this step, you'll need to return to Stage Six. Learning to fly requires new balance skills. As a side note, poor posture is a sign of an inability to control gravity in you. When you slouch, gravity is winning. If you're going to transcend gravity, you must cultivate good posture.

Homework 2: Going into Your Alchemy Cave

At the end of the day, find your inner sanctuary, your retreat. This is your Chamber of the Will, that safe inner chamber that's deep inside you, where you receive faith. Visualize the Alchemy cave from the outside in as much detail as you can. Now enter into sanctuary to be alone, just the way the Alchemists did when they went into their caves.

Close your eyes and take some time to imagine yourself in your inner cave. When you are ready, ask yourself what still feels broken in your life. Is there a relationship problem? A health issue? Does something feel like it can't be repaired? Stage Seven is your opportunity to transform and repair whatever still bothers you in this lifetime that is keeping you blocked and unable to truly fly.

Now begin to see and feel yourself as whole and complete. Take time with this. See an image of yourself as whole and then begin to gather around you any fragmented and troubling images you still have from previous lives or old periods in this life. Let the wholeness of you take up and embrace the broken parts of you.

If you have difficulty loving the parts of you that are broken, imagine a time in your life when you did feel whole and loved yourself. Often children are whole, healthy, happy, and giggling. Imagine yourself as a little child standing in front of you. Let that child embrace the current you. Let the remnants of the past heal inside you now.

This is a powerful meditation. It lets the Divine and its light hold you. You find the wholeness in yourself and receive redemption. What really causes us to soften is our self-love and self-acceptance. Most spiritual paths require going on retreat. There are also people in the world who can make others feel held in the same way that happens when we retreat. You can look into their eyes and find security, love, and healing. They've become "all-healing." Home is right there in their eyes.

> **NOTE**: This meditation is also helpful for people who are feeling suicidal. When you find love, safety, and wholeness, you've invited healing into your life.

The dark stone
looks as
though a tiger
is crouched behind
it.

The tree root seems
as though it
conceals a dragon.

- Yu Xin (513-581)

Stage Eight: Invisibility

The phrase *Crouching Tiger, Hidden Dragon*, made popular by the movie title, is a phrase that in Chinese refers to the fact that people with extraordinary talent or abilities, like the Immortals, are hidden from normal people's view. Thus the tiger is crouching and the dragon is concealed. In other words, the true masters go unnoticed.

Stage Eight is the art of the Ninja. You are learning how to become invisible. You learn to crouch and hide. You become the lurker. Your power is stored, a latency that is either not fully developed yet or is hidden away.

The key word for this stage is Hidden. Hidden also refers to the Akashic records that were hidden away. Our own records of our past lives were hidden from us when we were born. Many people go to oracles and psychics to find out their past life stories. In Stage Eight, we don't need a psychic to learn about our past lives. We are able to go into ourselves to find the truth.

The Immortals are able to transcend time and space. They transcend the confines of this physical world. They can time travel and fly. From times past, there are countless stories of sightings of many Immortals. One of the gifts of immortality is that by transcending space, you can be invisible. People can't see you unless you allow them to. Many of the stories describe that one second you see them, then the next second, they disappear. If you can't see them, you are not yet at the level in your self-cultivation to be *able* to see them. You aren't able to unveil their presence.

The Immortals are immaterial, meaning they are pure spirit without body. Saint Germain is one of the most famous Immortals of the West. There are many legends of how he became immortal through the use of Alchemy.

Stage Eight does not require a treatment or Qi Gong exercises to complete. You can still use acu-points to get acquainted with the energy of the treatment, but you don't need a "method" anymore because you have Divine Love. Your entire body is saturated with Divine Love, like the love of the Virgin Mary or Quan Yin.

Stage Eight is about circulating your Qi through visualization and meditation. Your goal is to open the crown chakra at the top of your head so that your spirit can enter and exit your body while your body stays intact. This is how you can dematerialize and re-materialize. You learn how to disappear in Stage Eight, and you learn how to reappear in Stage Nine. This is physical immortality.

This Stage is about the number *four*, which represents time and space in Chinese Numerology. There are Four Directions and Four Seasons. This Stage is about transcending both time and space. You are no longer confined by them. You can drop out of space and become invisible, and then you can reappear in any time you choose, as a time traveller.

In Stage Eight, you are no longer attached to short-term memory. You don't need it in order to be in the present moment. You don't need to be so attuned to your bodily sensations. This doesn't mean breaking off from your mental database of memories however! That would be a personality disorder. You cultivate the loss of short-term memory. It's a practice. You are already enlightened and have obtained the primordial Qi, which allows your body to sustain itself indefinitely. You now have access to the Dao, which is the number One. If you can do this, you can forget all your other cultivation practices. You are simply being.

The treatment is the meditation. Meditation is a practice. You are no longer practicing because there is nothing more "to do." You do nothing. So the homework is Stage Eight itself.

Step One: Ascension

At this moment in this lifetime, you no longer have any unfinished business. We reincarnate over and over again because we die with unfinished business. We come back to finish that business with a new curriculum. Your soul is already immortal and continues to refine itself lifetime after lifetime. It's an evolutionary process.

Inside you is your own library. It's a tower or pagoda that reaches toward heaven. It's the container for all your past-life experiences, and each new lifetime has the goal of reaching heaven, of evolving to a higher place. By opening this past-life library and accessing your pagoda, your past lives will be revealed to you so that you know what your curriculum was, and why you chose it, in each past life.

In this visualization, you imagine your own personal library or pagoda filled with books. This library has been locked, but now you have the key. You open it up and your past lives are revealed to you. This means you can access your curriculum of the past. But the pagoda is more than just a library. It is a tower, an axis point, to help you return to heaven. The tower is your soul. You ascend.

Step Two: Accessing the Memories

The record keeper of these past lives is in your spine. Like striations in stones that tell the story of the past, your spine holds the striations of your past. Each striation is a line that carries information. It's like there's a grid of past-life stories in the spine.

Now you meditate on the spine, at the area between your shoulder blades to discover these striations. This method was traditionally done by adding moxibustion to this area to increase the ability to consciously access these areas on your back.

Step Three: Opening Your Doors

Now that you're ascending upward, you visualize opening up like a lotus flower. You're opening all the doors to the clouds. You become like the wind. The wind is change, which is impermanence. Typically you don't want any wind to enter your body. Wind in the body causes resistance. However, when you work with this step in Stage Eight, you now have the ability to let wind enter and leave your body through a portal.

Moxibustion that burns the skin, called scarring moxibustion, was traditionally used at the base on the neck to open this portal. By leaving a small burn mark, the area stays activated long after the treatment. This helps you to visualize the area afterwards. It helps bring back the memories and improve concentration.

Even fear itself is frightened by the bodhisattva's fearlessness.

—Chögyam Trungpa

Stage Nine: Cold

After learning how to achieve the state of invisibility in Stage Eight, in this stage you are able to materialize again. You emerge out of the mists of invisibility (which is how a fetus emerges into the womb) using the process of condensation through cold. Cold causes solidification and you become solid or material. When water begins to freeze, it solidifies into a stable form —it takes shape. Now you can disappear and reappear at will. This is a resurrection and the ultimate redemption. You come back with a new curriculum. You come back new and different instead of perishing.

When the early Alchemists created an alchemical elixir for this stage, they used a lot of ice water. However, you can emerge out of the mists of invisibility through meditation and visualization alone.

So the important question is "Why would you want to be immortal?" Your new curriculum is different than previous ones. In this curriculum, you have no unfinished business. So why learn to become visible again? Why stay? To answer those questions, we bring you back to the beginning of the book and to the same questions we originally asked you. Do you want to live longer than the "normal" number of years? And if so, why?

Alchemy is not for everyone. At this Alchemy Stage, you come back not because you have unfinished business of your own, but because you are helping others with their unfinished business. You become an authentic, fully realized human being. You become a *Zhen Ren*, a Bodhisattva, a Quan Yin. You are able to help others with their suffering and so you do.

There are many famous Immortals throughout history who come back to help the suffering. All over the world, people relate accounts of the miracles of compassion performed by the Virgin Mary and by Quan Yin. They are here helping others and being of service to humanity.

Stage Nine is that service. At this point you're no longer practicing anything. This is simply an opening. The Earth is a new basin, containing the water. In earlier stages, you softened your physical essences and your karma. Then in Stage Eight, you developed the ability to see the hidden information about your previous lifetimes so that you're able to understand fully how to fulfill your life. You reach completion. And then, even though you're complete, you come back to be of service to others. For you, there's never the necessity of "the end." You always can come back.

There is a wonderfully simple and humorous story about the famous Daoist philosophers, Laozi and Zuangzi. They were walking along a small lake with a disciple following close behind. They began to walk upon the water's surface to cross the lake. The disciple tried to follow them as they effortlessly travelled across the water and quickly fell face first into the lake. The big splash made the masters stop for a moment. They looked at each other and said, "Do you think we should show him where the stepping stones are?" The stepping stones are the Stages of Alchemy that are laid out in this book!

In Stage Nine, you step with a sense of knowing and assurance and the stones are simply beneath your feet. As an invisible immortal, you are dematerialized lightness. To return, you need to condense yourself down in order to re-materialize. The story goes that you come back down to Earth from the Big Dipper. You concentrate on the top of your head, just above the forehead, where the frontal lobe controls all the highest level brain functions. It's the intuition center of the brain that houses psychic abilities and the seat of determination, will power, and faith. It's the part that creates projects, which then become realities. From this place, you return from the constellation far out in the cosmos like water from the clouds.

Your Metal spirit, which is called the Po, is the part of you that draws down the moisture from the cloud form of you. Now you must solidify the water into a solid, human form. At this point, you concentrate on your lower abdomen where your uterus is located. Metaphorically, we all have uteruses, even those assigned male gender at birth. This is the central axis or pole around which your body will re-materialize. It's the point between Yin and Yang. Your spirit has to inhabit your essences again, just like at the moment of conception when the spirit enters the egg.

Sometimes, there are problems. Ghosts are said to have difficulty materializing the lower half of their bodies. Usually they come back only as the face and upper torso and instead of being able to connect their feet to the earth, they "wander." To truly re-materialize into the human form, you have to concentrate on the lower body. The Earth Element in you has to trap the Water Element of you which is condensing and "coming down." The Earth Element functions as a bowl, where the mists can concentrate and consolidate into the physical form. You have to call the water into the bowl using your ankles and the bottom of your feet. You place yourself back on the ground, solidifying your presence and the ability to walk again on the earth. It's as if you simply appear from this different dimension. You condense, descend, and return back to earth.

By staying in your truth at each of the other Eight Stages of Alchemy, taking the time that is needed to release all past suffering, you will have the will power to intuitively project yourself back into something that becomes form— human form. And in this way, you can appear where you are needed to help end the suffering of others.

If you think about this Stage metaphorically (not just the physical disappearing and reappearing), once you have intuition and the ability to recreate yourself, then your senses, sensory motor skills, and sensuality return. You have a new level of self-awareness and self-learning. You have your attention span so that you can pay attention to yourself. You have the will and determination to manifest yourself and learn more about yourself. This is your self-worth. You have to have faith that you can Flow with whatever may happen, and let your mind be free: Stay centered by accepting whatever you are doing. This is the ultimate.

–Zhuang Zhou

Ling Shu Alchemy Treatments

L ife is challenging at times for almost all of us. A few of us had idyllic childhoods that provided an environment where we could easily thrive. But very few people make it through to age thirty without any trauma or serious negative experiences.

For this reason in Alchemy, we like to begin the Nine Stages of Alchemy with a clean slate. That means, we use treatments that help the client let go of these serious traumas that are held in the body or the heart before embarking on the path of Alchemical transformation. Often if we don't release these experiences first, they will make the Alchemical journey come to a grinding halt later, when they rear their ugly heads.

There are a number of Alchemical Treatments that have been developed by Alchemists over the centuries that are used for specific purposes. There are several kinds of major blocks to beginning Alchemy, including what Chinese Medicine calls *possession* and *obsession*. Trauma and negative experiences cause most of us to have difficulty being our authentic selves in the world. Much the way Leta struggled to be her outgoing, happy self in life after being bullied in grammar school, we all have ways of coping with our negative experiences as we make our way through life. If these coping mechanisms involve possession and obsession, they must be dismantled before we can make real progress in Alchemy.

Spiritual Pivot

It's best to get professional support to help you clear these kinds of issues before proceeding. It's not impossible but extremely difficult to clear them by yourself. It might take your entire lifetime, and beyond.

At the Alchemy Healing Center we often do some special *Ling Shu* treatments with new clients to help return them to their authentic selves. *Ling Shu* means spiritual pivot. We decided to give these types of treatments this name because we do them in half-day sessions which are four to six hours long, with the idea that a huge spiritual pivot or transformation will occur as a result. You can't rush this kind of transformation. Often the person has been stuck for a very long time, so it's unrealistic to attempt to shift that level of pain in an hour. The treatment's goal is to reestablish a person's true Qi. The result of the treatment is a sense of feeling lighter, like a heavy weight has been lifted away. These treatments are typically done in a single session, but in certain difficult cases of severe life trauma, they can be repeated.

Because we reference these *Ling Shu* treatments throughout the book, here is a summary of each treatment type. Each one really deserves an entire book on its own. Perhaps this will be the subject of a future book! But for now, this summary will give you some context for understanding the different treatments we've mentioned in this book.

The Ghost Points: Obsession

When a person has obsessive thoughts about anything, whether it's past traumas, negative ideas, rational or irrational fears, or patterns of negative behaviors, accidents, disagreements, or undesirable outcomes, we say that the person is *haunted* or *hooked*, like a fish on a fishhook. You can only become haunted if you have an opening for it. You have to have a receptor in order for that thing to be able to hook into you, whether it's a negative idea that got into your head, or a trauma-based fear that leaves you vulnerable. Even if the problem is that someone is stalking you in real life, the point is that *you* have an energetic opening for that issue to attach to you.

The Thirteen Ghost Points Treatment clears old trauma and removes the hooks that are stuck in you that can cause obsessive thinking and unwanted cellular patterns. The points of the treatment work on a deeper level to heal that vulnerability so that whatever strange or difficult issue you may be having can no longer affect you.

There are 20 Ghost Points in total, but the legendary King of Medicine, Sun Si Miao (581-618 C.E.) created a specific treatment for these kinds of issues called The Thirteen Ghost Points. This specific series of points helps to cleanse the soul of guilt, shame, and trauma. It cleans all the skeletons out of the closet.

When past experiences of any type still haunt you today, we say you're not really free to be yourself. We've all had the experience of having something bad happen and then wanting to prevent it from happening again. Some events are so big that they continue to haunt us throughout our lives: the loss of a lover, the death of a loved one, depression over lost dreams, or even a physical trauma, like a sudden accident, or coming into contact with some kind of parasite. All of these things can impact our energy and hamper our ability to grow and succeed in our lives.

The word ghost in Chinese contains the word for "hook" in its character. A ghost is anything that haunts you or has a hook in you. When you're hooked, the ghost convinces you not to be true to yourself, and then you're not free to be authentic and do what you want to do.

A Ghost Point Treatment releases all the areas where you may be hooked, for example:

- **Your eyes**—how you see the world

- **Your heart**—how you love

- **Your trust in yourself**—how much you believe in yourself

- **Your official rules**—whose rules you're following

We recommend Ghost Point Treatments in the following situations:

- When life just feels like too big of a struggle and you're working too hard to overcome it.

- When you don't feel free in your life.

- When you are living in a toxic situation.

- When you have past trauma that haunts you.

Typically we recommend a ghost point treatment with anything that feels very hard to overcome. If you are working very hard and not getting any results, that usually means there is something blocking you or haunting you. Most adults have some skeletons in their closet, so it is a good treatment to start with when embarking on a healing path.

We have been working extensively with The Thirteen Ghost Points for over fifteen years, doing them as a ritualistic, half-day treatment that includes music, and they have been nothing short of mind-blowingly amazing. We have hundreds of stories of people being set free from either their own emotional prisons or from very real and serious scenarios in their external worlds. Whatever strange story they may be carrying, what happens is the Thirteen Ghost Points Treatment is able to shift something that frees them to make new choices. It *makes available* choices they never had before.

We've seen this magical treatment work miracles to create deep personal transformation, to unravel unwanted cellular patterns, to break down emotional blocks, and to uncover and free a person's true nature, true essence, or what we like to call their true Qi.

Living life causes many ups and downs. After you've been living this life for many years, it's pretty much impossible to avoid having a few skeletons in your closet. The Ghost Points help to clear them out and return you to your original state of open potential.

For this reason, we at the Alchemy Healing Center usually do the Ghost Points before helping a person embark on the Nine Stages of Alchemy. Or, if there doesn't seem to be any major blockage, we sometimes do the treatment when the person reaches Stage Two. Stage Two has a natural affinity to the Ghost Points because it's about getting rid of the baggage of this lifetime.

Here are some examples of how Ghost Point treatments have helped our clients transform their stuck patterns and blocks.

> **NOTE:** The role of music in these ritualistic treatments is profound! We use a music playlist with 20,000+ songs on it, and shuffle them. You will notice in many of our stories that the music and the information it delivered played an integral part in the person's transformation.

Case Study: Lyme Disease

We mentioned Jade earlier in the book. She came to us at her wits end. She had spent the past four years getting sicker and sicker, until she was unable to work. Her Lyme disease was not responding to traditional antibiotic treatments, and she'd been searching for alternative cures for a couple of years. These cures were not making her feel better. In fact, she was feeling worse and worse. She was weak and plagued with intense dread and anxiety. Her nights were marked with sleepless bouts of terror.

One of the first things we do for anyone with Lyme disease or any parasitic condition, which is called *Gu* in Chinese Medicine, is the Ghost Points. These are not meant to instantly cure the condition, but rather to work on the cause or root of the condition.

What was the terrain that allowed the seeds of disease to flourish? We always say that if twenty-five people ate the same tainted food, only about three people would actually get really sick. The other twenty-two people would immediately eliminate the offending material and be done with it. This actually happened to Leta when she was stationed in West Africa in the Peace Corps. There were twenty-five volunteers eating the same exact meals, and twenty-two were just fine. But three had to be sent home to the USA with a parasitic infection. What made those three susceptible and not the rest of the volunteers? They had an opening for the parasites to attach into them.

Usually we think of such an opening as a fear of that thing happening. But it's not always that specific. Sometimes it's just being unhappy with your current life situation, or not fully inhabiting yourself or your life because of past trauma or pain. That is a common thread among people with Lyme disease. In Chinese Medicine we say you can only be sick, ever in your life, if you have an opening in your mind for sickness. If you only embrace and embody your health and your perfection, there is no opening for *ghosts* to get in.

Jade had a lot of ghosts that haunted her. She was given up for adoption at birth and was eventually placed with a family that had very little love in it, for themselves or for her. While they cared for her physically, she was emotionally bereft in the new environment and was incessantly bullied at school and home.

The Ghost Point treatment began to resolve many of these pains she'd carried into her present day, and helped her recognize the same patterns unfolding in her current life so she could make changes.

Over the next two years, she not only healed physically and was able to enjoy a more active way of life again, but also emotionally and spiritually as well, even to the point where she could feel happiness in the presence of her family. She is still working on her life's challenges and has worked through several Stages of Alchemy.

Case Study: A Son Haunts His Mother

A woman came into the clinic after her son's death, claiming that he was haunting her in the real sense of a ghost haunting. The reported ghost, which in Chinese Medicine is called a *Gui*, made noises in the house and even at times became visible to her. This was very disturbing to her, and she was very afraid about the possibility that either the ghost was real, or that she was losing her mind because her son was appearing to haunt her as a ghost.

> *The Ghost Points don't discriminate about what kind of torture someone is going through. We often say there is no hierarchy to trauma. Every person suffers not according to the severity of the trauma but according to their reaction to it.*

This client's reaction was very fearful in the extreme. Her Ghost Point treatment was quite magical. She went from being in a state of terror to the realization that she was blessed with the ability to stay connected with the spirit of her son. She came in wanting to cast out demons and left wanting to truly connect with the spirit of her son. When she came into the clinic for a follow-up, she was at total peace. She said she was able to feel his loving, caring presence always, and from there she was able to move on in her life. She never saw any sign of the ghost haunting again.

Case Study: Woman's Infant Dies

A woman came to us at the age of forty trying to decide whether to attempt to have another child. Her second child had died a short time after childbirth, which dealt a devastating blow to her and her husband. They had one amazing boy, already ten years old, but they had very much wanted another child. She came to us at a time when she knew she had to decide whether to try to get pregnant again or to give up trying due to her age.

During the treatment, there were many magical moments that reminded her of the baby she had lost. The music spoke to her. Three butterflies literally landed on the window sill of the room where we were doing the treatment. Butterflies had been the symbol she used for the baby in her mind. But then an even more amazing thing happened toward the end of the treatment just as we were talking about her having another baby. A children's song came up on the music shuffle. We have very few children's songs in our 20,000+ song playlist, and this one was remarkable. The lyrics were: "Mommy and Daddy and Baby make three. Three is a magic number."

She gasped and said, "Is this a sign that I shouldn't have another child?" It certainly was a strong coincidence, but it could maybe be chalked up to "chance." Still, she left feeling a sense of relief. Perhaps she could imagine her future without another child and be at peace.

When she came back a few days later for her follow-up treatment, she was in a different treatment room with a different stereo system, so it was different equipment. We don't always play music in the follow-up treatment, but for some reason, she wanted the music on. When the music began a new shuffle, the first song that came on, miraculously, was: "Mommy and Daddy and Baby make three. Three is a magic number!"

She squealed! How could it happen again? It must be a message from the universe, the Divine, or whatever she thought was out there. Whatever doubt she was still carrying was gone. She was completely at peace about the perfection of her family as it already was.

We like to call the musical component of the sessions the *Divine D.J.* because this kind of synchronicity happens quite frequently. It feels like undeniable messages come through from beyond. Pure magic!

She never had another child and seemed quite happy and satisfied with that decision, which in a way seemed to affirm the wisdom of the strong message she had received from her Divine DJ.

Case Study: Hospitalized Woman with Severe Psychosis

This is the story of a woman who was referred to us by a friend. By all accounts of her life beforehand, she had seemed completely normal, though depressed and perhaps drinking a little too much. Then she suddenly became quite delusional, and was found naked, babbling, and destroying the bedroom that she rented in a shared household.

After a week in the hospital, no one could find a cause for this sudden shift in her mental state. Her brain was operating within a medically normal range, but she had lost her connection to the normal dimension of reality.

Her friend called us, and the hospital staff was supportive and allowed Leta to come and do a session with the woman in the hospital. Leta began with the idea that it might be an Entity Possession and she did the appropriate treatment for that. However, nothing shifted. The woman was still babbling and not making any sense. She seemed to be getting increasingly agitated.

As Leta began the Ghost Points treatment next, the woman was fidgeting around and even tried to pull at Leta's clothing. Leta always travels with a fully packed iPod player and luckily this day was no exception. Leta brought out the little speaker and began to go through the points of the Ghost Point treatment. At first, nothing shifted with the woman. After about an hour, the song "Mrs. Robinson," by Simon and Garfunkel, from the soundtrack to the movie *The Graduate*, started to play. Suddenly the woman sat up and turned to Leta and said, "That's my name!" It was like a switch had been flipped in the woman's head. She smiled and began having a normal conversation with Leta, talking all about her life, where she worked and lived. It was a stunning shift. Leta actually didn't even know the woman's last name before the treatment began, since the friend that had called her only referred to her as Gabby.

Gabby left the hospital within a week. Leta saw her again soon after, and her friend has occasionally told her that Gabby is doing just fine. She never speaks of the incident, and it's as if it never happened.

Case Study: Bringing Your Mother to the Treatment

It's generally not recommended to bring anyone in your immediate family to a Ghost Point treatment. It could be difficult to speak freely about someone you have a long-term relationship with, if they're sitting in the waiting room or waiting to have lunch with you when you're finished.

However, one woman showed up for her treatment with her mother in tow, and asked if her mother could wait for her in the waiting room. The treatments are sometimes over four hours long, so this was a very unusual request. Leta tried to explain this to the two of them, however, the mother couldn't leave on her own, so she ended up staying in the waiting room area of the clinic.

The client's main complaint was that she had so much anxiety and stress in her life that she couldn't work. She'd always secured amazing jobs but if she got overwhelmed, she could have panic attacks that would leave her hiding in the closet at work so that no-one would know. This was a chronically repeating pattern.

Another problem was that she couldn't date anyone. For some reason, the anxiety and panic attacks only happened when she was involved with someone romantically. She really wanted to get married and have a family, but she couldn't stay with anyone due to this issue of romantic relationships bringing on another round of debilitating anxiety attacks. The woman had tried everything under the sun and had visited countless doctors, who prescribed various medications; she had bottles of them. But nothing made her feel like herself, and the drugs only held off the attacks for a short time.

About an hour into her Ghost Point treatment, the woman began describing a story her mother had recounted to her. Her mother told her that as a baby she had screamed constantly for the entire first year of her life. Other than that story about the crying though, she had no memory of any trauma occurring in her childhood. While she was telling this part of her childhood story, the woman paused, and suddenly, the wind blew open the treatment door! Leta was shocked to see her mother sitting in the waiting room in full view of the treatment. It's important to note that the wind had never blown open the treatment door before, and never ever blew it open again after that treatment. The door latch was very secure.

Leta looked at the woman, the woman looked at Leta, and they were both speechless. The mother sitting in the waiting room, quietly got up, walked over, and closed the door. Leta continued the treatment. About 15 minutes later, the door blew open again, and the mother came and closed it. That was the only remarkable part of the treatment, but it was truly unusual. There's no denying the presence of Mystery and Magic in the Ghost Point treatments!

After the treatment that day, the woman's anxiety vanished. She began dating a new guy and is now happily married with children.

Case Study: Two Sisters Reunite

The reason Laurie thought she had come for her Ghost Point treatment was because she became deeply anxious about driving her car long distances on the highway. Whenever she drove fast, she would break into a full body sweat and start hyperventilating. This caused a lot of frustration and consternation for her and her family.

During the treatment itself, she ended up talking very little about her anxiety. The topic that kept surfacing was actually about her sister. She and her sister had been very close growing up, but a few years prior, they had had a serious falling out and hadn't spoken since. This was incredibly upsetting to Laurie, and she talked about it as if it was going to be like that for the rest of their lives. In her mind, the relationship was permanently broken.

Laurie returned for her follow-up session a few days later with a big smile on her face. The very same night after the treatment her sister called her to apologize. The next day they went for a long walk together and patched up their relationship. Laurie also reported being able to drive on the highway the following day without any anxiety.

The Mystery of how the Ghost Points can positively affect relationships is fascinating. In our opinion, the points open up doors that were shut tight inside the person. Once these doors open up again, some kind of shift occurs that other people in the person's life somehow sense and they begin to behave differently towards them.

Case Study: A Boy's Evil Vanishes

Ellis was scaring his mother and his teachers at school. He'd been an active boy, but not someone who acted out towards others. However, his parents had gone through a very difficult, spiteful, and angry divorce, and Ellis had just started going through puberty.

His mood was becoming increasingly dark. Almost daily his teachers were calling home worried about him. He'd begun drawing very frightening pictures of death, murder, and other eerily violent acts. This is somewhat normal for boys, especially Water Element boys because Waters love the drama of scary things. However, a lot of teachers are used to that. They claimed that this boy's drawings were of a much darker nature than what they normally saw.

His mother brought him in with a sense of desperation. He had come with audiobooks to play instead of music because it was difficult to get him to agree to stay for so long.

When he arrived, Leta recognized that there was something seemingly dark about the boy, but it was difficult to explain what it was. The treatment was fairly uneventful. But Leta did notice that the treatment seemed somehow to be in sync with the drama of the books he had chosen to listen to.

During the treatment break, the boy went outside to get some fresh air and ended up playing basketball with a few boys who were visiting in the yard. He was aggressive and angry while playing. Then he came back in and Leta continued the treatment. At the end of the treatment, he played basketball again with the same boys while waiting for his mother.

The change was significant. The boys were laughing and seemed to be having fun. When Leta asked the other boys later how it was to play with Ellis, the boys said he was really weird at first but then he was "cool" the second time.

His mother brought him back in for his follow-up session. She told Leta privately that she had her beautiful boy back. He had returned to the child she'd always known before the darkness had come. She was deeply grateful and has encouraged many other parents of children who've had similar disturbances to get the Ghost Points Treatment.

Two Case Studies: Competition-Related Panic Attacks with Asthma

Here are two very similar stories of athletes who struggled with panic attacks during their games and with asthma.

Ben had played lacrosse in high school, but when he got to the college level, he found that his nervousness about the competition became so intense that he would have panic attacks during the games that ended up causing his stress-related asthma to activate. After he graduated from college, this symptom continued whenever he tried to play.

During his Ghost Points treatment, Ben talked a lot about his father and the difficulties he had with their relationship. This didn't seem directly related to his problems, but after his session, he reported being able to play sports without any issues again. Evidently he had released his past trauma.

In a similar case, Silvia came to us at the time when she was the captain of her college sports team. She lived for sports and loved her games. She was so sad and frustrated that she would invariably end up side-lined about halfway through the game, hyperventilating and having to lie down on the ground. In her Ghost Point treatment, she talked about the death of her father at an early age and how she didn't deal with the grief she'd felt at the time. Her way of coping had been to bury herself in her sports. After the treatment, the panic attacks subsided, and she was able to fully engage throughout her games as normal and with a much deeper sense of joy.

The Ghost Points often get to the emotional and not-so-obvious roots of problems like anxiety and its related symptoms.

The Nine Heart Pains Treatment

The Nine Heart Pains treatment is an appropriate choice to address addiction issues and life-long feelings of loneliness, isolation, and self-hatred.

Heart pain is an intrinsic component of life. We experience heart pain when someone hurts our feelings or our dreams cannot be fulfilled. Maybe we are disappointed that we weren't able to rise to the very top in our chosen career. Or maybe it's the pain of not having become wealthy or prosperous. Here it's helpful to review the Nine Palaces, which in Chinese Medicine relate to the nine areas of our lives that must be flourishing in order for us to be happy.

Each palace can be a huge source of heart pain when it's not fulfilled or working properly.

To review, the Nine Palaces are:

• Career/Knowledge

• Love/Relationship

• Health

• Wealth/Abundance (having enough)

• Home (a sense of belonging)

• Travel/Global

• Children/Creativity

• Wisdom

• Prosperity (having more than enough)

Whenever one of these palaces in your life is majorly struggling, you will often experience and accumulate heart pain. The pain of failed relationships and a sense of not belonging or loneliness are two of the most common heart pains.

The Chinese believe that heart pain is unavoidable. In fact, one of the twelve meridians of the body is called the *heart protector*. One of its major functions is to heal heart pain.

Heart Pain Treatments are used in the following situations:

- When you are trying to overcome an addiction

- When you have trouble with low self-esteem, self-loathing, or the inability to love yourself. We also call this "The Loving Yourself" treatment.

- When you've never felt "at home" in your life.

Internal Heart Block Treatment

When a person has had emotional trauma, they can build a wall around their heart over time. They can become so blocked inside themselves that they can't access their own heart. We say it's like the person has a wall of cellophane wrapped around the heart, and no one can get in, and the person can't get out.

Trauma or long-term emotional pain can sometimes have such a damaging effect on a person that the person gets lost. According to Chinese Medicine, the heart has a void inside it where our emotions, spirit, and Qi can move freely, via the blood. But when the heart is blocked, all of that gets stuck; nothing can move freely. This is how the true aspects of a person can become trapped and lost.

If this happens, they cannot proceed with Alchemy. There's no way to move forward if their heart is not under their control.

Another possible reason for this kind of block can be that something else has set up residence in the heart so that the person's spirit is no longer in control of their being.

If the person suspects some kind of entity possession, we don't even need to fully understand the nature of that block, but only to recognize that the person's blocked heart must be released before proceeding with Alchemy. You can't practice Alchemy if you have a roommate in your heart trying to manifest some other curriculum that is not your own.

The treatment is helpful in the following situations:

- When you feel like you are inaccessible to yourself and/or to others

- When nothing you try has seemed to help

- When you feel walled off from the world

- If you've never felt the same after a traumatic event

- If you've never felt the same after a long-term emotional upset

What does an Internal Heart Block feel like inside? You feel like you are not at home in your own body. You may behave and function normally, but you feel vacant or vacuous inside. Or sometimes you might feel too intense inside, like you're buzzing. Even though not everyone is trained in Chinese Medicine, we all have an inherent sense of when something is "off" with a person's spirit. Our eyes are the windows to our soul and since Internal Heart Blocks are caused by deep, soul-level pain, we can easily see this pain in a person's eyes.

Will Block Treatment

If you've been subjugated to another person's will for a long period of time, especially as a child or in an abusive relationship, your will can become blocked. In that case you can't move forward in your life in any way. You may try, but the forces of your will cannot be summoned to help you take the next steps. When a person is unable to move forward in life, no matter how hard they try, they most likely have a Blocked Will.

The Chinese believe your *Will*, meaning the will to survive and take action, is housed in the kidneys. And it's the kidneys' job to help you know how to do what you need to do. A person may be completely accessible to their own heart, and they may even have many good ideas of things they want to do, but movement forward in life still somehow seems impossible.

We generally recommend Will Block treatments in the following situations:

- When you have a good sense of what you want to accomplish but you are unable to do it.

- When you feel like you can't get anything done in your life.

- When someone in your life has blocked you from doing what you want and need to do over a long period of time, such as, your parents.

This type of block is uncommon in societies that encourage children to determine their own future, as in much of the United States. It's more common with people who grow up in oppressive situations.

Ma Dan Yang's Twelve Starry Sky Points Treatment

Ma Dan Yang created the Twelve Starry Sky Points Treatment for people who are out of alignment due to the effects of long-term emotional trauma. The treatment realigns the person with the cosmos, with the constellation of the Big Dipper. Ma Dan Yang believed this treatment was the root treatment for all diseases. It especially clears emotional trauma that has lodged in the chest.

In the clinic, we usually consider it after we've done the Thirteen Ghost Points Treatment.

Grieving Treatment

This treatment helps a person move through the blocks that can arise after a loved one dies. It is suggested in the following situations:

- Any recent, significantly difficult loss of a loved one

- Anyone struggling to get over this kind of loss

- The first anniversary of a loss, a key time for moving out of the stages of grieving

- Anyone still strongly impacted by the death of a loved one even years afterward (along with the Ghost Points treatment)

The loss of a loved one is one of the hardest things any of us ever has to face.

The Chinese believe that it's very important to walk through specific stages of grief in order to fully recover from the loss of a loved one, which is a process they believe should take approximately one year to complete. They believe that grief gives us a chance to contemplate what we have lost and, as a result, grow and change. For these reasons, they have specific energetic treatments to help anyone who feels caught up in that process.

A

nd, when you want something, all the universe conspires in helping you to achieve it.

–Paul Coelho

Afterword

Alchemy is a road less traveled. If you're attracted to Alchemy and to the ways it can transform your life, you must ultimately walk it alone. But we like to say you can have friends along the way, who will share the path with you. Many Alchemists retreated to the mountains in the old days, to practice in small groups. This is a tradition of living life differently than people do in mainstream modern culture. The focus is on self-cultivation.

We've been practicing Alchemy for many years now. We are also lucky to have found and built a community of others who want to practice with us.

The Alchemy Learning Center is our virtual mountainside where we've created a place for Alchemists all over the world to come together. The Alchemy Sanctuary is a vision we have for a future physical home, perhaps in the mountains, where modern day Alchemists can find a touchstone, and a safe place to practice Stage Seven in retreat from the busy world. For right now, please visit us at AlchemyLearningCenter.com.

Suggested Reading List

After the Ecstasy, the Laundry: How the Heart Grows Wise on the Spiritual Path by Jack Kornfield. Publisher: Bantam, 2001.

As You Thinketh by James Allen. Publisher: Top of the Mountain Publishing, 1989.

Ask and It Is Given: Learning to Manifest Your Desires by Esther and Jerry Hicks. Publisher: Hay House, 2007.

Blessings, Wisdom, and Hurt by Gregg Braden. Publisher: Hay House, 2005.

Change Your Thoughts, Change Your Life by Wayne Dyer. Publisher: Hay House, 2009.

Cultivating Stillness: A Taoist Manual for Transforming Body and Mind by Eva Wong. Publisher: Shambhala, 2012.

Healing Anxiety: A Tibetan Medicine Guide to Healing Anxiety, Stress and PTSD by Mary Friedman-Ryan. Publisher: Born Perfect, 2016.

Lao Tzu: Tao Te Ching: A Book About the Way and the Power of the Way by Ursula K. Le Guin. Publisher: Shambhala, 2019.

Life and Teaching of The Masters of The Far East by Baird T. Spalding. Publisher: DeVorss & Company, 1986.

Matrix Energetics: The Science and Art of Transformation by Richard Bartlett. Publisher: Atria Books/ Beyond Words, 2009.

Plant Spirit Medicine: A Journey into the Healing Wisdom of Plants by Eliot Cowan. Publisher: Sounds True, 2014.

Qi Gong for Total Wellness by Dr. Baolin Wu and Jessica Eckstein. Publisher: St. Martin's Griffin, 2006.

Rooted in Spirit by Claude Larre. Publisher: Barrytown/Station Hill Press, Inc., 1995.

Sastun: One Woman's Apprenticeship with a Maya Healer and Their Efforts to Save the Vani by Rosita Arvigo. Publisher: HarperOne, 1995.

Secrets of the Lost Mode of Prayer: The Hidden Power of Beauty, Blessing, Wisdom, and Hurt by Gregg Braden. Hay House, 2016.

Tales of the Taoist Immortals by Eva Wong. Publisher: Shambhala, 2001.

The Alchemist: A Fable About Following Your Dream, 25th Anniversary Edition by Paul Coelho. Publisher: HarperOne, 2014.

The Cosmic Serpent: DNA and the Origins of Knowledge by Jeremy Narby. Publisher: Jeremy P. Tarcher/Putnam, 1999.

The Diamond in Your Pocket: Discovering Your True Radiance by Gangaji. Publisher: Sounds True, 2007.

The Disappearance of the Universe by Gary R. Renard. Publisher: Hay House, 2004.

The Master Key System by Charles F. Haanel. Publisher: Filiquarian Publishing, LLC., 2006.

The Power of Now: A Guide to Spiritual Enlightenment by Eckhart Tolle. Publisher: New World Library, 2004.

The Power of Vulnerability: Teachings of Authenticity, Connection, and Courage by Brené Brown. Publisher: Sounds True, 2013.

The Power of Vulnerability by Brené Brown, TED Talk. https://www.ted.com/talks/brene_brown_the_power_of_vulnerability?language=en

The Science of Being Well by Wallace D. Wattles. Publisher: Wilder Publications, 2008.

The Secret of the Golden Flower: A Chinese Book of Life translated by Richard Wilhelm. Publisher: Houghton Mifflin Harcourt Publishing Company, 1970.

The Secret Teachings of Plants: The Intelligence of the Heart in the Direct Perception of Nature by Stephen Harrod Buhner. Publisher: Bear Company, 2004.

The Tao of Healing: Meditations for Body and Spirit by Haven Trevino. Publisher: New World Library, 1999.

The Wandering Taoist by Ming-Dao Deng. Publisher: HarperCollins, 1986.

The World Is a Waiting Lover: Desire and the Quest for the Beloved by Trebbe Johnson. Publisher: New World Library, 2005.

More from the Authors

Connecting Your Circle: How the Five Elements Can Help You Be a More Authentic You by Leta Herman and Jaye McElroy. Publisher: Born Perfect Ink, 2014.

The Big Little Gua Sha Book: Learning (and Loving) the Ancient Healing Art of Gua Sha by Leta Herman and Jaye McElroy. Publisher: Born Perfect Ink, 2016.

The Energy of Love: Applying the Five Elements to Turn Attraction into True Connection by Leta Herman and Jaye McElroy. Publisher: Llewellyn Publications, 2014.

Made in the USA
Monee, IL
16 April 2021